Praise for *Stewarding Our Bodies*

"By rightly situating perspectives about stewarding the body in biblical theology, the authors set our thinking and our practice on solid ground. Each chapter contains well-researched insights and thoughtfully developed recommendations. In a time when moral development and spiritual formation of our students is so critical, this resource will inform my direct work with students and the leadership of my student life team."

—Edee Schulze, Vice President for Student Life, Westmont College

"Perry Glanzer and Austin Smith have put together an invaluable resource for those working with college students. This volume is very thorough and provides great insights into some of the more difficult issues college students are facing. It provides a biblical framework, a thoughtful understanding, and practical approaches to help engage students in these important topics. The authors included represent a great mix of scholars and practitioners. This book will quickly become a must for anyone working in Christian Higher Education. Thanks for a job well done."

—Skip Trudeau, Vice President for Student Development and Intercollegiate Athletics, Taylor University

"In the current raft of research books for Student Affairs professionals, stewardship of the body as God's temple seems dimly distant in the shadows. Glanzer and Smith pull together a collection of lively and accessible essays that brightly turn the lights on to a theologically grounded and comprehensive understanding and practice of stewarding the body. This book is a must-read for Christian higher education scholars, student affairs professionals, administrative leaders, and their students!"

—Steve Ivester, Dean for Student Engagement, Wheaton College

Stewarding
Our Bodies

Stewarding Our Bodies

A Vision for Christian Student Affairs

Edited by
PERRY L. GLANZER and
AUSTIN T. SMITH

Abilene Christian University Press

STEWARDING OUR BODIES
A Vision for Christian Student Affairs

ACU
PRESS

All Scripture quotations, unless otherwise indicated, are taken from the Holy Bible, New International Version®, NIV®. Copyright ©1973, 1978, 1984, 2011 by Biblica, Inc.™ Used by permission of Zondervan. All rights reserved worldwide. www.zondervan.com The "NIV" and "New International Version" are trademarks registered in the United States Patent and Trademark Office by Biblica, Inc.™

Scripture quotations marked (ESV) are from the ESV® Bible (The Holy Bible, English Standard Version®), copyright © 2001 by Crossway, a publishing ministry of Good News Publishers. Used by permission. All rights reserved. The ESV text may not be quoted in any publication made available to the public by a Creative Commons license. The ESV may not be translated in whole or in part into any other language.

Scripture quotations marked (NRSVUE) are from New Revised Standard Version, Updated Edition, copyright © 2021 National Council of the Churches of Christ in the United States of America. Used by permission. All rights reserved worldwide.

Scripture quotations marked (RSV) are from Revised Standard Version of the Bible, copyright © 1946, 1952, and 1971 National Council of the Churches of Christ in the United States of America. Used by permission. All rights reserved worldwide.

Scripture quoted by permission. Quotations designated (NET) are from the NET Bible® copyright © 1996, 2019 by Biblical Studies Press, L.L.C. http://netbible.com All rights reserved

Scripture quotations marked (KJV) are from the King James Version.

Scripture quotations marked (RGT) are from the Revised Geneva Translation © 2019 by Five Talents Audio.

Library of Congress Cataloging in Publication Data is on file at the Library of Congress, Washington, DC.

Cover design by Bruce Gore | Gore Studio Inc.
Interior text design by Scribe Inc.

For information contact:
Abilene Christian University Press
ACU Box 29138
Abilene, Texas 79699
1-877-816-4455
www.acupressbooks.com

22 23 24 25 26 27/ 7 6 5 4 3 2 1

Contents

Part Two
From Fall to Redemption

Acknowledgments

This volume would not have been possible without significant support financially and intellectually. We would first like to thank the Association for Christians in Student Development (ACSD) for their enthusiasm and financial support for this project. While finances are a necessity to completing a project such as this, ACSD's enthusiasm for this project has been an incredible encouragement that this volume is meeting a real need within the field. Additionally, we would like to thank each of the authors who agreed to share their wisdom and experience to contribute to this volume. It is a better book for the wisdom each of you has shared.

This book is dedicated to those who faithfully serve students, encouraging them to become more the people who God has created them to be. It is our hope that this volume provides encouragement and reminds you of how valued your ministry is.

Perry—I dedicate this book to my friend Matt Burchett, who demonstrates what it means to engage in Christ-animated student affairs. He is willing to address the difficult issues whether it comes to those related to the body or other areas of student life. Thanks for our weekly meetings and your deep, soul-nourishing friendship.

Austin—I dedicate this book to the students I have encountered during my time in student development work, particularly the resident advisors and spiritual life advisors with whom I had the pleasure of serving alongside at Pepperdine. Though you have all graduated by now, you continue to inspire me and convince me of the importance of this work. Additionally, this book is dedicated to my colleagues and friends in student development at Taylor, Pepperdine, Baylor, and other institutions across the country. Thank you for entertaining my musings on the philosophy and theology of student development work.

Introduction

Stewardship of the Body and the Christian University

The State of Situation

Perry L. Glanzer and Austin T. Smith

Christian student affairs professionals currently neglect students' bodies. How do we know? I (Perry) recently led a mixed-methods study of Christian student affairs. In a survey of three hundred student affairs leaders (SALs), we gave them sixteen different themes that they might emphasize on their campus. Educating students about stewardship of the body as God's temple finished dead last. The next most neglected theme was teaching students a Christian view of time (e.g., Sabbath rest, thanksgiving, and celebration)—a theme that also relates to stewardship of the body. Overall, as described in the book summarizing the findings, *Christ-Enlivened Student Affairs: A Guide to Christian Thinking and Practice in the Field*,[1] we found stewardship of the body woefully neglected.

This neglect also came out in our examination of other topics. SALs noted that discussions about alcohol and sex were missing. For example, over half of the SALs indicated their campus lacked

---

1 Perry L. Glanzer et al., *Christ-Enlivened Student Affairs: A Guide to Christian Thinking and Practice in the Field* (Abilene, TX: Abilene Christian University Press, 2020).

a resource with regard to sex education. They also indicated they needed more communication and education as the following SALs indicated:

- "[We need] more training and more conversations about sexuality in our campus community and with other student affairs professionals."

- "We don't talk about it enough."

- "The conversation is lacking."

- "I think that we are lacking the courage to have a real conversation about sexuality issues and how they are impacting our students."

- "[We need] more time and space to discuss these topics."

- "It's not addressed in large-scale ways, so it feels at times like it's a 'secret group' or issue that can't be discussed publicly. I think we would benefit from bringing it into the mainstream conversation more regularly."

Even when we found sex education, it did not give attention to how Christ animates sex education, as one SAL complained regarding sexuality: "Our campus educates us on how to handle things from a professional standpoint but not a spiritual one." Another SAL wrote, regarding their campus's needs, that they need "everything. We don't really have any resources provided to us on campus." This problem is backed up by the research findings from one of the coauthors, Britney Graber, who found via her PhD dissertation interviews with eighty-eight Christian Title IX directors that not one of their campuses had formal sex education through the curriculum or a significant cocurricular sex-education program.[2]

We found this neglect of stewardship of the body in numerous areas remarkable. After all, the misuse of the body is what makes

2 Britney N. Graber, "Incompatible? How Christian Faith Informs Title IX Policy and Practice" (PhD diss., Baylor University, 2021).

major headlines today, whether it be regarding sexual assault, binge drinking and all the behavior that goes with it, the current mental health crisis on campus, or other student-related crises. Much of student life is spent seeking to deal with the negative effects of these problems. What we need to do is set forth a positive vision for students of what it looks like to use their bodies properly.

Some educational leaders and their respective campuses have already begun to recognize this need. For example, in 2019, the *Chronicle of Higher Education* reported about Michelle Lampl's new course, Health 100. An anthropology professor at Emory University, Lampl became concerned about students' health, even declaring that the health of late adolescents "is a national emergency."[3] Thus, Lampl designed a required course for students that is basically about what it means to be an excellent steward of your body, or as the *Chronicle* described it, it "aims to get students to make healthier choices to improve their well-being, including diet and mental health."[4]

Our interviews also brought this need to the forefront. Numerous SALs identified stewardship of the body as a neglected theme. In fact, one SAL noted this absence and observed that what her students needed was "a clearly articulated sexual ethic that's a high level." She then went on to inspire the unique theme for this book by noting, "I actually do like stewardship of the body, because I think it relates to women struggling with body image, I think it relates to pornography, I think it relates to sexual addictions. I think it relates to relationships. I think that we could build on that. If I could wave a magic wand and say, 'Let's build on that,' and that's sort of how we talk about this, other things flow from that, that would be great." This book seeks to build on this important theological theme.

This book is meant for two audiences in particular. First, we are writing for current Christian student affairs professionals throughout higher education. This audience includes both those working in Christian institutions and those in pluralistic institutions. Second, we

3 Vimal Patel, "Why Colleges Are Keeping a Closer Eye on Their Students' Lives," *Chronicle of Higher Education*, February 18, 2019, https://www.chronicle.com/interactives/Trend19-InLoco-Main?cid=wcontentgrid_2Trends.
4 Patel.

are writing for students who will be involved in the world of student affairs, such as resident assistants or leaders of student groups.

The book is organized into two parts. Part One focuses on a Christian vision rooted in what has traditionally been called the "doctrine of creation." It centers on the positive view of the body that results from this foundation as well as the positive views of food, drink, rest, play, and sex that extend from it. Part Two discusses the journey "From Fall to Redemption." It describes the ways that the Fall corrupts the stewardship of our body—which includes our bodily thinking, affections, and behavior—and how Christians understand the redemption of the body in areas such as clothing, social media, mental health, and disordered sexual desires. It is our hope that this volume can provide a starting point for the discussion and transformation of how Christians—particularly those in the college setting, whether faculty, staff, or students—understand and practice what it means to steward the body.

Part One

Foundational Christian Vision

Chapter 1

The Body in the Biblical Narrative

Foundations

Perry L. Glanzer and Julia D. Hejduk

(Perry) remember teaching Sunday school to a young married class decades ago and talking about the goodness of our bodies. I read out this quote from Mike Mason's well-known book *The Mystery of Marriage*, which he wrote as a young newlywed:

> As for me, I still haven't gotten used to seeing my own wife naked. It's almost as if her body is shining with a bright light, too bright to look at for very long. I cannot take my eyes off her—and yet I must. To gaze too long or too curiously is, even with her, a breach of propriety, almost a crime. It is not *like* watching a flower or creeping up to spy on an animal in the wild. No, my wife's body is brighter and more fascinating than a flower, shier than any animal, and more breathtaking than a thousand sunsets. To me, her body is the most awesome thing in creation. . . . I catch a small glimpse of what it means that men and women have been made in the image of God. If even the image is this dazzling, what must the Original be like?[1]

---

1 Mike Mason, *The Mystery of Marriage: Meditations on the Miracle* (Multnomah, OR: Multnomah, 2005), 125.

Whenever I use this quote in class, I am struck by how uncomfortable it makes people. I understand that this discomfort may arise from past wounds regarding their bodies or problematic objectifying messages from others that "your body is for our admiration." Yet if I ask people to peel back the scars from early lifetime wounds and fallen messages, I often find something else occurring. They are running from their bodily glory.

The glory of our bodies can scare and overpower us. As Edmund notes to Fanny in *Mansfield Park*, "You seemed almost as fearful of notice and praise." Thus, he must tell her, "You must try not to mind growing up into a pretty woman."[2] If there is something we should embrace from the very start of the Christian story, it is that our bodies are good and, yes, glorious. We need to start with a clear understanding of this biblical foundation. Only then should we proceed through the rest of the biblical story.

Bodies Are Part of Being Made in God's Image

Though Christians sometimes shy away from this fact, part of how we image God takes place through our created bodies. This truth is the first thing the Bible tells us about ourselves: "Then God said, 'Let us make humankind in our image, according to our likeness . . .' So God created humankind in his image, in the image of God he created them; male and female he created them" (Gen. 1:26–27 NRSVUE). That we are made in God's image—including our bodies—is the most important component of our identity. Our bodies are good.

More specifically, our female and male bodies are good. As Beth Felker Jones reminds us, just because there is a lot of cultural baggage associated with masculinity and femininity, "that doesn't stop maleness and femaleness from being created goods. Male bodies are good. Female bodies are good. God made them and God loves them."[3]

---

2 Jane Austen, *Mansfield Park* (1814; Project Gutenberg, 2022), chap. 11, https://gutenberg.org/files/141/141-h/141-h.htm#link2HCH0011.
3 Beth Felker Jones, *Faithful: A Theology of Sex* (Grand Rapids, MI: Zondervan, 2015), 33.

We are "fearfully and wonderfully made" (Ps. 139:14b). Our bodies are bearers of this truth.

The First Great Commission: Stewardship of the Body

Immediately after declaring that we are made in God's image, God bestows upon us the additional identity and responsibility of being rulers or stewards of all creation. We often tend to think of this verse as referring simply to nature, or "every living creature," and we fail to remember that our own bodies are part of God's creation (Gen. 1:28). God has also charged us with stewarding our bodies. Indeed, as every parent knows, part of raising children involves helping them steward their own bodies, all the way from potty training to learning how to eat healthy, exercise, get enough sleep, and not take stupid risks with the great gift they've been given.

That education also includes teaching the young the ultimate reason for bodily stewardship. The world and all it contains have a *telos*, a final end *for* which God created them. In a mystery that will always exceed our understanding, the triune God is simultaneously *One*, the unified ground of all being, and *Three*, a community of Love consisting of the Father, the Son, and the life-giving love between them we call the Holy Spirit. The *telos* of every human being is *to share for all eternity in the divine nature of God*, or what theologians from various Christian traditions call *divinization* (Catholic), *sanctification* (Protestant), or *theosis* (Eastern Orthodox; see 2 Pet. 1:4).[4] C. S. Lewis makes this point forcefully in *Mere Christianity*:

> The command Be ye perfect is not idealistic gas. Nor is it a command to do the impossible. He is going to make us into creatures

---

4 There are some subtle and important differences among the terms, but they share a basic core. On "divinization" as a staple of the Christian tradition from its earliest days, see Gregory Popcak, *Broken Gods: Hope, Healing, and the Seven Longings of the Human Heart* (New York: Image, 2015), 3–7. A helpful primer on theosis can be found in Daniel Clendenin, *Eastern Orthodox Christianity: A Western Perspective* (Grand Rapids, MI: Baker Books, 2003).

that can obey that command. He said (in the Bible) that we were "gods" and He is going to make good His words. If we let Him—for we can prevent Him, if we choose—He will make the feeblest and filthiest of us into a god or goddess, a dazzling, radiant, immortal creature, pulsating all through with such energy and joy and wisdom and love as we cannot now imagine, a bright stainless mirror which reflects back to God perfectly (though, of course, on a smaller scale) His own boundless power and delight and goodness. The process will be long and in parts very painful, but that is what we are in for. Nothing less. He meant what He said.[5]

All that has ever happened or ever will is for the purpose of teaching us to receive God's love—which is sweeter, more passionate, and more tender than we can possibly imagine—and then allow it to flow through us to others. Nothing less can satisfy the infinite cravings that God, who made us in his image, has placed in the human heart. This end is the ultimate purpose of bodily stewardship.

To begin this stewardship, we must recognize that our core bodily desires are good. This truth is tricky to understand correctly. We instinctively feel that our sinful desires—especially the ones that cause us to use other people as instruments for our own gratification—must be *bad*. Yet while Eastern philosophies such as Buddhism seek to eliminate desire, Christianity sees desire as the essential fuel for divinization, sanctification, or theosis. Our bodily desires for food, health, relationship, sex, and more are inherently *good*, even though they have become disordered by sin.

Although this stewardship has these important common elements, God created our sexually differentiated bodies with certain kinds of natural powers and gifts. One does not need research to reveal that, on average, men are created physically stronger than women. Young boys should be taught to celebrate and steward their strength as part of the first Great Commission. Women are also created with unique forms of physical power, most obviously the ability to nurture

5 C. S. Lewis, *Mere Christianity* (New York: Macmillan, 1952), 205–6.

new lives both within and outside of their bodies. This superpower should be celebrated.

Of course, one additional bodily relationship celebrated in the Creation story is marriage, through which a man and a woman "become one flesh" (Gen. 2:24). Marriage is a kind of joint bodily stewardship, the ultimate opening and uniting of one's body to another person's. Through becoming one body, the married couple also helps fulfill God's commission to produce new bodies: "Be fruitful and increase in number; fill the earth and subdue it" (Gen. 1:28). Together, they form an image of the life-giving, creative love of the triune God. Finally, the Creation story ends by focusing upon humans' self-perception of their bodies in marriage, noting that Adam and Eve "were both naked, and they felt no shame" (Gen. 2:25b). What a glorious beginning for wiser and older Christians to pass along to children and young emerging adults!

The Fall and Our Bodies

Since the Fall, our desires have been "disordered," which means we desire good things in the wrong way. Satan is an expert sniper: he targets and twists those desires that, if rightly ordered, would bring the greatest glory to God and flourishing to ourselves. Unfortunately, Satan especially attacks our bodies and our view of our bodies. In the following section, we will mention a few distortions of our desires and thoughts that have negative implications for college students.

Shame, Contempt, Covetousness, and Competition. The Fall consisted of a bodily act (eating), and its very first consequence was a change in the view of our bodies. Immediately after Adam and Eve ate the forbidden fruit, "the eyes of both of them were opened, and they realized they were naked; so they sewed fig leaves together and made coverings for themselves" (Gen. 3:7). Shame entered the world.

The shame you feel about your body comes from the Fall. To say "I hate my body" or "My body is ugly" is to internalize a lie from Satan. Of course, others often help us magnify this shame. I (Perry) can still remember comments made about my body from the fifth and sixth grades (one positive and one negative). Sometimes it starts earlier. I (Julia) also remember a remark about my tummy—I was probably in third grade at the time—that led to years of dieting and obsessing about food, though it fell short of a full-blown eating disorder. Through the grace of God, and meeting at age eighteen the boy who would become my husband, I eventually was able to develop a saner relationship with food. Many girls are not so lucky.

Sometimes the shame comes simply from our own critical eyes. In her book *More Than a Body*, Lindsay Kite talks about how, at age eleven, a fixation with a dimple on her thigh started her on a preoccupation with her body. Her friends were no different, as it led them down a path of covetousness and bodily abuse: "One of our most popular friends cut out dozens of lingerie models from a *Victoria's Secret* catalog and stuck them all over the back of her door for 'motivation.' Another friend, a cheerleader, bragged to everyone that all she had eaten in days was five Doritos."[6] Women are not alone. I (Perry) recently talked with someone who has conducted a marriage ministry for three decades, and he noted that in the last decade, he has found men increasingly preoccupied with how they will look to their wives on their wedding night. Critiques and images from others and ourselves distort our views of our bodies and our expectations of them.

These negative, fearful views of one's body can even become integral to one's worldview or religion. In fact, much of the philosophical enterprise throughout the ages has involved freeing the soul from the prison of the body. This "Gnosticism," summarized in the Greek jingle *sōma sēma*, "the body is a tomb," holds that the intellectual and spiritual is the realm of enlightenment, while the corporeal is base, dirty, and confining. The spiritual is associated with masculinity and the corporeal with femininity; the Gnostic *Gospel of the Egyptians* has Jesus say, "I have come to destroy the works of the feminine."[7] As the second-century Greek philosopher Celsus argued with Christians, "If

6 Lexie Kite and Lindsay Kite, "From Body Anxiety to Body Image Activism: Our Story," More Than a Body, accessed September 28, 2022, https://www.morethanabody.org/body-anxiety-to-body-image-activism/.

7 Quoted in Joseph Cardinal Ratzinger and Hans Urs von Balthasar, *Mary: The Church at the Source* (San Francisco: Ignatius, 1997), 41.

you shut your eyes to the world of sense and look up with the mind, if you turn away from the flesh and raise the eyes of the soul, only then will you see God."[8] The modern offspring of this philosophy is the idea that we can be whatever we think we are because our bodies are merely disposable wrappers for our souls.

Furthermore, this negativity often takes gender-related forms. There are some men who despise physical strength and others who despise physical weakness. Some women despise feminine beauty or fertility, while others despise those without these gifts. This shame and contempt leaves some to rage against God or themselves for the body God gave them. They long for extensive plastic surgery and enhancements.

Stewardship Failures. Beyond the shame and contempt we have for our bodies and the covetousness we have for other bodies because of the Fall, we also simply fail to steward them. Going to college is for many young people the first time they have primary control over their bodily stewardship. Parents are not monitoring their food, and high school sports coaches are not encouraging them to steward their bodies a certain way. The all-too-frequent result is the "freshman fifteen."

I (Perry) remember how, during my first year in college, I started breakfast many mornings with a ham and cheese omelet, a bowl of Cap'n Crunch cereal, and a doughnut. It was glorious freedom. My mother did not allow us to buy sugared cereals growing up. The closest we could get to cheating was the slightly sweet Honey Nut Cheerios. I (Julia) had a more dismal cereal experience still—our mainstays were Total and Product 19 (Who ever thought that was a good name for a food?)—but we always had ice cream around, which is still my go-to comfort food. In my freshman dining hall, there were ten-gallon bins in a variety of flavors available at every meal. You can fill in the rest.

The Body as a Weapon, Idol, and Decaying Vessel. One of the first things we see happen after the Fall is that the body is used as a

---

8 Origen, *Against Celsus* 7.42, quoted in Robert Louis Wilken, *The Spirit of Early Christian Thought: Seeking the Face of God* (New Haven, CT: Yale University Press, 2003), 9.

weapon. Whether it be Cain, who attacks his brother and kills him (Gen. 4:8), or Potiphar's wife, who seeks to seduce Joseph (Gen. 39:7–18), the fallen stewardship of the body involves using it to hurt others. The body's power or beauty can also become an idol: as Ezekiel says of God's chosen people, Israel, "But you trusted in your beauty" (Ezek. 16:15a). Christians are no different. As a result, men and women must take seriously the training and stewardship required to resist those who would use the body in these ways.

Of course, God has a way of teaching us not to make an idol of our bodies. One very effective method is age: "At the end of your life you will groan, when your flesh and body are spent" (Prov. 5:11). Yet even in our aging, we still fall prey to covetous sin. As one famous line notes, you spend the first forty years wishing you looked like someone else and the next forty wishing you looked like your former self.

Early Bodily Betrayal. Even worse than aging, our bodies sometimes betray us before their time. My wife and I learned that our second child in her womb was dead—a miscarriage. As is often the case, we did not know why. We simply grieved together silently and cried. Later, when our youngest child was three years old, I got a call from my wife asking me to rush home. Our son had just been screaming in pain. By the time I arrived, the screams had stopped, but my wife was exhausted. Later, we would finally learn that he has Crohn's disease. Now he lives with chronic pain. Bodily betrayal.

My wife and I also live in chronic pain. Her pain comes from the nerve damage she experienced from contracting a debilitating disease known as Guillain-Barré syndrome fifteen years ago. For a year, she had to stay in bed. She has since recovered, but she still experiences constant and chronic nerve pain that is barely controlled by medicine. She can no longer walk more than a mile or do any extensive activity without having to recover by lying in bed the next day.

My bodily betrayal happened in 2017 because of multiple factors (particularly taking two doses of an antibiotic close together that the FDA warns attacks ligaments and tendons and then having a particular medical procedure). As a result, I endured painful spasms and could not walk or sit for more than twenty minutes at a time.

I have now recovered, but I still experience other bodily betrayals and have had to retire from the sports I love, such as basketball, racquetball, tennis, and jogging. God, who can save us from the fallen ways we view and use our bodies? Who can save us from bodily sin and betrayal?

Redeeming the Body Now

"The Word became flesh and made his dwelling among us" (John 1:14a). To appreciate the mind-boggling absurdity of this statement, you need to remember how the ancient world understood the body and the soul. To them, the prologue of the Gospel of John (1:1–14) at first would have appeared congenial to soul-body dualism: "In the beginning was the [*Logos*]"—word, thought, rationality—"and the [*Logos*] was with God, and the [*Logos*] was God." The Greek Platonist would have been at home with the light of the *Logos* shining in darkness and the assurance that the saved were born "not of blood, nor of the will of the flesh, nor of the will of man, but of God" (John 1:13 KJV). So far so good.

But then "the [*Logos*] was made *flesh* and dwelt among us" (John 1:14 RGT—emphasis added). That one Greek word, *sarx*, explodes Platonic metaphysics. The transcendent Form of the Good, the *telos* of all philosophical contemplation, became *flesh*? Even worse, as Eamon Duffy points out in "The God of History," every woman mentioned in Matthew's genealogy of Jesus is "sexually compromised" in some way.[9] Their bodies had been used and misused. Yet God became a flesh-and-blood body to redeem us through this genealogical line of fallen bodies.

Although we are told to imitate Christ in particular ways in the New Testament, all of them involve enacting virtues through our bodies (e.g., love, humility, forgiveness, service, acceptance). In fact, Christ becoming flesh is used as the model of humility in what is known as the "kenosis hymn," or "hymn of self-emptying" (Phil. 2:5–7):

---

9 Eamon Duffy, "The God of History," in *Walking to Emmaus* (London: Burns & Oates, 2006), 153–63.

> In your relationships with one another, have the same mindset
>   as Christ Jesus:
> Who, being in very nature God,
> did not consider equality with God something to be used to his
>   own advantage;
> rather, he made himself nothing
> by taking the very nature of a servant,
> being made in human likeness.

Jesus, as God in the flesh, came to wash his disciples' dirty, smelly, fleshy feet. He commands us to do the same: "Now that I, your Lord and Teacher, have washed your feet, you also should wash one another's feet. I have set you an example that you should do as I have done for you" (John 13:14–15). Christ showed us how to fulfill what it means to be made in God's image.

Indeed, God not only became flesh but offered his body as a sacrifice for us! Jesus took bread and said, "This is my *body* given for you" (Luke 22:19—emphasis added). The same God who chose to hide himself in a human embryo in a Jewish girl's womb chose to have us remember him through a fleshly, bodily act. For Protestants (such as Perry), the Lord's Supper is a memorial. For Catholics (such as Julia), the Mass is both a memorial and the consumption of the body and blood, soul and divinity of Christ, though they retain the physical properties of bread and wine. In either case, Jesus commanded us to eat and drink: "Very truly I tell you, unless you eat the flesh of the Son of man and drink his blood, you have no life in you. Whoever eats my flesh and drinks my blood has eternal life, and I will raise them up at the last day" (John 6:53–54). Christ's body and blood are the instruments of our salvation. And to prove his triumph over evil and the ultimate bodily betrayal of death, he rose *bodily* from the grave.

The implications of this sacrifice for our bodies are manifold, but we want to focus on one of the most important ones. Through Christ, Christians are now what God intended for humans in the Genesis 1 story: temples of the Holy Spirit that are to grow in our reflection of God's image. When writing to the Corinthians, Paul noted that their sexual immorality came from a Gnostic view of the body: "You say,

'Food for the stomach and the stomach for food, and God will destroy them both'" (1 Cor. 6:13a). In contrast, Paul made it clear that we have a different view of the body, since "by his power God raised the Lord from the dead, and he will raise us also. Do you not know that your bodies are members of Christ himself?" (1 Cor. 6:14–15a). Paul explained regarding this new story for our bodies, "Do you not know that your bodies are temples of the Holy Spirit, who is in you, whom you have received from God? You are not your own; you were bought at a price. Therefore honor God with your bodies" (1 Cor. 6:19–20).

In this verse, we see the key motivations God gives us for bodily stewardship. It is not done simply to look good, live longer, and feel better. We should honor God with our bodies for three reasons: (1) Christ died for our bodies; (2) Christ rose bodily from the grave, and we will too; and (3) as a result, we are members of Christ's body, and God's Spirit lives within us. The most compelling reason for taking care of ourselves is that we house God's Spirit! Our bodies are more valuable than the greatest cathedrals ever built, and in stewarding them well, we show gratitude for Christ's sacrifice.

Beyond 1 Corinthians, the book of Romans spends the first eleven chapters outlining what God has done for us. The climax of the book is found in the transition in Romans 12:1–2, which gives the command we should follow in light of God's generosity: "Therefore, I urge you, brothers and sisters, in view of God's mercy, to offer your *bodies* as a living sacrifice, holy and pleasing to God—this is your true and proper worship" (Rom. 12:1—emphasis added). The temple was not just an impressive worship space but the place where the literal sacrifice of animals took place. The obedience to which we are called as living "temples" may come at a great price, but honoring God in this way is always redemptive. God used Christ's body to save us. Now we're asked to sacrifice something of value, our bodies, for something of greater value: Jesus.

The lives of the saints only make sense if we realize this bodily sacrifice. A famous anecdote about Saint Mother Teresa of Calcutta, who devoted her life to serving the poorest of the poor, nicely illustrates this exchange. As a man watched her plucking maggots from the rotting flesh of a leper, he remarked, "I wouldn't do that for a million dollars." She replied, "Neither would I. But I would gladly do it for Christ."[10] We too worship God by giving him our bodies.

Bodily Suffering and Death— God's Reaction and Ours

It started to rain as we drove to the funeral. My (Perry's) oldest son, who was six years old at the time, commented with words that summed up the heavy grief: "Look, God must be crying for Paul." Paul was the six-year-old son of my colleague to whose funeral we were driving. Tears welled in my eyes, and I agreed, "Yes, Bennett, I think God's crying." Six-year-olds should not die of cancer.

"Jesus wept" (John 11:35). That God cries remains one of the most profound and comforting mysteries of the faith. While throughout the Old Testament we may get the sense that God continually wants to wring some necks, it is always because he grieves over his people's infidelity and yearns to woo them back (e.g., Hos. 2:14–23). In Jesus, who reveals the true face of the Father to us, we see even more clearly the way God weeps for the suffering caused by the Fall. He wept for Lazarus, whose body he would raise and then allow to die again. God weeps for the bodily death we all must face.

Remembering that God weeps saves us from one of the biggest temptations we face as we grow older: to think that God does not care. When my (Perry's) wife came down with Guillain-Barré syndrome, my biggest temptation was not to yell at God and ask "Why us?" It seemed like a selfish question. I also was not tempted to deny God. The atheistic reaction has never been the least bit intellectually, morally, or emotionally persuasive for me. No, my biggest temptation was to think that God doesn't care. That he's the passive deistic God. Sure, I believe he created the world and established a particular moral order. But does God really give a rip about our pain right now? I found myself not praying because I didn't expect much from God.

---

10 James Martin, *My Life with the Saints* (Chicago: Loyola University Press, 2006), 164.

I have constantly faced this temptation throughout my life. My brother-in-law has spent decades of his life in bed fighting horrible pain. He often was not able to play with and hold his daughters. He could not attend their music recitals and sports events. It became hard for me to pray for him; nothing had seemed to help—the latest drug, technology, or procedure always failed. I want a God who will act, who will do something. My brother-in-law himself said that one of the primary ways he copes is to remember that Christ is crying with him. Jesus weeps.

I do not want God to cry, though. I want God to fix it. Oddly, my wife tells me the opposite at times in our relationship. She does not want me to always try to fix a certain kind of problem. She wants my heart and my tears. A lover does not always want things to be fixed but simply longs for the beloved's tears. God weeps. And God somehow made us to reflect his image and his glory. Sometimes we reflect the image of God in us just by shedding tears for others' bodily maladies.

The Meaning of Suffering

Since God is infinitely powerful and infinitely loving, we know he permits us to suffer only in order to bring about a greater good. Sometimes, suffering has an obvious corrective purpose, showing us a failure in our stewardship of our bodies that needs to be changed. It hurts when you put your hand on a hot stove, and when you eat or drink too much, and when you otherwise engage in behaviors that are harmful to you. The usefulness of that kind of suffering can be seen by everyone from the smallest child to the greatest philosopher, religious or not.

The suffering that mystifies us is the kind that is undeserved and serves no obvious corrective purpose. Why would a loving God allow anyone, let alone an innocent child, to experience a lifetime of chronic pain with no discernible cause or cure? Here is where modern heresies such as the prosperity gospel and moralistic therapeutic deism, which treat God like a cosmic vending machine or urgent-care doctor, show themselves to be of no use whatsoever. The only satisfying answer is to be found in the cross.

Our bodily sufferings, though not a good in themselves, are permitted by God in order to bring forth the greatest good of all. The cross is where Jesus embraces us most tenderly, where we experience a foretaste of the intimate communion with him that is our *telos*. He said that we need to take up our cross daily (Luke 9:23) but also that his yoke is easy and his burden light (Matt. 11:30). That is because he goes beside us as we carry his yoke (a cross-shaped beam used to join cattle). It is *his presence with us* that is a good infinitely more valuable than any worldly success or comfort. We know this from the Beatitudes, which call "blessed" those whom the world would call cursed (Matt. 5:1–12, and even more clearly Luke 6:20–23).

When we join our sufferings to his, he also grants us the dignity of participating in his saving sacrifice. Remember that his "stewardship of the body" meant not only poverty and celibacy but allowing himself to be mocked, whipped, and tortured to death! Paul followed in his Master's footsteps joyfully, recognizing that ultimately, the "body" he was stewarding was the *body of Christ*: "Now I rejoice in my sufferings for your sake, and in my flesh I complete what is lacking in Christ's afflictions for the sake of his body, that is, the church" (Col. 1:24 RSV).

Christians, with their understanding of the cross, are in a unique position to imbue suffering with meaning. Not only can our sufferings bring *us* closer to Jesus, but they also, in an ineffably mysterious way, help us join with Christ in redeeming *others*.

Restoration: No More Tears, No More Pain

The great promise of Christianity, the one through which it transformed and continues to transform the world, is that the cross is the gateway to the resurrection of perfect, eternal joy. The year my (Perry's) body betrayed me so that I could not sit or walk for more than twenty minutes, I began attending a house church, since I had to lie down to worship. I remember crying when I heard the lyrics to a particular song speaking of the coming promise—no more tears, no more pain. We know the end of God's great story: "He will wipe every tear from their eyes. There will be no more death or mourning or crying or pain, for the old order of things has passed away" (Rev. 21:4). The fallenness of our bodies will be no more.

Our bodies will eventually betray all of us. That certainty is in fact a great gift. It reminds us that compared to heaven, our true home, this earthly life is merely, in Saint Teresa of Avila's wonderful metaphor, "a bad night in a bad inn." It helps us say, "Dear Jesus, I may not be very happy about *my* body right now, but I am grateful to be a living member of *your* body!" We remember the promise of bodily glory proclaimed by Paul: "But our citizenship is in heaven. And we eagerly await a Savior from there, the Lord Jesus Christ, who, by the power that enables him to bring everything under his control, will transform our lowly *bodies* so that they will be like his glorious *body*" (Phil. 3:20–21—emphasis added). Come, Lord Jesus.

Chapter 2
Savoring and Stewarding Food

Lisa Graham McMinn

D inner at Fern Creek—the little farm my husband, Mark, and I tend together—provides a diverse sensory experience. It is not unusual for "hmmm"s and sighs to accompany our savoring of, let's say, roasted acorn squash stuffed with wild rice, chanterelles we foraged from forests not far away, dried blueberries from the summer harvest, roasted hazelnuts, sautéed onions and garlic from the root cellar, and herbs from the kitchen garden. The colors, aromas, flavors, and textures of good food consumed in good company turn eating into a communion of sorts that feeds our bodies and relationships with tangible, nutritious gratitude. When we mindfully expand what makes food "good" to include what encourages the flourishing of the soil, plants, and animals from which our food comes, then we are humbly reminded that we belong to and depend on something bigger than ourselves for our well-being.

We all steward our bodies (and our collective "body") with daily food choices. It is, after all, required that we eat to keep going at all. Since many of Mark's and my meals come from what we grow and then preserve in one way or another, savoring and stewarding food comes relatively easily for us. Not many have—or want—our kind of life, and so making connections and giving honor to the mostly invisible processes, people, and animals that provide the food that fuels our bodies takes more intention.

Caveat: I'm a sociologist who can't think about personal well-being without considering social contexts. Take an illustrative journey with me, if you will, to get into my head. Imagine being lost in a forest on day ten without food (since you've never been taught to eat what the forest offers those lost in the woods). You happen upon a fishing pole and bait beside a lake and manage to catch a trout that jumps and splashes and fights, sending ripples to the grassy bank at your feet (the ripples are more poetic than relevant, although we might all be served by attending to ripples caused by our actions). Your weak and hungry body will be made stronger by the trout, who must die so that you might live. Aquatic and terrestrial insects, smaller fish, crustaceans, leeches, and worms must die so that the trout might live. Algae and zooplankton must die so that the insects and small fish might live, and so it goes. Something has to die for you to live.[1] Something has to die for anything to live. Even some algae live off decaying dead things—a necessary cleanup crew joining dung beetles, slugs, vultures, and hyenas, to name a few other members of this important tribe. Old trees eventually fall, making room for and feeding new ones, and they feed a myriad of other beings besides—both when they are living and after they die. Death makes room for life.

That is worth pausing over. Something sacred and holy surrounds that truth.

This is also worth pausing over: we need the algae, worms, and leeches—the whole of the lake—to stay healthy that we might stay healthy. If we eat a trout made toxic by junk dumped into the lake, it's not going to contribute to our wellness. In fact, it may make us *unwell*. While self-interest isn't my primary argument, it sometimes provides a necessary nudge—a starting place.

You may be ready to quit this chapter, not wanting a guilt-inducing excursion down the food chain. *This will not be that.* Rather, I invite you to take a different look at what it means to be stewards of our

---

1 Yes, a vegetarian or vegan argument can rightly be made that humans don't have to eat animals to live, and yes, animals and plants are different types of creatures. But stick with the notion that something has to die for other beings to live.

bodies around food. How might Christian thoughtfulness about the body fuel we consume to keep breathing, thinking, loving, and doing contribute to our spiritual, emotional, and physical well-being? How might bringing intention to our eating contribute to joy and hope and healing? How might it also, inadvertently or intentionally, contribute to the well-being of the whole shebang?

Eating Well for One's Own Sake

Books containing knowledge about eating well for one's own sake sit on shelves of every bookstore and library. Michael Pollan offers a good three-point summary of those I've found most helpful: "Eat food [real food, not heavily processed foodstuff unrecognizable by your grandmother], not too much, mostly plants."[2]

By now we all know that sugar is bad, but so are artificial sweeteners. We shouldn't eat white flour, too many saturated fats, and too much salt. We know vegetables and fruits are good, especially ones that don't come in cans and aren't heavily sprayed with pesticides, herbicides, and petroleum-based fertilizers. Whole grains are good, as are lean meats. We know all this, but culturally we also consider eating a private matter and one that is not particularly relevant to our faith. Given those two cultural assumptions, we resist being schooled in how to eat.

So how does one get inspired and maybe inspire one's house- or roommates to make different choices? Perhaps by examining our norms and traditions with a soft and curious light rather than a piercing spotlight of inquisition. My hope is to invite you into a conversation about our assumptions and relationship with food because optimistically—deep down for some and near the surface for others—I believe our souls hunger for something better, something that is good not only for the palate and gut, heart and liver, but also for our near and distant kin.

---

2 Michael Pollan, *In Defense of Food: An Eater's Manifesto* (New York: Penguin, 2009), 1.

Eating: A Private or Public Matter?
Relevant to Faith or Not?

Wendell Berry (who is unapologetically *not* invitational in his approach) challenged the assumption that eating is a private matter when he called it an agricultural act, which is by nature communal rather than private.[3] What might change if we knew how choices we made with our food dollars impacted our local economies, farmers and food producers in our region, and farmers and food producers in ever-widening circles that cross continents and oceans? What if we chose to learn one story about how a food we eat gets to our plate? Maybe we start with bananas. John Soluri[4] offered a six-minute TED-Ed talk that summarizes the darker side of the banana trade's history, though much has been written about it as well. Chocolate, coffee, sugar, tomatoes, wheat, corn—any one of these can be explored with an internet search that pairs words such as "story of" with "environmental justice" or "socio-economic justice." Once you walk down the path of one story, you may feel inclined to look at others. Eventually, you may look behind the curtain at the misery of chickens, pigs, and cows in our industrial food complex and feel compelled to make different choices regarding who supplies you with the animals, milk, and eggs you eat as well as if (or how often) you consume them.

While eating may be a private choice, humble curiosity can help us connect the rippling between our private choices and their public impacts. If we come to see that our membership, and thus obligation, is to something broader than our own self-interest, the conversation shifts to include matters of our faith.

---

3 Wendell Berry, "The Pleasures of Eating," in *The Art of the Commonplace: The Agrarian Essays of Wendell Berry* (Emeryville, CA: Shoemaker & Hoard, 2002).

4 John Soluri, *Banana Cultures: Agriculture, Consumption and Change in Honduras and the United States* (Austin: University of Texas Press, 2021); or watch Soluri's TED-Ed talk, John Soluri, "The Dark History of Bananas," TED-Ed, November 2, 2020, YouTube video, 6:02, https://www.youtube.com/watch?v=esvycD1O3cM.

Western Christians have not much considered a theology of eating. Theologian Norman Wirzba invites us to consider how food and faith belong together beyond respecting and tending our bodies as God's temples. Wirzba provided a foundation for that conversation in *Food and Faith: A Theology of Eating*, where he invites readers to consider food as one of God's abiding ways of expressing divine provision and care: "We don't really understand food until we perceive, receive, and taste it in terms of its origin and end in God as the one who provides for, communes with, and ultimately reconciles creation. Created life is God's love made tastable and given for the good of another. The mundane act of eating is thus a daily invitation to move responsibly and gratefully within this given life. It is a summons to commune with the divine Life that is presupposed and made manifest in every bite."[5] Every time we eat of God's tastable love we have an opportunity to pause in gratitude and to allow that place of gratitude to lead us toward living and eating responsibly in response.

Eating can remind us of God's earthy, immanently present grace. All that is required is waking up to it, paying attention. After reflecting on the wonder of eating foraged mushrooms, lamb, and simple green and yellow beans, poet Mary Oliver remarks, "How calmly, as though it were an ordinary thing, we eat the blessed earth."[6] To pay attention is to eat with intention, recognizing that what we easily take for granted, while seemingly ordinary, is a manifestation of God's grace in the world.

What if we saw eating as a sacred partaking of God's goodness? Maybe if we curiously explored the wonders, as well as the hard particulars, of the food chain, we might ultimately bow our heads in awe of and gratitude for God's web of life that feeds us all.[7] The hard particulars, as I've hinted at already, stay largely invisible because

5 Norman Wirzba, *Food and Faith: A Theology of Eating* (New York: Cambridge University Press, 2011), xii.
6 Mary Oliver, "Beans Green and Yellow," in *Swan: Poems and Prose Poems* (Boston: Beacon, 1994), 16.
7 Lisa Graham McMinn, *To the Table: A Spirituality of Food, Farming, and Community* (Grand Rapids, MI: Brazos, 2016).

only a sadistic person would be eager to learn about the magnitude of animal and human suffering that is an integral part of big agribusiness, which developed to feed the Western world cheaply and efficiently. We don't have to drill down far in that direction to be compelled to steward our bodies through food differently. It turns out that when we eat in ways that are good for the blessed earth and good for our neighbors, it is also good for us.

Savoring and Stewarding Community through Food

The autumn equinox comes on or around September 21, the date when the night and day are equally long on account of where Earth is in her annual journey around the sun. The autumn equinox corresponds with nearing the end of the harvest, and Mark and I, not unlike generations of human cultures before us, celebrate it with autumn foods and friends. Some years this is a simple gathering and some years (one in particular) a memorable extravaganza. That year, Kara, one of our farm interns, wanted to celebrate the wrapping up of our farming season by sharing some of the bounty in a meal with friends. Kara helped me pull off a dinner for nine in the tree house, which meant ascending and descending the wood ladder with card tables, chairs, linens, dishes, lights, lanterns, and three magnificent courses of food. We started with a kale, pickled beet, hazelnut, and feta salad, drizzled with a balsamic vinegar reduction and olive oil. Sautéed heirloom cherry tomatoes with basil and homemade butternut-squash ravioli topped with sage browned butter followed the salads, and pumpkin bread pudding with dulce de leche (simmered down for hours a couple days before) completed our meal. We ate slowly and with purpose, savoring our food and one another's company. Conversation flowed, and we brought intention to how we leaned and listened to one another. At one point, one of the guests—who had had a hard week—interrupted the table conversation to say, "This is feeding my soul in a very significant way. Every. Single. Bite."

Something happens when we share a meal with another or others. Not surprisingly, multiple studies have demonstrated links between eating together and physical, emotional, and social well-being.[8] In part, we discover a grace-filled gift that comes with making room for others and having others make room for us. We accept responsibility for another's well-being and have others do the same for us. The sense of belonging and being cared for provides scaffolding to help us negotiate the trials and challenges that come with living. Eating together around a common table where we have been welcomed to come, take our place, sit, and be filled, seen, and heard reminds us that we belong to something bigger than ourselves. We are not alone. Eating involves a pleasurable way of communing. We are invited to let others care for us, which renews and reminds us that we have the capacity to care for others.

Imagine again being ten days lost and hungry in the forest. What shifts in your sense of aloneness and despair when, rather than coming across a fishing pole and bait, you come across someone who has already caught, cleaned, and cooked a trout and asks you to join their meal by the fire?

In her history of Christianity, Diana Butler Bass argued that unlike most contested ideas in the early church, "the unanimous witness of the ancient fathers and mothers was that hospitality was the primary Christian virtue."[9] Hospitality involved caring for the sick, orphaned, and widowed as well as welcoming the stranger. Such hospitality always involved feeding people.

Stewarding community through hospitality, through the feeding of one another, runs deep in the bones of our faith. Communion painted in broader strokes depicts a *membership*, as Berry and Wirzba are fond of saying. Eating in community acknowledges various memberships: we belong to God, are members of the *Homo sapiens sapiens* clan (wise humans), and share God's created and good Earth with other animal and plant clans. All of Earth's members depend on being able to sup from a global table that offers good water, clean air, and

8 Nicole Visnic, "Never Eat Alone! The Benefits of Eating with Others," Brain-World Magazine, last modified July 30, 2019, https://brainworldmagazine.com/never-eat-alone-the-benefits-of-eating-with-others/.

9 Diana Butler Bass, *A People's History of Christianity* (New York: HarperOne, 2009).

fertile soil. Wirzba[10] invites us to get to know and appreciate these memberships and then to live sympathetically and compassionately into them.

That invitation moves us beyond hospitality extended to a table of our peers. We begin to consider how we steward the commons when it comes to our assumptions about eating, which sends ripples to members living out their lives lower on the food chain.

Savoring and Stewarding the Commons: Eating with Gratitude

In *Braiding Sweetgrass*, Robin Wall Kimmerer, an environmental biology professor and member of the Citizen Potawatomi Nation, writes about the Onondaga school, where students learn the values and the way of life of their ancestors. The students begin and end their school week as a community pledging gratitude together, with different grades reciting different verses. This gratitude pledge, or Thanksgiving Address, offers the "Words That Come Before All Else" and begins by naming the people's duty to live in balance and harmony, ending each stanza with "and now our minds are one."[11] It is a long recitation.

The Onondaga begin with thankfulness to the Earth, who gives everything needed for life, and offer gratitude toward the waters of the world, the fish life in the water, the vast fields of plant life, the medicinal herbs of the world, the families of trees, all the animal life, the birds, the powers of the four winds, the sun and moon and stars, the teachers, and the Creator. The final verse before the conclusion of the Thanksgiving Address ends with this: "For all the love that is still around us, we gather our minds together as one and send our choicest words of greetings and thanks to the Creator. Now our minds are one."[12] Christian community builders could learn from the common grace demonstrated within this community.

---

10 Wirzba, *Food and Faith*.

11 Robin Wall Kimmerer, *Braiding Sweetgrass: Indigenous Wisdom, Scientific Knowledge and the Teachings of Plants* (Minneapolis, MN: Milkweed Editions, 2013), 107–17.

12 Kimmerer, 115.

How might it shape one's sense of membership, obligation, generosity, contentment, and belongingness to be guided by words known by memory and spoken in community regularly? How might it shape how we harvest? Or how we shop for the food we will consume?

Gratitude permeates Kimmerer's work. She describes relationships of reciprocity between people and other members of our earthy community. She writes about harvesting honorably and offering a gift in return for a plant or animal taken. She speaks of trees as neighbors, plants and animals as teachers, and all of it as a beloved community. *Braiding Sweetgrass* made it to the *New York Times* Best Sellers list in January 2020. (As of November 2022, it had been on the list for 132 weeks.) In an interview about her six-year-old book making it to the *New York Times* Best Sellers list, Kimmerer said, "When a book with a message like that hits the best sellers list I can only be hopeful that means that these ideas have adherents. . . . There are places in *Braiding Sweetgrass* where I ask, 'Aren't we a better species than this?' and for the book to be doing so well gives me the answer that 'Yes, yes we are.'"[13] Yes. We can be more grateful and compassionate. The success of Kimmerer's book suggests a groundswell of people want to be a better species than we've been, to live and eat with more gratitude, less entitlement, and more reciprocity. And we can get there graciously, through curiosity that seeks greater understanding rather than through blanket judgment on our—and our parents' or grandparents'—prior choices. Of course, our grandparents and parents would have been attracted to foods that cost less money. For starters, they would have argued they were being "responsible consumers" for shopping the bargains. They didn't know what they didn't know.

Our parents and grandparents *did* know farming and husbandry had become more efficient, and that efficiency saved them money at the grocery store. Agribusiness developed and expanded gradually and outside the purview of the public eye. For example, until concerned,

---

13 Karen B. Moore, "Dr. Robin Kimmerer's Braiding Sweetgrass Hits *New York Times* Best Selling List," SUNY College of Environmental Science and Forestry, last modified February 5, 2020, https://www.esf.edu/communications/view2.asp?newsID=8595.

inquisitive people began investigating concentrated animal feeding operations (CAFOs), we did not know the profound animal misery required for us to eat eggs, chickens, pigs, and cows so cheaply. Pleading ignorance to that information is a choice to look away from what is known more than an inability to know. Choosing to be a better species—to be compassionate and responsible eaters—is borne out of embracing and understanding our connections and memberships and moving, living, and eating with gratitude for them.

As we gain awareness about the great and invisible cost of those bargains, we have the choice to be, as Kimmerer, Berry, and Wirzba suggest, a more neighborly species. A growing awareness around health and food ethics has exploded our options, making it more possible to be intentional about reciprocal relationships and to approach eating with a deep and broad gratitude.

"Fair Trade," "organic," "GMO-free," and "free range" are terms that have become familiar to most of us. Although more compassionate and intentional options are available, there is controversy about whether plant-based eating is on the rise. Some evidence suggests that it is,[14] though with varying definitions (e.g., if one eats turkey on Thanksgiving, is one still a vegetarian? If one eats fish?), it's hard to measure trends. Still, the number of self-identified vegetarians has been on a slow rise since 2013.[15] When asked why they changed the way they eat, people offer explanations including personal health, a growing concern about climate change, and food-related ethics. I'd like to think some would also say they are motivated by gratitude for the gift of life and want to eat in compassionate, neighborly ways. As the mostly invisible stories around our food get told, our capacity to care, to feel gratitude, and to want to be compassionate eaters has an opportunity to get expressed. Humans have more choice over how and what we eat than squirrels, vultures, and bobcats. Given our

14 Caryn Ginsberg, "Is the Number of Vegetarians on the Rise?," Faunalytics, last modified September 26, 2018, https://faunalytics.org/is-the-number-of -vegetarians-on-the-rise/.
15 Saulius Šimčikas, "Is the Percentage of Vegetarians and Vegans in the US Increasing?," Animal Charity Evaluators, last modified August 16, 2018, https:// animalcharityevaluators.org/blog/is-the-percentage-of-vegetarians-and-vegans -in-the-u-s-increasing/.

capability to choose, we can be a better species. A good number of food-related companies have taken that aspiration on with intention.

Theo Chocolate, a Seattle-based chocolatier, is an example of a company committed to being neighborly at every step of their operation. The website mission statement says, "From the cocoa farmer in the Congo, to the truck driver in Seattle, and the chocolate lover in Philadelphia, we believe there is a thread that runs through us all. The choices we make here in Seattle touch lives across the planet in real and lasting ways. That knowledge, and that responsibility, drives us to do things in ways that contribute towards a more compassionate and enduring world."[16] The website details their commitment to third-party verification (for wages, working conditions, and environmental impact), stable pricing (opting out of the global-commodity market guarantees the cocoa farmers with whom they work a stable price for their cocoa rather than subjecting them to the global market's volatility), and full transparency along their entire supply chain.

As consumers of food, we communicate our Christian convictions by how we spend our dollars. Once awakened to what we didn't know, we can spend differently; recognize our memberships; and choose gratitude, honor, and compassion over efficiency, low prices, and ignorance. Our daily food choices not only influence our health; they also shape what kind of people we become, what kind of assumptions and entitlements we claim, how we see ourselves in the world, and how we behave in our relationships to near and distant kin. Our ordinary choices shape our spiritual selves and the spiritual well-being of other members—visible and less visible—in our earthy membership.

Conclusion

I offer a final image and claim in closing. Paul and John assume in the New Testament that Christ created all things, gives life to all things, fills all things, is *in* all things, *and holds all things together* and that, as the psalmist declares in Psalm 139, "there is nowhere that God

---

16 "Mission & Values," Theo Chocolate, accessed June 9, 2022, https://theochocolate.com/mission-values.

is not." One could then surmise that the Living Word, Christ, is in our bodies—in all bodies—infusing all creation with life. The Eastern Orthodox tradition holds that everything is a reflection of God, making all creation sacred.[17]

This is not pantheism, which would assert that the oak tree in my backyard (for instance) is God. Rather, this version of panentheism seeks to embrace the difficult mystery that God transcends this created universe, existing outside of it *while also* being deeply immanent within it. Steven Bouma-Prediger suggests that God's relatedness to us *depends* on God being other than us[18] and also that Christ is *in* and holding every atom and subatomic particle of creation together. The tendency of Western Christianity has been to focus overly much on the transcendence of God over creation rather than the immanence of God within all of it—that God holds all things together. Scholarship in evangelical ecotheology encourages us to hold a healthy emphasis on both.[19] My invitation is to let yourself be enchanted by this mystery and to imagine how that might change the way you live, including how you eat.

So here's the image: What if you saw yourself as God's only chance to experience life in you, as you? What if you are, in more than a figurative sense, truly a temple, a home of God? What if God gets to delight in the taste of a fresh crisp apple when you eat one? Might God experience the bellyache that comes from eating too many apples, or too much beef, or food that has come from unnecessary suffering?

Christians hold that humans have a particular way we bear the image of God and are the temple of the Holy Spirit. A deep immanence, as reflected by the Eastern Orthodox tradition and newer work in ecotheology, would also have us imagine that something of God is *in* the green bean, the chicken, the cow, the cocoa, the sugar

---

17 John Chryssavgis, *Creation as Sacrament: Reflections on Ecology and Spirituality* (New York: T&T Clark, 2019).

18 Steven Bouma-Prediger, *The Greening of Theology* (Atlanta: Scholars Press, 1995).

19 Daniel L. Brunner, Jennifer L. Butler, and A. J. Swoboda, *Introducing Evangelical Ecotheology* (Grand Rapids, MI: Baker Academic, 2014).

beet, holding them together; they too reflect something of God and, as such, are sacred.

God called this astounding universe into existence and sustains it. Everything in this wildly extravagant world would cease existing if God turned away. But God doesn't turn away and won't turn away. Our proper response to that kind of relational love is gratitude.

Holding to that, here's my (maybe) audacious claim: compounded goodness and well-being showers down on our own physical selves and the selves of whatever we eat when we eat with a gratitude that recognizes how our consumption is interwoven with the plant, animal, and human communities with whom we share our common home. The more our choices help them flourish, the more we will also flourish. When we eat with gratitude for the God who called all this into being, and sustains it with God's lovingkindness, our eating can become a form of grateful participation in living.

Come to the table and eat ("real food, mostly plants, not too much"[20]) and drink and be satisfied and filled with gratitude and joy.

---

20 Pollan, *In Defense of Food*, 1.

Chapter 3

Stewarding Our Limitations

Receiving God's Gift of Sleep

Lisa Igram

I sat in a large circle with the students, sharing findings from our first issuance of the National College Health Assessment (NCHA) in over fifteen years. We had initiated the assessment to better understand our students' physical and emotional well being, as recommended by an external review of our student health center. The results confirmed what many of us had suspected over the last several years: high numbers of our students reported experiencing feelings of anxiety, depression, stress, and being overwhelmed.[1]

We needed to hear what our students were thinking when they saw the data and considered their own experiences. As I sat with this group of senators in our Student Government Association, I was reminded that this data was sobering. Our staff worked with struggling students daily, and I had become used to these realities. As I asked questions about what this bright group of student leaders noticed in the data, I struggled to generate conversation—they found the information meaningful but were unsure of what to say beyond affirming that the data resonated with them. I began to worry I was

---

1 Note that these items did not elicit self-reporting of clinical diagnoses but rather asked students to self-report feelings of anxiety, depression, stress, overwhelm, and sadness over a set period of time.

contributing to these students' anxiety by sharing how overwhelmed their peers were!

And then I clicked to the slide on students' experiences of sleep—or, rather, their lack thereof. After a brief pause, the room *lit up*. Conversation rippled around the circle as tangibly as if we were doing "the wave" at Friday's baseball game. Affirmative groans, side comments to neighbors, and knowing laughter filled the room. I watched the ripple for a moment or so and then asked, "OK, tell me what's going on here. What are you seeing?" What followed was a rich discussion on the world of sleep among students at Biola University. And I learned something critical that day: students *love* talking about sleep.

My mind whirled: that year, I had been charged with starting a new "Student Wellness" area at our institution and championing proactive, preventative strategies to support student well-being at all levels of institutional policy and practice. Our vice president wisely encouraged me to look for "low-hanging fruit" along the way. The research suggested that focusing on sleep education might help moderate our increasing number of emotional care cases and offer proactive support for academic success.[2] In an effort to capitalize on student eagerness to talk about sleep, our annual Sleep Week was born.

Following that conversation, an internal qualitative study on our students' perceptions of sleep and well-being, and three annual Sleep Weeks since, we have learned a few things about our students and their relationships with sleep. What follow are just a few observations around the value of and barriers to sleep among students, theological implications that are integral for those of us at faith-based institutions, and possible next steps to consider in how student life professionals can help address students' sleep deficits on our college campuses.

---

2 Monica E. Hartmann and J. Roxanne Prichard, "Calculating the Contribution of Sleep Problems to Undergraduates' Academic Success," *Sleep Health: Journal of the National Sleep Foundation* 4, no. 5 (October 1, 2018): 463–71, find that sleep difficulties are just as, if not more, detrimental to student academic success than stress and binge-drinking, both of which are more often the focus of wellness programming on university campuses.

Sleep and Holistic Well-Being

When it comes to healthy sleep habits, undergrads at my university (and I would guess at your institution) are not much different from students across the nation. The best research indicates that college students (ages eighteen to twenty-five) need seven to nine hours of sleep each night.[3] Nationwide results from the 2021 National College Health Assessment indicate that 46.9 percent of undergraduate respondents receive six hours or less of weeknight sleep, and 22.7 percent indicate that sleep difficulties impacted their performance in a class.[4] Students also indicate a desire for sleep education; two-thirds of respondents marked "sleep difficulties" as a health-related topic they wanted to learn more about from their institutions.[5] The research is clear on the value of good sleep for fostering the holistic health and well-being of our college students; what follows is a *very* brief review of sleep's value for physical, relational, and emotional well-being, as well as academic performance.

Sleep Supports Mental and Emotional Health

Sleep recalibrates the chemicals in the brain (especially norepinephrine) that determine our ability to engage well emotionally. Insufficient sleep can lead to stress, anxiety, risky behavior, anger, confusion, depression, fatigue, and a higher likelihood of using

3 Nathaniel F. Watson et al., "Recommended Amount of Sleep for a Healthy Adult: A Joint Consensus Statement of the American Academy of Sleep Medicine and Sleep Research Society," *Sleep* 38, no. 6 (June 1, 2015): 843–44.

4 American College Health Association—National College Health Assessment III, *Undergraduate Student Reference Group Data* (Silver Spring, MD: American College Health Association, 2022), https://www.acha.org/documents/ncha/NCHA-III_FALL_2021_UNDERGRADUATE_REFERENCE_GROUP_DATA_REPORT.pdf.

5 American College Health Association—National College Health Assessment II, *Undergraduate Student Reference Group Executive Summary Spring 2018* (Silver Spring, MD: American College Health Association, Spring 2018), https://www.acha.org/NCHA/ACHA-NCHA_Data/Publications_and_Reports/NCHA/Data/Reports_ACHA-NCHAIIc.aspx.

prescribed and over-the-counter stimulants.[6] Research indicates that students who get less sleep present "more symptoms of psychological maladjustment."[7] In a study on the impact of sleep on brain functioning, scans of amygdala activity suggested that "a night of sleep may 'reset' appropriate brain reactivity to next-day emotional challenges."[8] One study assessed the efficacy of a cognitive-behavioral sleep program against a cognitive-behavioral stress and resilience program. When comparing students in both groups whose pretests revealed poor sleep scores, those participating in the sleep program demonstrated "greater improvements in sleep quality *and* greater reduction in depressive symptoms" than those participating in the resilience program.[9] Sleep can be a powerful protector and moderator of our emotional well-being. Given the rise in mental health concerns, both prior to and exacerbated by the COVID-19 pandemic, education about and behavior change toward quality sleep will likely be helpful strategies in supporting students' emotional well-being.

Sleep Supports Relational Health

Sleep enhances our ability to engage well in relationships, and healthy relationships are something for which our students long. A fascinating series of studies indicates that good sleep correlates with healthier

6 Hannah G. Lund et al., "Sleep Patterns and Predictors of Disturbed Sleep in a Large Population of College Students," *Journal of Adolescent Health* 46, no. 2 (February 2010): 124–32; Gabriel Natan Pires et al., "Effects of Acute Sleep Deprivation on State Anxiety Levels: A Systematic Review and Meta-analysis," *Sleep Medicine* 24 (August 2016): 109–18.

7 W. Kelly, K. E. Kelly, and R. Clanton, "The Relationship between Sleep Length and Grade Point Average among College Students," *College Student Journal* 35, no. 1 (2001): 84.

8 Seung-Schik Yoo et al., "The Human Emotional Brain without Sleep—a Prefrontal Amygdala Disconnect," *Current Biology* 17, no. 20 (October 2007): 877–78.

9 Mickey Trockel et al., "An E-Mail Delivered CBT for Sleep-Health Program for College Students: Effects on Sleep Quality and Depression Symptoms," *Journal of Clinical Sleep Medicine* 7, no. 3 (June 15, 2011): 276–81.

relationships—and, in particular, romantic relationships.[10] Given the value of sleep to help foster a positive outlook and resiliency in facing emotional challenges, it makes sense that our relationships benefit from a good night's rest!

Sleep Supports Physical Health

Sleep is critical to the work of our immune systems; not getting enough sleep results in a decrease in white blood cells that help fend off viruses such as the cold or flu.[11] Over time, physical health risks of sleep deprivation include hypertension, increased possibilities for heart attack and stroke, and the development of type 2 diabetes.[12] Adequate sleep supports the physical health needed for students to be well enough to attend classes as well as meaningfully engage in learning through class participation, exams, and papers.

Sleep Supports Academic Performance

Sleep impacts students' academic performance in that it improves the consolidation and encoding of memories, supports the ability to sustain attention, and "facilitates generalization of knowledge."[13] One study found that "sleep disturbances were found to be a signifi- cant independent predictor of academic problems; on average, each additional day per week that a student experienced sleep problems

10 Studies on the correlation of sleep and healthy relationships reviewed in Joshua W. Madsen et al., "Romantic Relationship Satisfaction Is Associated with Sleep in Undergraduate Students," *Couple and Family Psychology: Research and Practice,* June 3, 2021, 1–16, https://doi.org/10.1037/cfp0000163.

11 Hui Liu et al., "Effects of Sleep and Sleep Deprivation on Blood Cell Count and Hemostasis Parameters in Healthy Humans," *Journal of Thrombosis and Thrombolysis* 28, no. 1 (July 2009): 46–49.

12 Francisco Lopez-Jimenez, "Sleep Deprivation: A Cause of High Blood Pres- sure?," Mayo Clinic, accessed October 25, 2022, https://www.mayoclinic.org/ diseases-conditions/high-blood-pressure/expert-answers/sleep-deprivation/ faq-20057959.

13 Björn Rasch and Jan Born, "About Sleep's Role in Memory," *Physiological Reviews* 93, no. 2 (April 2013): 681–766; K. Ahrberg et al., "The Interaction between Sleep Quality and Academic Performance," *Journal of Psychiatric Research* 46, no. 12 (December 2012): 1618–22, 1618.

raised the probability of dropping a course by 10% and lowered cumulative GPA by 0.02."[14] Another study reports that students who got more sleep (nine-plus hours) maintained or achieved higher GPAs than students who got six hours or less.[15] On realizing that education about a matter does not necessarily shift behavior, one Baylor faculty offered extra credit to prompt students to get eight hours of sleep each night during finals week. After statistically correcting for students' prior average grades, "sleeping 8 hours was associated with a four-point grade boost—even prior to applying extra credit."[16]

Connections between sleep, holistic well-being, and academic performance—alongside students' desire for information on sleep hygiene—tell us that providing education on healthy sleep habits and intervention for those with sleep disturbances will be fruitful for our students' personal growth and academic success.

Barriers to Sleep

Students seem to love talking about sleep; the research is clear that good sleep supports emotional and physical health as well as academic success. What, then, are the barriers to receiving a good night's rest? Space does not allow for rich description of the nuances of individual student lives, but a few broad themes may provide a helpful starting point in discussing our students' experiences and needs.

14 Hartmann and Prichard, "Calculating the Contribution," 463–71.

15 Kelly, Kelly, and Clanton, "Relationship between Sleep Length," 84–86.

16 Baylor University, "Students Who Met '8-Hour Sleep Challenge' Got Extra Points—But They Didn't Need Them, Thanks to Superior Snoozing, Baylor Studies Find," news release, December 3, 2018, https://www.baylor.edu/mediacommunications/news.php?action=story&story=205058; Michael K. Scullin, "The Eight Hour Sleep Challenge during Final Exams Week," *Teaching of Psychology* 46, no. 1 (January 2019): 55–63.

The Triangle Meme: A Multiplicity of "Goods"

As our conversations around this theme of sleep developed with students, one particularly astute student asked, "Have you seen that one triangle meme?" I had not, so they shared: each of the triangle's points was given a title: "Good Grades," "Social Life," and "Enough Sleep." The caption read, "College: You Can Only Choose Two." This meme, they said, reflected their peers' thinking: students come to school to learn, get ready to land a good job, and build community. There isn't time to sleep for one-third of each twenty-four-hour day and accomplish their goals for college.

Later that day I found a number of memes carrying a similar message—there are many, and some are outright funny. But one in particular stopped me in my tracks, as it illustrates succinctly what this bright student observed and what I have heard from overwhelmed students over the years. The same triangle meme was titled "How People Think It Is." But next to the triangle was a decagon titled "How It Really Is," with its ten points listing friends, class, work, family, homework, sleep, hobbies, food, extracurricular activities (resume builders, volunteering), and love life. The caption read, "Attempt to do everything until stress takes over and things start slipping and you end up crying in your bed deciding to do none of it and just watch T.V. to attempt to escape to somewhere else."

A multiplicity of "goods," promoted to our students by university culture and broader culture, compete for our students' attention, time, and energy. In our faith-based context, these goods are often overlaid with a spiritual imperative, fostering a perception that a "good Christian" should be able to do all these things and more, especially for the sake of the Kingdom. A vague sense of guilt can plague those who don't or can't do it all. The challenge of balancing so many needs (some of our students need to work to pay for school or carry responsibilities for siblings at home) and values (there is no end to what can be done to spread the Kingdom of God) is overwhelming. Throughout each day, as our students struggle with competing priorities and a fear of missing out (FOMO)—focusing on classes, jobs, internships, ministry, and friends—sacrificing sleep to write that paper or study for that exam can seem like an easy choice. All-nighters, suggests one study, lead students to *think* they are performing well, even though adequate sleep would have allowed them to demonstrate higher levels of cognitive performance in their studies.[17] No wonder one student shared that getting good sleep feels like a luxury.

Racing Minds

For many of our students, the answer to getting more sleep may not simply be our enthusiastic exhortation: "Sleep is good for you! Go to bed!" Feedback from our first Sleep Week highlighted another significant theme that keeps our students awake at night: racing minds. One student confided, "There are a lot of people who wake up all the time at night because they have so much going on that their brain doesn't shut off." Racing minds manifest in tense, tossing-and-turning bodies that are unable to relax as to-do lists, problems with friendships or family, or concerns over landing a summer job or internship bubble to the surface. Racing minds are a natural outcome of the sheer number of pressures facing students throughout the day as well as the developmental realities of emerging adults who are learning to navigate relationships, daily choices, and life decisions.

For some students, racing minds may be a product of how they manage day-to-day demands. For others, racing minds may be indicative of clinical mental health diagnoses such as anxiety or depression.[18] God created us as holistic beings: our sleep, mental and emotional well-being, and the ways we choose to live during the day all impact one another. Other chapters in this book are important elements of conversations around healthy sleep habits, particularly as we consider

---

17 June J. Pilcher and Amy S. Walters, "How Sleep Deprivation Affects Psychological Variables Related to College Students' Cognitive Performance," *Journal of American College Health* 46, no. 3 (November 1997): 121–26.

18 Depression may also be associated with *too much* sleep, though such sleep may not provide the rest one actually needs. Students who regularly sleep far more than the recommended seven to nine hours should certainly be seen by a physician or a counselor, depending on the situation.

sleep-promoting practices and resources for our campuses. Mental health concerns are skillfully addressed in Stephen Beers and Lea Hart's chapter on anxiety, Connie Horton's on depression, and Steve Conn's on mental health and the spiritual disciplines, and they are well worth taking into account for this conversation.

For those students who struggle with racing minds but may not meet the criteria for mental health diagnoses, conversations around mindfulness practices, exercise, play, rest, and/or Sabbath may be in order. Exercise has long been understood as beneficial to quality sleep,[19] and research indicates the benefits of exercise for college students during stressful times of the semester: to both reduce stress *and* enhance sleep.[20] For more, Andrew Borror's chapter on exercise is worth the read.

During our pandemic iteration of Sleep Week, a colleague wisely suggested that we may not need to focus on sleep as much as the larger concept of rest, which helps our bodies slow in preparation for nightly sleep. In our remote learning environment, where most of our students were stuck at home (as were we), the time needed for sleep was less of an issue; yet many still lacked consistent quality sleep.[21] They (and we) needed rest—breaks from the urgency and emergency of news headlines, a pause from screens to look out windows or take walks in fresh air, or intentional connections with loved

19 Christopher E. Kline, "The Bidirectional Relationship between Exercise and Sleep: Implications for Exercise Adherence and Sleep Improvement," *American Journal of Lifestyle Medicine* 8, no. 6 (November 2014): 375–79.

20 Kathrin Wunsch, Nadine Kasten, and Reinhard Fuchs, "The Effect of Physical Activity on Sleep Quality, Well-Being, and Affect in Academic Stress Periods," *Nature and Science of Sleep* 9 (April 2017): 117–26, http://dx.doi.org/10.2147/NSS.S132078.

21 Our anecdotal observations were affirmed in this study, which found that "students in the 2020 remote instruction semester slept later, less efficiently, less at night and more in the day, but did not sleep more overall despite online, asynchronous classes and ~44% fewer work days compared to students in previous summers." Andrea N. Smit et al., "Impact of COVID-19 Social-Distancing on Sleep Timing and Duration during a University Semester," *PLoS ONE* 16, no. 4 (April 26, 2021): 1.

ones. We needed to pause and breathe; we need the same in our postpandemic life.

In teaching on the spiritual disciplines of silence and solitude, I often bring along a closed jar of mud and water, carried carefully to the lecture hall or dorm lobby so that the water remains clear above a layer of settled mud. As I share what students might expect to experience as they enter into silence and solitude, I prompt them to write a quick sixty-second list of every activity that has filled their day or to-do list. I then ask them to point at the jar and shout each activity they wrote aloud, together in a glorious din, as I shake the jar with all my might. I place the jar on a desk, point at it, and say, "It's time for silence and solitude NOW!" As the muddy mess swirls, we guess how long it will *actually* take for the dirt to settle, for the water to become clear again (it is usually more than twenty-four hours).

And then we ponder this little illustration together. We run straight into the disciplines of silence and solitude and are surprised that we do not experience the peace we hope for; we crash into our beds at night and are surprised that our minds are racing, keeping us from falling asleep or waking us in the middle of the night. Our hearts, minds, and bodies need time to settle. Weekly Sabbath or cultivating a few daily moments of rest prepare us for a good night's sleep. Justin Whitmel Earley's chapter on Sabbath taking may be a helpful resource for students and staff who need to consider this rhythm as a way to address racing minds. Others may find that needed moments of rest and pause are cultivated in a structured bedtime routine, which is key to healthy sleep hygiene—closing curtains or lowering blinds, putting technology away at least fifteen minutes before bed, keeping consistent sleep times on weekdays and weekends, having a warm cup of herbal tea, and/or showering before bed. Over time, routines involving these kinds of practices signal to the body and mind that it is time to sleep.[22]

---

22 The Sleep Foundation offers suggestions for helpful sleep routines at "How to Build a Better Bedtime Routine for Adults," Sleep Foundation, January 8, 2021, https://www.sleepfoundation.org/sleep-hygiene/bedtime-routine-for-adults.

Reframing Limitation as a Spiritual Good

In a sense, these barriers stem from the foundational concept this book intends to address: the stewardship of our bodies as God's good gift to us. I am convinced that the *need* to steward our physical bodies through sleep, rest, food, exercise, and healthy relationships is not necessarily part of the Fall; rather, our physical limitations are part of God's good created order, and bodily stewardship is part of our calling as God's creation. Kelly Kapic wrote that Jesus incarnate is God's "yes" to our bodies and our bodies' limitations; after all, even Jesus slept and ate.[23] Even as God proclaimed the rest of his creation as "good," he proclaimed the human person—dependent, limited, and finite—as "*very* good" (Gen. 1:31—emphasis added).

And yet, we are products of a culture that promotes *conquering* bodily limits, pushing beyond whatever threatens to hold us back. Messages saying that we can "have it all" or exhorting "no limits," "Just Do It!" "You can sleep when you're dead," or "mind over matter" fill our earbuds and screens. After all, YOLO (you only live once), so no regrets! Tish Harris Warren wrote, "In our increasingly technological, workaholic, image-barraged, caffeinated, entertainment-addicted, super-charged culture, remembering our limited, embodied creatureliness is a difficult and necessary part of discipleship." In her work with graduate students, she noted that often the most spiritually helpful advice is to take care of their physical bodies and get more sleep.[24] One of my wise colleagues explicitly points out that giving our students permission to do *less* is a critical piece of the puzzle.

As culture tempts us to overlook the gifts of our creatureliness, we neglect to live within the interconnectedness of our minds, souls, and bodies as God's intention for creation and as a gift to us. We miss the ways that caring for our physical bodies allows God to form our

23 Kelly M. Kapic, *You're Only Human: How Your Limits Reflect God's Design and Why That's Good News* (Grand Rapids, MI: Brazos, 2022).
24 Tish Harris Warren, "The Well," *Spiritual Direction: Get More Sleep* (blog), October 29, 2013, https://thewell.intervarsity.org/blog/spiritual-direction-get -more-sleep.

souls. Jason McMartin suggests, "The spiritual significance of the physical act of sleep ought to be a relational trust that recognizes my place as a creature who depends on the grace of a self-sufficient provider."[25] When we sleep, we enter the eight hours of our day in which we cannot control outcomes or be productive; we leave our bodies to self-repair and replenish as God created them to do without our oversight; we leave God to take care of our daily worries and concerns. When we steward our physical bodies with sleep, we also engage in a spiritual practice of dependence on our Creator God, who needs no sleep (Ps. 121:4).

Strategies

God's gift of sleep is a means to refresh our bodies, minds, and souls. But how do we help our students address their own distorted views of sleep, much less help them move toward practices and habits that promote healthy sleep? There is no simple solution; processes of personal and communal growth and behavior change are layered and complex, and each of our campus cultures differs in context and need. We have found that promoting good sleep in discipling, mentoring, and/or clinical conversations with individuals and small groups is effective. Such conversations are most impactful when a student recognizes their need and, in relationship with others, considers next steps in the context of their whole lives. However, the following principles and strategies might be helpful to consider in your own context: attend to practical education, foster cross-campus collaboration, implement sleep promotion at multiple points of education and intervention, and together celebrate the gift of sleep.

---

25 Jason McMartin, "Sleep, Sloth, and Sanctification," *Journal of Spiritual Formation & Soul Care* 6, no. 2 (2013): 256.

Practical Education

I have noted throughout this chapter some educational elements that are helpful for many of our students. First, education around the value and God-given gift of sleep for our emotional, physical, academic, and spiritual well-being is invaluable to helping students understand sleep as an essential component of holistic well-being rather than a luxury. Second, students need practical skills, such as time management techniques and development of healthy sleep hygiene habits. Time management is a critical skill for getting good sleep; one of our students observed that homework or social connections not done or made during the day are accomplished in the late evening hours. Many of our students need to be guided through the basics of calendars and to-do lists. Skills for healthy sleep habits can also be developed. For example, encouraging students to make small changes toward a bedtime routine will help them foster good sleep.[26]

Cross-Campus Collaboration

Educating students is a campus-wide effort, and similar conversations around student concerns are often happening in multiple places on campus. Identify your on-campus experts, resources, and allies around students' experiences of sleep, and find ways to collaborate across departments and academic units. Several areas working together, even in small ways, can make a significant impact on campus culture.

Invite cross-departmental conversation on sleep with student life, the health center, the counseling center, and faculty colleagues whose expertise relates to holistic well-being (such as physical education, public health, psychology, nursing, or similar fields). What sleep education might students already be receiving in the classroom? What formal assessments might have been done by any of these areas that

26 Sleep Foundation, "How to Build."

offer insight into students' experiences of sleep? What individual conversations around sleep are faculty and staff already engaging in with students, and what might you be learning about your students' sleep habits? What themes emerge from these conversations that you can begin to address?

Draw on your campus experts to consider the following: What evidence-based strategies from professionals in the health center, counseling center, or relevant academic units may be helpful for your students? What small shifts can various departments make to help create a sleep-promoting culture on your campus? For example, faculty may be willing to adjust due times in your campus's learning management system, which is likely set to a default due time of midnight. Student health centers or counseling centers might offer "sleep kits" containing sleep information cards, lavender oil, sleep masks, and herbal tea. What can student life professionals glean from evidence-based strategies for larger-scale programming, and how might this programming reinforce the messaging and education students are receiving in other parts of the university?

Sleep Promotion at Multiple Points of Education and Intervention

The Institute of Medicine (IOM) Continuum of Care Model encourages practitioners to classify interventions aimed at various subgroups within a population—in part to clarify hoped-for prevention and treatment outcomes in a variety of contexts.[27] Following this model, addressing sleep concerns on our campus might include the following.

---

[27] Fred Springer and Joel Phillips, "The Institute of Medicine Framework and Its Implication for the Advancement of Prevention, Policy, Programs and Practice," Center for Applied Research Solutions, 2006, http://ca-sdfsc.org/docs/resources/SDFSC_IOM_Policy.pdf.

Universal Interventions

Universal interventions include campus-wide educational programming for the general student population as well as faculty and staff who are in positions to make adjustments to classroom practices. Embed education around the value of sleep and tips for healthy sleep hygiene in multiple areas on campus, such as chapels, orientation, awareness weeks, and residence-life programming. Repeated education and messaging, especially from peers, can be particularly valuable at this prevention level.

Selective Interventions

More selective interventions include targeted educational programming for particular groups that may be more "high risk" for sleep deprivation based on what you know of your campus. These may include student leaders, students in intense academic programs, or first-year students, many of whom may experience the need to say "yes" to many opportunities due to FOMO or are learning to care for themselves for the first time. Targeted education that includes opportunities to practice sleep-promoting behaviors together with small groups of peers may be embedded in areas such as student-leader training or first-year student courses or programming.

Indicated Interventions

Indicated interventions include targeted interventions for individual students who have identified sleep as a concern. The "stages of change" concept[28] indicates that students who come to you with sleep problems are positioned to make and sustain lifestyle changes to foster good sleep. In your conversations with these students around basic tips and tricks to foster healthy sleep, be attentive to more extreme concerns, such as whether a student struggles with recurring insomnia over time. Do not ever hesitate to refer

---

28 John C. Norcross, Paul M. Krebs, and James O. Prochaska, "Stages of Change," *Journal of Clinical Psychology* 67, no. 2 (2011): 143–54.

students to a health professional for further evaluation and directive conversation.

Celebrate God's Gift of Sleep

Finally, *celebrate* God's gift of sleep! Crafting tone and messaging around the celebration of sleep can be tremendously helpful in avoiding framing sleep as yet another thing to add to an already-long to-do list for hurried and harried students. Celebrating sleep as a gift from God that nourishes us spiritually, emotionally, physically, and academically has been a helpful tone for our campus.

Practice Good Sleep for Yourself Too!

If you are anything like me, you may have resonated with a point or two reviewed in this chapter. I have experienced the physical, emotional, and cognitive toll sleep deprivation takes, and I have experienced the energy and renewal of a good night's rest. We in student life have chosen careers that involve loving, helping, and supporting people, and it can seem that the work will never be done. Our professional and personal lives are just as full as our students'—if not more! But God's gift of sleep is for us too. When we practice stewarding our own bodies, minds, and souls by receiving God's gift of sleep, we also model for our students that it can be good to reach out for professional help when sleep struggles come, say "no" to yet another responsibility, accept our God-given limits, and practice trust in God's care for us and our world's needs.[29]

---

[29] P.S.: It is tempting to think that writers work alone as they put pen to paper around thoughts and ideas. This could not be further from the truth. This chapter reflects several years of conversations with colleagues who are experts on organizational leadership, sleep, public health, and our current generation of students. Without ongoing conversations with and learning from André Stephens, Suzanne Welty, Jen Fanning, Sarah Templeton, Debrianna DeBolt; colleagues in our Student Health and Wellness Collaborative (SHAWC); and students like Elliott Sutter, Lauren Decker, Kelsie Thompson, and KateMarie Fitzpatrick (and more—there are too many to name), this chapter could not have been written. It is a joy to work with them all!

Chapter 4
Sabbath Taking

Justin Whitmel Earley

ust before turning·sixty-one, the award-winning author Anne Lamott gave a short speech on the TED stage sharing her lifetime's reflections on writing and more. In a top-ten-list style and with her characteristic pithiness, Lamott dispensed gem after gem to a hungry audience. Her second point was "almost everything will work again if you unplug it for a minute. . . ." The crowd laughed for a good while before she added, "including you."[1]

I watched this speech sometime just after my fourth son was born: a streak of time where I was particularly exhausted; I spent many evenings letting him sleep on my lap while I caught up on my lawyering work or researched a book I was writing. I think it stuck out to me because I felt in such need of true Sabbath rest.

As good writers are wont to do—she makes the point backward so that the technological (and exhausted) crowd at a TED conference and the millions and millions since who have watched this short talk on the internet have all instantly understood something important about themselves—their need for rest. By comparing humans to machines, she makes the obvious point that we are not. I call this an obvious point. But the truth is that increasingly, it is not so obvious. In fact, the TED crowd, along with the rest of us, understand and treat our bodies like machines.

1 Anne Lamott, "12 Truths I Learned from Life and Writing," Filmed in 2017 in Vancouver, BC, TED video, 15:45, https://www.ted.com/talks/anne_lamott _12_truths_i_learned_from_life_and_writing.

But we are not machines. We are bodies: created bodies that are endowed by their Creator with a soul.

Anne Lamott's quip remains a splendid way to point us to our need for rest. My hope in this chapter is to extend the metaphor. Exploring the ways that our bodies are *not* machines actually tells us a lot about our bodies and their need for Sabbath rest.

•

I am pleasantly amazed by the increasing popularity of Sabbath. Not so many years ago, I wrote a book called *The Common Rule: Habits of Purpose for an Age of Distraction.*[2] (This is the one I was working on with my fourth son napping in my lap.) My thesis was that the modern world is a habit-formation machine and by not doing anything in particular we were doing something very significant—going along with the default American way of life that was forming us into the busy, exhausted, anxious, and overworked people that we are.

In the book, I proposed four daily and four weekly habits as a counter-formational program for the regular American. My goal was to help readers understand that they were not limitless; they were not autonomous; they did not need more choices; and, in fact, they were generally (like me) pretty bad at making day-to-day choices for themselves. Thus, they needed a better program of spiritually formational habits.

I was pleasantly surprised by two things. First, the vast majority of readers responded very well to being told what to do. I have found that despite the cultural buzz of autonomy, most Americans actually do realize that "normal life" is neither normal nor neutral but rather dangerous. These people are looking for a way out, but they genuinely do not know what to do and are far more receptive to being told what to do—even open to adopting new weekly habits like Sabbathing.

---

2 Justin Whitmel Earley, *The Common Rule: Habits of Purpose for an Age of Distraction* (Downers Grove, IL: InterVarsity, 2019).

Second, I was surprised that something as (at least I thought) "stale" as Sabbath, arguably the most ignored of the Ten Commandments, was then and still is now one of the chapters from which I get the most engagement and questions. My recollection of reading the Ten Commandments in high school and college was a lot of whataboutism regarding the "rules" of Sabbathing. Instead of hearing a gracious invitation to rest, my reaction was a lot of "What about doing this? What about doing that?" I'm amazed that by and large, no reader has asked me that. The question no one, not even once, has asked me is "Why?"

What they do ask, over and over, is a short and eager "But how!?" The richest and most productive country in the world has thus found itself begging to be told how to stop. We no longer need to be convinced that rest is good—we simply need to be told how to do it. Because we have no examples—or, rather, no human examples.

We have great examples from technology. When Anne Lamott tells us that we—like our computers—need to be turned off and unplugged, we have an epiphany worth a million views on YouTube. This realization is shocking. And it runs deep.

•

As a business lawyer, I swim in the waters of exhaustion and overwork. In my profession, the words "work-life balance" and "burnout" are as common as "statute of limitations" and "indemnification." As smart as we are, we can't seem to solve the professional puzzle: *Why are lawyers two or more times as likely as the general public to abuse alcohol, wrestle with depression, commit suicide, and engage in so many other destructive behaviors?* We suspect that we overwork ourselves. Yet what I continue to notice about our collective attempt to understand out predicament is—again—the language of technology.

When lawyers look to describe what we need, we draw on mechanical language. Are the scales balanced with work and life? Such an idea presupposes that work and life are things that could be separated, measured out on scales, and finely tuned. Burnout literally suggests we are out of fuel. We've used it all.

I suggest that the reason we like the machine analogy is that it connotes a possibility of solving the problem without confronting our weakness. In other words, if we are machines, we can be tinkered with, reprogrammed, and hacked to a more perfect form. This analogy allows us to avoid sticky and less-definable words like "idolatry" (*Why do we want to be limitless?*) or "pride" (*Why do we use work to prove who we are?*).

If we are machines, we can find a more neutral flaw. Even the best machines need to be debugged and maintained. Such is our predicament. Some cleaner fuel and bit more fine-tuning and we'll be on our way to optimal production, avoiding the need to rest altogether.

So it is that the machine analogy is part of what perpetuates our problem. The most radical *and* most Christian thing that we need to hear is this: "You are not a machine; you are a created body—and you were made to rest." If anyone can hear this, the next questions to ask might be "Well, what's the difference between a body and a machine? And how do we rest?" Those questions are related, and I would like to spend the rest of this chapter showing how one answers the other.

I'm much more practitioner than academic. But sometimes lives are the best research. And I think I'm probably more like the typical overworked American than not, so perhaps I'm a particularly good lab rat. So I'll share mostly what I've learned in practicing a Sabbath, exploring along the way how being *unlike* a machine is precisely one way humans like us figure out how to rest.

Here are my main discoveries:

- Machines need maintenance—but we were made for rest.

- Machines need no people—but we were made for community.

- Machines need fuel—but we were made for food.

- Machines need no awareness—but we were made for worship.

Machines Need Maintenance—
but We Were Made for Rest

I have four boys in the house who are just a little bit prone to breaking lots of things most of the time. So I often find myself passing along a little piece of wisdom I learned from my father. When I see them trying to kill a fly with a baseball bat or playing tug-of-war with their mom's scarf, I am quick to ask them, "Hey, what was that made for?"

It's a wonderful question. Because as it turns out, when you use something for a purpose it wasn't made for, something is going to break. It might be the thing, it might be you, or it might be someone else. But someone or something is going to be hurt. Because what we were made for matters. This is philosophy 101 put into kid language—teleology on the most practical level.

I believe our renewed interest in Sabbath is because we are tired of breaking. Rightfully so. At some point, we must communally realize that the culture of overwork not only *does not work* (we get less, not more, done), but it is also miserable. Why? Because we were made for rest. Let's explore that way of putting it.

Humans were made in the image of a God who rests. We could say that like a fish is made for water, so we were made to live in rhythms of work and rest. Of course, we could use the machine analogy and say that we were programmed for such rhythms, but we should be careful with programming language. Machines are made to perform tasks, and only as an act of service to that productivity do they need to, occasionally, shut down for maintenance. But in a true sense, we were made for rest just as much as we were made for work. Rest isn't something for the work. It's for us. *We were made for it.*

Jesus uses such language when he says that man wasn't made for the Sabbath, but the Sabbath was made for man (Mark 2:27). In other words, the Sabbath was fashioned by the Creator to satisfy one of the innate purposes of his creation: *rest*. This distinction between "needing maintenance" and "being made for rest" is the beginning of learning how to Sabbath. A machine needs to "turn off" so maintenance can be performed. If we were like machines, then to rest we would simply need to be "unplugged" or "off." This notion is problematic. Not only for the obvious reasons—we don't have plugs or off switches—but, worse, because it suggests that to do nothing is to rest. That definition may be true for machines, but not for the created bodies of human beings.

Rest for a human being is something entirely active. We know this physically. Good fitness coaches will tell you that rest for an athlete means not just sleeping but also stretching, hydrating, and performing light movements.

Rest is something we do *on purpose*. In exploring what this purposefulness of rest means, I've always been drawn to the quip attributed to civil rights leader and rabbi Abraham Heschel: "A man who works with his hands should sabbath with his mind, and a man who works with his mind should sabbath with his hands."[3] The wisdom here is that rest is not what happens when we *don't do* anything else. Rest is what happens when we *do certain things on purpose*.

I am a lawyer and a writer. I work with my head all day, every day. As much as I love reading and writing, I have found that it is usually better for me to Sabbath without books and paper. Recently I have come to love doing handyman projects at my mother's house on the Sabbath precisely because it is *not* what I do for work, and it is *not* something I need to do. But it is something I can do to get out of my head and into my body—which is *restful*. In the past couple months, I have rehung a door, rescreened parts of the porch the dog had torn up, fixed drawers, rewired a thermostat, and done a couple other odd jobs. And it's tremendously restful to me. However, my wife, who unlike me is *not* paid to read Monday through Friday, often finds it restful to sit and read on the Sabbath. Try Heschel's approach across vocations. Students and academics might consider resting their minds and getting into their bodies. Construction workers and stay-at-home parents might consider resting their bodies and getting into their minds.

---

3 This quip is often informally attributed to Abraham Joshua Heschel but likely traces back to a common Jewish saying.

But don't think of this approach so much as a rule but as a clue. Learning to Sabbath is less about what we *have to do* and more about what is true of being created bodies. When we move out of the realm of what we *must* do and into the realm of other things we *can* do, we begin to learn something about what it means to be a created human. Everyone's greatest fear is being a cog in the machine—the dehumanizing idea of being made for a singular purpose. You are *only* a mother. Or *only* a student life worker. Or *only* a technology consultant.

But Sabbath liberates us from such machine language. We don't just do one thing. We are people who were also made for hiking and handyman projects, we were made for reading and wrestling, we were made for studying and swimming. To live with an intention toward the world is the beginning of realizing that we were not made to be turned off; we were made to rest. Rest is always running to—not from—the world.

Machines Need No People— but We Were Made for Community

It is perhaps obvious that machines are autonomous creations. Unless they are programmed to work in a line—and they certainly don't have to be—they need no company. It is perhaps less obvious that we are communal creations. But one of the most remarkable parts of the creation story, from which I will continue to take most of my biblical cues on Sabbath, is the communal creation of Adam and Eve.

By communal creation, I mean that Adam was created from community. The image in which he was created was plural. Eve was made *out* of Adam, and for Adam, because God—in a verse that almost sounds blasphemous to the modern Christian ears—tells Adam that it is *not good* that he is alone. Keep in mind he is standing in the Garden of Eden *with God*. But God's understanding of his creation was that God plus one human was insufficient for that human. In other words, we need others to live and worship properly.

I think it's helpful to dwell on this startling claim. It is one of those truths that seems blasphemous at first: you and God are not enough. This is *not* a sign of God's insufficiency. It is a sign of his artistic generosity: *God actually designed us to need people in order to experience him the way we were meant to.* I find this insight as practically true as I find it spiritually true, and it has plenty of practical and spiritual implications for Sabbath.

Spiritually speaking, being communal creatures tends to suggest that we are not truly at rest until we are at rest with others. Sabbath in ancient Israel was, of course, a radically communal command—a way of living as a human society, not just as an autonomous unit. Practically speaking, I can attest that figuring out how to Sabbath communally has really been the foundation of developing an enduring rhythm of Sabbathing. Previously, I mentioned fixing things at my mother's house on Sundays being a part of my rhythms of rest. That is part of my rhythm because my whole family—six of us kids, five of our spouses, fifteen of our collective offspring, and four dogs—all gather on Sunday afternoon to Sabbath at my mom and dad's house. This gathering, which has become an absolute gift to our family's Sabbath rhythm, happened almost totally by accident.

Years ago—in 2015, I believe—the family began this weekly Sunday afternoon gathering at my parents' home in Richmond, Virginia, but *not* because we were looking for a way to Sabbath. In fact, I don't think any of us thought it would be particularly restful at all. We were just a family living in the same city who wanted to find a time to gather. But with the six of us grown up, married, and working different jobs, we just found it tremendously difficult to schedule a time when the family could actually be together. Not only was it a nightmare of texts and emails, but also the time we would finally land on never quite worked for everyone. We were a family living in the same city on purpose, because we longed to be together, but any gathering was incredibly hard to pull off—until we stumbled upon the power of rhythms. Finally, we decided the thought that went into planning a family gathering was impossibly difficult, and we all had space in our schedule Sunday afternoon—so why not just create a standing time that everyone could come together? As it turns out, something about having a large, communal gathering was utterly different from the rest of the week.

In a world where everything from transportation means to household architecture tends to separate us into our small, individualistic domains, coming together for a bustling meal and afternoon of conversation is dramatically different from the rest of the week. That difference is part of what sets it apart or, in the words of the Bible, makes it holy.

Recall that we already established that rest is not about *not* doing anything but about doing things differently in order to enter into restful activities. When my kids are playing with all the other kids, and when my family shares the work of preparing a lunch for them and entertaining them, I find true rest from the work of parenting. Playing a game of tag football in the street with my nieces and nephews is actually fun—even when we still have to parent them all the while. Keep in mind that my family started this just as a small rhythm of actually seeing one another, but here is the thing about small rhythms; they grow.

And this too is part of the wisdom of Sabbath: we were made to live into rhythms, including rhythms of rest, and when we start to conform our collective lives to these created patterns, there is a resonation that seems to multiply our efforts. I think of this as the common grace following God's created order. If you eat healthy, generally you get stronger and you feel better. If you establish a *communal* rhythm of Sabbath, it grows into something you never could have planned on any single Sunday and certainly something you never could have done alone. Truly, it has snowballed. Now nearing a decade later, it's difficult *not* to Sabbath because I am expected at family dinner for the afternoon.

What's more is that once the communal rhythm of Sabbath begins turning, there is a center of gravity that tends to pull people in. It's not unusual at all to have an extra guest or extra family at our Sunday Sabbaths. I cherish these moments of hospitality because I feel like we can offer a unique communal rest to all those who long for it.

This is a unique feature of being an embodied human being: we develop and change in community. Unlike machines that are pre-destined to do the one, solitary thing they do, we grow and have the constant opportunity to become something new. This process is not just better with people, it *requires* people. Like the rest of life, you cannot really move toward rest without the help of others.

Anyone in (or who remembers) the young years of parenting knows this. Unless you have significant wealth, no one is going to take your kids to let you rest from the work of parenting by doing something else. But in community, obtaining this rest is possible.

Of course, you do not need a large family to do Sabbath communally. My point is simply that I think it takes community to really Sabbath. Many of my friends around Richmond—particularly ones without family in town—do something similar but with one another. They often gather together in the afternoon or evening to share the work of parenting and the gift of conversation. They cook or order food, and that communal effort transforms what would otherwise be the work of housekeeping into the work of Sabbathing.

That is the power of community: to transform something that would have otherwise been inadequate into something complete. This is what the second human, Eve, did of course. And it's what God intended her to do: to create the plural of community where the singular individual was not enough.

I imagine that Sabbath could be done alone, in theory. I just wouldn't recommend it as a habit in practice. To really find what we were made for, we need other people.

Machines Need Fuel—
but We Were Made for Food

In 2014, some fledgling entrepreneurs in a San Francisco apartment complained that the trouble with food was that it was too expensive and burdensome. In searching for ways to optimize their life (so as to work more and get their startup to succeed), they developed a vitamin and nutrient shake. As a group prone to extremes, they then claimed this chemistry lab concoction could become the sole substance for survival. A new company was born.

They named it Soylent, and it became their big entrepreneurial break. Advertising the "end of food," the company took off and raised millions upon millions in investments.[4]

Why? Because we want to be liberated from our needs. Including the need to eat. We may want to eat, but we don't want to *have* to eat.

This is the vision of food as fuel, which is ultimately sensible if you think humans are machines. If we are simply trying to preserve and fuel the body, then why waste time and energy on anything more than is necessary? We should be looking for the simple and most renewable resource.

Almost a decade later, Soylent is still thriving, but not on their original promise. Now they are more of a meal replacement shake and nutrition company. They dropped the "end of food" shtick. As it turns out, it seems that when they thought twice about it, most people don't like the idea of ceasing to need food—and probably for good reason.

Somewhere in our spiritual DNA, we may sense that more is going on when we eat, and we would be right. Ironically, while products such as Soylent claim to set us free from the burdensome needs of the body, God gave us food to tie us to our dependence. Hunger is not just about the body being low on fuel; it is about the soul needing something *other than itself.* We were built with a hunger for God, a hunger for creation, *and* a hunger for others. All these desires come to play in needing to eat. This is why I believe that eating together as a Sabbath activity is a holy thing, and I mean holy in all its senses, including the "set apart" sense. When it comes to how to Sabbath, my strong suggestion is that you include a communal meal that is in some way "set apart" from the other meals of the week.

There is some truth to the Soylent struggle. Gathering, preparing, and serving good and healthy food is an enormous task. It takes work. And many days of the week, we very well may find ways to

4 Lizzie Widdicombe, "The End of Food—Has a Tech Entrepreneur Come Up with a Product to Replace Our Meals?," *New Yorker,* May 12, 2014, https://www.newyorker.com/magazine/2014/05/12/the-end-of-food.

minimize that work. However, there is something in sharing that work in community over a Sabbath meal that reveals what God is doing in food. It reveals that our interdependence is the *source* of our joy, not the barrier to it. This reality is a stunning fact.

The human dream for machines is to see them maintenance free. Think about a solar-powered streetlight, for example. It is something that seems to work all on its own with endless clean fuel and no maintenance. An old car would be the opposite: it has an almost slovenly hunger for constant maintenance and gasoline. Insofar as machines go, this constant maintenance makes sense. But we are neither streetlight nor jalopy.

We are created bodies with the very breath of God in us. We remain dependent on God for each breath. Leaning into our dependence is therefore not inefficient—it is holy.

Food is a continual opportunity for us. To welcome our need for it is to welcome our need for God. It is also to embrace our need for creation (to provide the food) and our need for community (which helps us obtain and prepare it).

I am not suggesting reorienting our Sabbath in relation to food is easy. In fact, preparing a communal meal on the Sabbath would certainly offend the traditional Jewish notions of work on Sabbath, and it may be the last thing a stay-at-home parent would want to do. But I continue to recommend the idea of a communal meal as a Sabbath-keeping activity because an intentional movement toward food is a movement toward facing our need, *and Sabbath is all about our need*. When Jesus said Sabbath was made for man, he acknowledged that we are at a lack without it. Sabbath is given to teach us that we are not autonomous, we are not independent, we are not even hyperefficient—we have all kinds of interdependencies, and learning to embrace those is the process of learning to love.

In our family, we have a rotating schedule of potlucks and prepared meals so that each family only occasionally has the burden of preparing a large meal for everyone, and very often one gets to simply bring something and enjoy the food that someone else has prepared. I think we are blessed to have tremendous cooks in our family. If things get busy or one family who was supposed to be cooking is out of town, my dad will often throw together a soup or happen to have a pork shoulder he can slow cook. He will, overnight, produce a delicious meal that feeds seventy. And this is precisely what I'm grateful for: on Sabbath, I'm not only excited to eat a meal that tastes good; I'm also more excited to rest in what someone else has done for me (or excited to contribute my meal to their rest). When I think about those family meals, I think far more about savoring the conversation than I do the soup.

These meals are the one time a week my whole extended family gathers around a table. We pray. We present the food. We eat. We laugh a lot. We talk. We clean.

We hold a Sabbath meal because we need one another, and we need the God who made us. Food is not the fuel for the machine so our bodies can get on to the next task. It is not a pit stop. It is a mini sacrament to our neediness—just like the Sabbath is.

Machines Need No Awareness— but We Were Made for Worship

In a culture starved for rest, we are hungry for whatever trick can get us made right and back to work again. Enter the idea of "life hacks." We can trick our minds and bodies into thinking they're rested so that we can get on to the more important stuff: production. This is, of course, yet another way of thinking our bodies are like machines. The life-hack culture reveals one of the nasty implications of humans as machines: pride. In the life-hack analogy, we are the mechanic or the programmer, as if separate from our bodies and looking down into them and tinkering. It is *we* who are the masters of it, and we will put it to *our* service.

As it turns out, what we need is not to look down but to look up. We don't need new wiring. We need new worship. Sabbath teaches this need. In Sabbath, we don't look down into ourselves to figure something out—we look up to God to be awed.

On the seventh day, part of God's rest was to look in awe at what he had done—to be satisfied with his work—to gaze upon the beauty of it and be filled.[5] Given that we are made in the imprint of God, this too should be our goal; to make space in our weekly rhythm is to look at what God has done, be satisfied with God's work, and gaze upon the beauty of it. Gazing at the work of God is the task of worship, and it must be included in our Sabbath rhythm.

Most Christians would intuit that worship is a central feature of the Sabbath; it seems obvious. But if we're honest, it doesn't seem restful. For example, most of us, if we wanted to schedule out a day of rest, would not include trying to be at a large group activity around nine o'clock in the morning in clothes we don't normally wear and with a bunch of people who we don't necessarily enjoy. Whether you're a student and nine o'clock in the morning seems unconscionably early, or whether you're a parent and even leaving the house with half-dressed children is a Herculean feat, going to worship is not something we regard as relaxing. And that is OK. The Sabbath we need is not necessarily relaxing, but it is restful. As the world sleeps in, heads to brunch, or starts cutting the grass, they likely would look on all of us coordinating our Sunday morning to be at a group program as, frankly, very odd—and that's the point. The hustle of getting to church and being there is actually a signal of something greater that is happening. We are signaling that our lives revolve around something, and that something is worth reordering our schedule. Such a reordering is, in fact, the beginning of worship—before we ever arrive at the sanctuary. When we get there, we will see and greet people we are not exactly like and do not necessarily enjoy. To commit to such relationships with people despite the friction we feel is the seed of love and, as such, also worship.

Then comes the service, where, regardless of our tradition, we are going to be led into prayer, into song, into the word, and into the sacraments—all like the hand of a parent under the chin of a child saying, "Look up." Many of the important parts of Sabbath are happening when we don't think anything important is happening, and the hustle of worship is one of these. When we commit part of our

5 Genesis 1:31–2:2.

Sundays to worship, we are doing something far more important than a rewiring life hack that helps us work better on Monday morning.

Sure, we're being reprogrammed—but to remember that it is *not* about us. Sure, we're being rewired: to recall that we don't have to perform to be loved. Sure, we're being tinkered with: to remember that we need the forgiveness and love of God in order to face the difficulties of others and the world. But this language is not sufficient for what is actually happening, because we are out of the realm of hacks and machines and into the world of beauty, art, and what it means to be human. When the psalmist rejoices in the house of the Lord, what he thinks of is "to gaze on the beauty of the LORD" (Ps. 27:4). This is the heart of Sabbath, because it is what God does: gazing at the beauty of all that he has done and made. This is what we are also called to do. Beholding beauty is not really a matter for a checklist; it is an invitation to a different way of being. That is the call of Sabbath.

When we worship and get wrapped up, even just a little bit, in the beauty of God and what he has done, we are astounded. We are reminded once again that there is something more worthy of gazing at than us. There is something more compelling than a life of productivity. There is something more important than our task list: the God for whom we were made. We can throw out what we thought we were trying to achieve throughout the week; that was a circle we were trying to jam into the square-shaped hole of our hearts. In worship, we find the hole in our heart filled by God, and it is exactly what we did not know we needed.

And it is useful too. Working with a hole in your heart is the way to all the worst parts of the workplace: the cheating, the selfish gain, the criticisms and slights, the gossip, and the self-consciousness. Studying with a hole in your heart is the way to both laziness and overwork. You may have too little concern for the subject or too much concern for your grade. It is the way to zone out and to burn out. Parenting with a hole in your heart is the way to shame your kids, feel like you're never enough, be short tempered with everything, and control rather than disciple your kids.

Whatever we are doing during the week, what we need first—and last—is a Sabbath where we gaze upon the beauty of God and remember there is more above us than we thought.

Children of God

At the beginning of this chapter, I mentioned that I came across Anne Lamott's words about unplugging at a time when I was particularly exhausted and spent a lot of time working while my fourth son slept in my lap. I actually learned a lot from him during that time too. I would often look down and think, "Wow, I wish I could just conk out like that." Anyone who looks at a baby learns a lot about Sabbathing, more than even Anne Lamott can teach you. Because trying to live as a machine is exhausting. But embracing our dependence is actually the key to Sabbath. Once you know that there is someone bigger than you and stronger than you who loves you and who is going to hold you, then you can really rest.

Lucky for us, that is true. His name is Jesus. And in his arms of grace, we can truly Sabbath.

Chapter 5
Attuning and Attending
Exercise and the Body

Andrew Borror

T ertullian was adamant that avoiding the gymnasium of his day was a trademark of Christian faithfulness: "We [Christians]," he wrote in the second century, "have nothing to do in speech, sight, or hearing with . . . the vanity of the gymnasium."[1] In other epochs, however, the fusion between fitness and faith has been more agreeable. Christian believers, at various points throughout history, have adopted fashionable attitudes toward the body and its development. For instance, following the revival of classical thought in the Renaissance, the Roman Catholic church erected statues of saints with perfectly proportioned bodies reminiscent of Greek gods. A few hundred years later, in response to growing fears about the ill effects of industrialization, so-called muscular Christians preached about the "maximal muscle development" of Jesus, "the manly man from Galilee," and the need for manly Protestant men to engage in physical exercise—to reform society through reforming their bodies.[2]

---

1 Tertullian, *Apology: De Spectaculis* 38.4, trans. T. R. Glover (Cambridge, MA: Harvard University Press, 1998), 173; Shirl J. Hoffman, *Good Game: Christianity and the Culture of Sports* (Waco, TX: Baylor University Press, 2010), 36.
2 G. Stanley Hall, *Jesus, the Christ, in the Light of Psychology* (Garden City, NY: Doubleday, Page, 1917), 36–37; I. H. Meredith and Grant Colfax Tullar, eds., *Manly Songs for Christian Men: A Collection of Sacred Songs Adapted to the Needs of Male Singers* (New York: Tullar-Meredith, 1910), 27, quoted in Clifford

Today, in the wake of the fitness boom, there is a whole world of Christian diet and exercise programs. Believers can participate in the Daniel Fast, the Take Back Your Temple initiative, Bod4God, F3, and Praise Fit aerobics.[3] Megachurches house six-million-dollar, state-of-the-art fitness facilities on their premises and offer Christian yoga classes with church-branded yoga mats.[4] There are even Christian fitness magazines encouraging exercisers to take Communion during their workouts.[5]

While some of these examples may be extreme, collectively they suggest a tendency for Christians to adopt cultural assumptions about the body and to live in response to the concerns of the times. In the sedentary Western world, exercise is becoming increasingly popular among Christians—and for good reason. The benefits of regular physical activity are well documented. Exercise can improve one's mood, sleep quality, and energy levels, as well as reduce stress, anxiety, and chronic-disease risk.[6] Exercise thus warrants consideration for Christians who are called to cultivate creation and care for the well-being of God's creatures.[7] But before reproducing the structures and ethos of mainstream fitness culture in our churches and Christian

Putney, *Muscular Christianity: Manhood and Sports in Protestant America, 1880–1920* (Cambridge, MA: Harvard University Press, 2001), 92, 96.

3 For an overview of such programs, see Martin Radermacher, *Devotional Fitness: An Analysis of Contemporary Christian Dieting and Fitness Programs* (New York: Springer, 2017).

4 Sylvia Small, "Church Gyms Offer Community Places to Exercise Body, Spirit," Reporter Newspapers & Atlanta Intown, March 10, 2011, http://reporternewspapers.net/2011/03/10/church-gyms-offer-community-places-exercise-body-spirit/; Erin Beresini, "Thou Shalt Work Out," Outside Online, October 3, 2016, https://www.outsideonline.com/health/wellness/thou-shalt-workout/.

5 Tim Cheux, "Are Holy Communion & Fitness Compatible?," *Faith & Fitness Magazine*, March 15, 2021, https://faithandfitness.net/are-holy-communion-fitness-compatible/.

6 George Brooks, Thomas Fahey, and Kenneth Baldwin, *Exercise Physiology: Human Bioenergetics and Its Application*, 4th ed. (New York: McGraw Hill, 2004).

7 A number of authors have made this point in recent years. For a popular-level example, see Gary Thomas, *Every Body Matters: Strengthening Your Body to Strengthen Your Soul* (Grand Rapids, MI: Zondervan, 2011). For a more academic argument, see Erik Dailey, *The Fit Shall Inherit the Earth* (Portland, ME: Pickwick, 2018).

colleges, it would be wise to probe the assumptions embedded within them—assumptions about what the body is, what it is for, and what constitutes sound bodily care.

Without losing sight of the merits of physical activity, what I want to suggest in this chapter is that in order to exercise faithfully in today's fitness climate, Christians need a more robustly *theological* understanding of what the body is. Mainstream fitness culture tends to view the body through a biomedical lens, as a machine to be optimized. Since the fitness lifestyle is deeply connected to particular images of success, it is easy for exercise to become a self-improvement venture carried out for the sake of worldly happiness.

I argue in this chapter that if Christians are to escape these cultural mores, we need to take more seriously the claim that our bodies are *not our own*. Additionally, I suggest that if exercise is to avoid becoming anxious toil, it must be oriented by God's Sabbath. I hope to show how this repositioning of exercise enables it to become playful. Playful exercise is the joyful work of attuning and attending to particular bodies, receiving their health as a gift from God with thanksgiving.

The Biomedical Body

In contemporary Western society, the predominant view of the body is biomedical. The body is perceived as an organic compound that is sharply distinguishable from the disembodied self. "Body" refers to the physical structure of a person: muscles, bones, sinews, flesh, and organs—material stuff that can be measured empirically and that functions similarly to a machine. Describing the body as a machine is commonplace in health care settings—from modern medicine (fixing the machine), to organ transplantation (replacing its parts), to nutrition (providing it fuel), to fitness (improving its efficiency).

While useful for research and teaching, overuse of the machine metaphor can be dangerous.[8] Thinking of the body primarily as a machine directs our attention toward certain aspects of it—like its

---

8 See Wendell Berry, "Health Is Membership," in *On Moral Medicine: Theological Perspectives in Medical Ethics*, ed. M. Therese Lysaught et al. (Grand Rapids, MI: Eerdmans, 2012), 421.

physiological functioning—while occluding other aspects, like its moral or spiritual significance. Consequently, discourse on the body exhibits a disproportionate emphasis on scientific description and technique in contrast to questions of meaning and purpose. This disparity is evident in college health and wellness curricula, which often begin with a short section on the importance of holistic approaches to health and well-being before proceeding to discuss, almost exclusively, physiological mechanisms and empirical research.[9]

It makes sense to introduce students to the basic tenets of physiology and the exercise habits that constitute a healthy lifestyle. But scientific knowledge needs to be framed within a broader context. I am shocked by the number of students I meet with who quite simply have not thought deeply about the fact that they have bodies or about what it means to be an embodied creature. The conventional conversation lacks serious reflection on what the body *is*, theologically speaking, and what it is *for*.[10] A biomedical lens can tempt us to think that the body *is*, fundamentally, an object of scientific examination, the significance of which can be discerned empirically. It can precipitate the assumption that the body exists *for* maximal health or efficiency (or beauty) rather than for love. To be sure, exercise can be an effective means of stewarding the body for those with sedentary vocations, but we must consider how overemphasizing the mechanical qualities of our bodies fosters reductionism. Our language orients our perception.

Perception is also oriented by material practices like bodily measurement. Biomedical fitness paradigms prioritize empirical data, often using quantitative measures to prescribe, monitor, and evaluate exercise. Workout machines at the gym are rife with metrics that quantify bodily movements and calculate caloric expenditure. The recent boom in wearable technologies has expanded the scope of this data gathering, making it easier to track metrics outside of the gym.[11]

---

9 For instance, David Peterson, Jeremy Kimble, and Trent Rogers, *A Christian Guide to Body Stewardship, Diet and Exercise* (Cedarville, OH: Cedrus, 2021).

10 Joel James Shuman, *The Body of Compassion: Ethics, Medicine, and the Church* (Boulder, CO: Westview, 1999), xvii.

11 Lin Lu et al., "Wearable Health Devices in Health Care: Narrative Systematic Review," *JMIR mHealth uHealth* 8, no. 11 (November 9, 2020): e18907, https://doi.org/10.2196/18907.

Once again, measuring the body is an expedient practice for those who want to set goals and track their progress. However, excessive measurement of the body can draw attention away from the subjective aspects of exercise, like its context and rationale. Moreover, when one adopts a metric-based approach, stewarding a body can devolve into making it a "normal" body as defined by statistical averages. Population statistics do not account for the natural diversity of bodies or the plurality of individual vocations.[12] Not to mention, exercise is about more than health; it is entangled with fitness (a potentially limitless ideal) and beauty (a notoriously context-dependent one). The unattainable and arbitrary nature of these ideals can lead to frustration with the uniqueness of particular bodies that do not conform to them. In my experience, this has been the case even among those who, from the outside, seem to most closely approximate such ideals.

Additionally—and this point is key—excessive data gathering makes physical activity primarily about self-monitoring and self-improvement.[13] This shifts the focus toward ourselves and our own progress and away from faithfully responding to the call of God. To put it bluntly, if Christians uncritically adopt a biomedical definition of the body and principally focus their efforts on improving their personal fitness data, exercise can quickly morph into a self-improvement venture that loses sight of its purpose.

Fitness culture is rife with narratives about what the good life entails and how one's body relates to it. The core of the message is that if our bodies look and function a particular way, we will be successful, productive, and happy. Sociological studies suggest that college students may be particularly susceptible to these temptations due to

---

12 Physician Jeffrey Bishop argues that defining a healthy body according to statistical norms exerts power over patients and "extinguishes the uniqueness" of the individual. Jeffrey P. Bishop, *The Anticipatory Corpse: Medicine, Power, and the Care of the Dying*, Notre Dame Studies in Medical Ethics (South Bend, IN: University of Notre Dame Press, 2011), 94.

13 Wearables create a feedback loop of self-monitoring and lifestyle modifications. Sam Jacob, "Body Building," *AA Files*, no. 70 (2015): 89–91.

their stage of life and social media habits.[14] College is a time that is full of potential. Students are faced with myriad decisions that will shape the trajectories of their lives, like what to study, where to live, and whether and whom to marry. The sheer scope of possibilities can foster a culture of continual self-improvement and resume building, whether to keep one's options open for the future or to demonstrate one's worth to others through past achievements. Moreover, in today's digital age, it is not enough to simply be successful. People must also display their success to the world, and since the fit body is an emblem of success in mass media, students (and staff!) immersed in the sea of fitness culture can get caught up in the tides.

Unfortunately, Christian rhetoric on exercise often fails to offer an alternate narrative. It both embraces the biomedical body and mimics the general ethos of fitness culture—which places the primary onus for living a worthwhile life on human effort. By emphasizing grit, discipline, and the need to make an impact with one's life, Christian accounts of fitness can fail to bear witness to the gospel. The Christian confession is that we have been liberated from the need to make our lives count and from the anxieties of bodily presentation. Fitness is not about self-justification or self-improvement. While the Christian life requires discipline, it is not about making ourselves; it is about creating space for Christ to remake *us* through the Spirit. Discipline is an organic response to the gospel, not a prerequisite for living a life that counts.

This is not meant to deny the need for disciplined stewardship or careful planning, but to relocate the accent of exercise theology on a different note in order to hear the melody of the gospel amid the piping chords of fitness culture. What I am suggesting is that a distinctly Christian account of fitness needs to be founded on two pillars: a theological understanding of the body and a posture oriented by God's Sabbath rest. The remainder of this chapter will address these matters in turn.

---

14 Francesca C. Ryding and Daria J. Kuss, "The Use of Social Networking Sites, Body Image Dissatisfaction, and Body Dysmorphic Disorder: A Systematic Review of Psychological Research," *Psychology of Popular Media* 9, no. 4 (October 2020): 412–35, https://doi.org/10.1037/ppm0000264.

The Theological Body

One of the most oft-cited claims in exercise theology is that our bodies are temples of the Holy Spirit (1 Cor. 3:16; 6:19–20).[15] References to this claim are often followed by the imperative: therefore Christians ought to exercise—it is their duty. What often goes unnoticed, however, is that in both passages, the crux of Paul's argument is that believers' lives are *not their own*.[16] Both references to the body being a temple are in contexts foregrounding that Christian bodies and Christian lives belong to God and, consequently, to others.

As believers, we are bound to Christ and to others whose bodily needs lay claim to our lives.[17] The things we do with our physical bodies are not private affairs but public ones that are deeply tied to the life of the church. This is why, after declaring the body to be a temple, Paul goes on to call believers to live out their individual vocations with the ecclesial health of Christ's body in view (1 Cor. 7). In this light, overly individualistic approaches to exercise may dishonor rather than honor the body and be harmful rather than healthful. The fitness buff with a rigid workout schedule may presumably be healthy in biomedical terms while being radically unhealthy in relation to his community. Proper stewardship through exercise needs to see the body not as a machine that belongs to an individual but as a gift that belongs to others through Christ.[18]

The fact that Jesus had a physical body—that the Word *became* flesh—is another prominent theme in exercise theology. It bears

---

15 Endless debates have ensued regarding the "your" in this passage—is it singular or plural? For a discussion and a way forward, see Nijay K. Gupta, "Which 'Body' Is a Temple (1 Corinthians 6:19)? Paul beyond the Individual/Communal Divide," *Catholic Biblical Quarterly* 72, no. 3 (July 2010): 518–36.

16 For a recent, popular-level book on this topic, see Alan Noble, *You Are Not Your Own: Belonging to God in an Inhuman World* (Westmont, IL: InterVarsity, 2021).

17 See Brian Brock, *Wondrously Wounded: Theology, Disability, and the Body of Christ* (Waco, TX: Baylor University Press, 2019).

18 See Bernd Wannenwetsch, "Owning Our Bodies? The Politics of Self-Possession and the Body of Christ (Hobbes, Locke and Paul)," *Studies in Christian Ethics* 26, no. 1 (February 1, 2013): 50–65, https://doi.org/10.1177/0953946812466491.

repeating that any Christian account of bodily stewardship must affirm the goodness of physical creation and our call to cultivate its flourishing. However, what often goes overlooked is the decisively outward orientation of Christ's life in the body, which ultimately ended in his death. Christ's vocation was to allow his body to be *broken*; he sacrificed it and its health for the sake of others. That is to say, in order to discover the vocational meaning of Christ's body we must look not only to the incarnation but also to the cross.

We are reminded of this when we come to the table: *this* is my body, broken for you (cf. 1 Cor. 11:24). The meaning of Christ's body, and so of our own bodies, is revealed in the breaking of bread. Like the disciples on the road to Emmaus, we cannot recognize the body's full meaning by simply perceiving its physical form (cf. Luke 24). Rather, we discover it as we partake of Christ's body broken for us. In Communion, our individual bodies—which have been bound to one another through baptism—are nourished to go out and be sacrificed for others. Not all of us are called to be physically crucified, but we are beckoned to die with Christ (and so participate in his sufferings; 1 Pet. 4:13; Phil. 3:10) and to offer our bodies as a living sacrifice to God (Rom. 12:1).[19]

Thus, glorifying God in the body—honoring God's temple—does not, in the *first* place, mean counting calories or frequenting the gym, though it may entail such behaviors later on. Rather, it means living as true members of Christ's body, which has many members (Rom. 12:4) and is called out to serve others. God undoubtedly cares about the health of his creatures, and ignoring the needs of your body is no way to honor it. However, bodily health is of no help if it is not used well.

In Christian discourse, the call for fitness to be "for the other" is not so much ignored as underemphasized. Some Christian accounts of fitness begin with a call to service, but it is more commonly mentioned after the fact as a post hoc rationale for exercise or an additional

---

19 Notice how our "bodies" (plural) are to be offered as a *single* sacrifice; we offer our bodies together as one community. Notice also the nondualistic implications of this verse: offering the *body* as a sacrifice is an act of *spiritual* worship.

perk (i.e., being fit to serve).[20] Even when it is addressed at the outset, it is frequently mentioned in passing before moving on to technical instructions about how to exercise effectively.[21] Consequently, it is easy for Christian exercisers to absorb the individualistic assumptions and achievement-oriented narratives that govern fitness culture. As a counterbalance, the call to become the "least of these" (Matt. 25:40, 45) and "the servant of all" (Mark 9:35) needs to be a constant refrain in any foundational account of Christian fitness.

The point is not that Christians should avoid exercise but that Christian engagements with exercise, rightly understood, ought to be expressions of thanksgiving (*eucharistia*) for the gift of the body—which is not one's own but to be received from God and, at once, offered back to him. However, lest we simply replace the call to self-improvement with a call to serve, Christian exercise needs to be repositioned within a radically alternative story: it must flow out of Sabbath.

God's Sabbath Rest

Life contains rhythms of work, rest, and play. At face value, rest and play seem more naturally aligned with a Sabbath orientation. This might lead us to wonder whether sports and games are preferable to the banality of going to the gym.[22] There is something to this line of argument—I doubt there will be strip-mall gyms lining the streets of gold—but I want to address the real possibility that exercise could have a place in our sedentary, industrialized society. Work, in addition to play, is part of God's intention for humanity. And it is reasonable to think that exercise could be part of God's preordained means for our faithfully receiving his abundant provisions.

The Sabbath is a reminder that all human work is a response to the prior work of God. Rest precedes and positions the human

---

20 For an example, see Kevin Vost, *Fit for Eternal Life: A Christian Approach to Working Out, Eating Right, and Building the Virtues for Fitness in Your Soul* (Manchester, NH: Sophia Institute Press, 2007), 48.

21 See, for instance, Tim Powers, *Fit to Serve* (Seattle, WA: YWAM, 2009).

22 Sports, of course, have their own challenges. See Hoffman, *Good Game*.

vocation. The first full day of humanity's existence, day seven of creation, was not a day of work but a day of rest (Gen. 2:2–3). Accordingly, as G. K. Beale observes, when Genesis says God "put" Adam in the garden to till and to keep it, the standard Hebrew word for "put" ("šŭm") is not used; rather, the word "nŭah" is used, which is typically translated "to rest."[23] To say that Adam's work in the garden is restful does not mean that Adam is inactive but that his activity is nested within God's activity.[24] Such activity can also be called "playful," suggested Brian Brock, "because it does not conceive itself as enacting self-salvation. Instead, it finds its meaning solely in following and witnessing to the work of God."[25] The good news of the gospel is that we do not need to "make ourselves" through our own sweat and effort; while we may be sanctified through our work, we are justified by Christ.[26]

A Sabbath posture reframes the task of bodily stewardship by making it playful rather than anxious or self-justifying. It is easy for work—even when it has a praiseworthy aim—to be animated by worry, greed, or envy rather than by faith in God's provision.[27] In his exposition of Psalm 127, Martin Luther went to great lengths to clarify this distinction, insisting that if a house is to be built, the Lord must be the one to build it. He wrote,

> God wills that man should work, and without work he will give him nothing.... Because God gives him nothing unless he works, it may seem as if it is his labor which sustains him; just as the little birds neither sow nor reap, but they would certainly die of hunger if they did not fly about and seek their food. The fact that they find food, however, is not due to their own labor, but to God's goodness. For who placed their food there where they can find

23 G. K. Beale, *The Temple and the Church's Mission: A Biblical Theology of the Temple* (Downers Grove, IL: InterVarsity, 2004), 69–70.
24 Brian Brock, *Formed for Freedom: A Theological Ethic of Creatureliness* (forthcoming; Grand Rapids, MI: Baker Academic, 2024), 197.
25 Brian Brock, *Christian Ethics in a Technological Age* (Grand Rapids, MI: Eerdmans, 2010), 318.
26 Brock, *Formed for Freedom*, 206, 305.
27 Brock, 203.

it? Beyond all doubt it is God alone . . . our labor is nothing more than the finding and collecting of God's gifts; it is quite unable to create or preserve anything.[28]

Luther's account suggests that playful bodily stewardship begins with prayer, thanksgiving, and praise. Measurement, prescription, and cardio workouts may come later, but these subsequent tasks will be loving responses to God's provision rather than fearful initiatives to procure good health. To put it differently, the temporal frame that orients Christian exercise is not the workout regimen but the rest day. And rest is meaningful not simply because it allows us to work harder tomorrow or because the rest cycle is when "gains" occur. Rest is meaningful because in it we remember who we are: creatures whose health comes as a gift from a loving God.

Recognizing that bodily health is a gift does not mean we can sit on the couch all day. God often works through so-called natural means to carry out his purposes. But it does remind us that the effects of exercise are not due to biological processes from which God is entirely absent. God *actively* sustains our bodies in his providence, often through, but sometimes in spite of, our actions.[29] Overprioritizing human action can conceal the reality that health is a gift. Emphasizing rest, by contrast, provides a freeing reminder that the fruits of our labor are not achieved but received.

This is a particularly salient point for busy students and for those in helping professions, where burnout rates are astronomical.[30] Caring for one's health may very well mean sitting on the couch some days. It may also mean saying "no" to opportunities out of respect for one's limits. Limits are intrinsic to embodiment and an essential

28 Martin Luther, "Exposition of Psalm 127," in *Luther's Works*, ed. Christopher B. Brown, Jaroslav J. Pelikan, and Helmut T. Lehmann, vol. 45 (Saint Louis, MO: Concordia, 1955), 326–27.

29 Martin Luther, "Lectures on Genesis Chapters 6–14," in *Luther's Works*, ed. Christopher B. Brown, Jaroslav J. Pelikan, and Helmut T. Lehmann, vol. 2 (Saint Louis, MO: Concordia, 1960), 76–77.

30 Patrick R. Mullen, Amanda Malone, Adam Denney, and Syntia Santa Dietz, "Job Stress, Burnout, Job Satisfaction, and Turnover Intention among Student Affairs Professionals," *College Student Affairs Journal* 36, no. 1 (2018): 94–108.

feature of human nature.[31] They are also peculiar gifts that allow us to be *us*, to experience love and relationships as the unique creatures that we are, and to receive God's grace.[32] Bodily exercise can be a healthy means of experiencing one's limits, and even pushing them at times, but it can also be used as an instrument of rebellion against them. Learning this difference is important for both students and staff at universities who wish to nurture God's gift of health.

Receiving bodily health well is the task of playful exercise. Playful exercise is about responding to and resting in God's work through actively attuning and attending to the gift of the body, whatever its state. To attune is to truly *see* and appreciate the gift of particular bodies, including our own. And to attend is to genuinely care for (i.e., to at*tend* to) those bodies with the recognition that we may be able to influence, but cannot manufacture, health. To build on the metaphor given in Genesis, Christian bodily stewardship is more like cultivating a garden than running an industrialized farm. The garden Adam was called to keep was already considered fertile and fruitful as a result of God's blessing.[33] Unlike commercial agribusiness conglomerates, Adam's stewardship was organized not around profit or the ideal of efficiency but around genuine care for material creatures. Thus, he was free to attune and to attend, to rest and to play, through his work.

Likewise, playful exercise is not a technique to improve a body and so *make* it valuable. Rather, it is an avenue for the loving cultivation of that which is *already* perceived to be valuable. The body is, fundamentally, a gift to be loved, even when it is physically unwell in medical terms or unattractive according to cultural beauty standards. This truth bears repeating in our highly aesthetic fitness culture that is prone to exalt the abstract, perfect body while scorning actual living bodies, scanning them for imperfections and "problem areas." A student recently told me that he does not work out regularly, but when he does, it tends to be in one of two situations: (1) just after the holidays or (2) when he is experiencing low self-esteem. In both

---

31 See Kelly M. Kapic, *You're Only Human: How Your Limits Reflect God's Design and Why That's Good News* (Ada, MI: Brazos, 2022).

32 Karl Barth, *Church Dogmatics* vol. 3, part 4 (London: T&T Clark, 1961), 567–73.

33 See chapter 9, "Worship and Work," in Brock, *Formed for Freedom*.

instances, he is motivated negatively: propelled to exercise out of guilt or shame. Playful exercise holds out the hope that he might instead be drawn to exercise out of love for his body and for God, to see it as a joyful duty and opportunity to participate in God's purposes for creation.

In our medicalized, sedentary world, the body is often seen as a problem—it limits us, contracts disease, and becomes obese. By contrast, the Christian tradition proclaims that the body itself is good; it is the body *as subject to sin* that is evil. It may be true that obesity is a problem today and that it is linked to physical inactivity, but rather than jumping to technological solutions for technological problems, perhaps we need to reframe our questions.[34] "What are we going to do about the obesity epidemic?" warrants a different response than "What does the obesity epidemic tell us about how we have misunderstood our bodies and God's ways of caring for the health of his creatures?"[35]

In practice, responding to God's provision might mean fighting off laziness to engage in exercise, or it might mean skipping a workout to help a classmate or colleague in need. In my own life, the latter has proved more difficult and has required its own kind of discipline and training. Learning one's own proclivities is necessary because playful exercise is not a determinate prescription. It is the natural outgrowth of a Sabbath people who are seeking to attune and attend to the body. Attuning and attending may look similar, on the surface, to other forms of bodily maintenance that are not grounded in Sabbath. A playful exerciser may be found running on a treadmill alongside others who are striving to improve their bodies for other reasons. Despite external similarities, however, the internal disposition, expectations, and goals of a playful exerciser will be distinct. The same action can be done in more ways than one. The gaze of an optometrist is very different from the gaze of a lover; though both stare intently into the eyes, one sees a retina while the other sees a soul.

34 "Controlling the Global Obesity Epidemic," World Health Organization, accessed March 15, 2022, https://www.who.int/activities/controlling-the-global-obesity-epidemic.

35 Brock, *Formed for Freedom*, 389.

Conclusion

Christian discourse on health and fitness often fails to bear witness to the gospel, reproducing instead cultural assumptions about the body and its care. The temptation today is to make fitness primarily about self-optimization and self-fulfillment. Many of us long to be fit, attractive, and successful Christians—who are faithful to God, yes, but who are also impressive by the world's standards. I have attempted to put forward a more theological account of fitness that recognizes the communal, sacrificial nature of the body as well as the need for stewardship to be oriented by Sabbath. There is no list of rules to ensure faithful engagement with exercise (e.g., "If you buy these machines or offer those programs, people will exercise playfully"). Our stony hearts need more than a well-designed exercise program; they need to be replaced with hearts of flesh! Thus, the way to maintain a distinctive witness in today's health and fitness culture is not to develop a novel strategy for personal fitness. It is to open ourselves up to the working of the Spirit and so be made fit for Christ.

Chapter 6

Sex

A Positive Christian Vision

Jonathan Grant

L et's be honest. Sex, sexuality, and relationships are massive topics, ones that a library of books would struggle to cover. Additionally, the area has become even more complex and challenging with the shifting sands of identity politics making even the most basic traditional claims about sexuality offensive within mainstream culture. It is within this confusing and controversial environment that I want to cast a positive Christian vision for living as sexual beings and followers of Christ.

Despite seemingly infinite perspectives, there are essentially two competing visions of human sexuality within our Western culture—a secular one and a Judeo-Christian one.[1] In order to steward our bodies well, we need to understand what each vision believes and why—what they offer us and what they sow into our future. Then we need to choose between them and set the course for our lives.

You might be wondering why we need to understand our culture's vision of sexuality. Isn't this chapter about a positive Christian vision? It's a good question, and the answer is that we are holistic beings who soak in the world as much as we think our way through it. In fact, a lot of what we believe is subconsciously absorbed from the

---

1 The other Abrahamic faiths share many of the core tenets of a Christian vision of human sexual identity.

thousands of messages we receive every day. David Foster Wallace began his famous Kenyon College commencement address with this story. There are these two young fish swimming along and they happen to meet an older fish swimming the other way, who nods at them and says, "Morning, boys. How's the water?" And the two young fish swim on for a bit, and then eventually one of them looks over at the other and goes "What the hell is water?"[2] The point is that a fish doesn't feel wet; it is simply conditioned to its native environment. We, too, are powerfully shaped by our native culture through movies, music, conversations, billboards, and social media. Whether we like it or not, we've already absorbed our culture's essential vision of reality, and so the first step in stewarding our sexuality well is to clearly articulate our culture's vision of sex as well as the Christian view. With this cultural reality in mind, let's explore these competing visions.

What Do We Mean by Sex and Sexuality?

With so many different definitions of human sexuality, it helps to first describe sexuality within a Christian framework. First, our sexuality is an essential and inseparable part of who we are: our personal identity. Although we might try to compartmentalize our lives, each of us is a psycho-socio-somatic whole, and our sexuality is an inextricable part of our whole selves. A bit like flour in a baking mix, our sexuality can't be extracted or separated from our mind, body, and relationships. But our sexuality goes deeper than just sex and other forms of physical sexual expression. Our sexuality reflects everything within our personality, consciousness, and "self" that has to do with our essential "maleness" and "femaleness."[3]

Connected to this idea is the Christian belief that there is no such thing as sex as a separate thing in itself. Sex, and even relatively

---

2 David Foster Wallace, *This Is Water: Some Thoughts, Delivered on a Significant Occasion, about Living a Compassionate Life* (New York: Little, Brown, 2009), 3–4.

3 Stanley J. Grenz, *Sexual Ethics: An Evangelical Perspective* (Louisville, KY: Westminster John Knox, 1990), 21–27.

detached forms of sexual expression like pornography, are always part of the package of who we are, and sex is always an aspect of our relationships.

A critical trend over the last sixty years or so has been the way that sex has become detached from the things that had previously given it meaning and purpose like marriage, children, relationships, and the guiding testimony of our own bodies. This progressive separation of sex from these meaningful contexts has been driven by the idea that sex should be set free from its restrictive cage so that we can use it like a consumer product or technology to fulfill our needs and desires. Just like the interchangeability of vitamin pills and vegetables, it does not really matter what form our sexual expression takes—what we do or with whom—as long as our basic sexual needs are fulfilled.

This simplistic view of sex plays out in the growing trend of people becoming sexually active at ever younger ages while delaying relational commitments and family formation until later in life or, in many cases, indefinitely. The basic cultural belief is that, while sex and relationships may coincide at times, they are not necessarily or intrinsically connected.

The various sexual revolutions of recent times were meant to set sex free to find its highest form, like Cinderella being let out to the ball to meet her destiny. In particular, this separation was meant to set young women free from the claustrophobic expectations of a patriarchal society that treated female sexuality as sacred, jealously guarded by taboos. One of the questions we will explore in this chapter is whether these sexual revolutions have really set us free and how we can respond positively as Christian stewards of sex and relationships.

So within the Christian vision of personal identity that we find in the Genesis 1 creation story, our sexuality is an essential part of who we are, and sex is always an aspect of relationships. Our sexuality is also largely social. I don't mean that in the sense of having multiple sexual partners, but I mean that most of our sexual personality and energy are expressed through our social relationships rather than our overtly sexual ones. That reality is why, despite our culture's obsession with sex as a fundamental form of self-actualization, we don't tend to think of single or celibate people as "unsexual beings" or less than fully human. One of the most countercultural Christian beliefs is that it is possible to fully express a person's sexuality without overtly sexual relationships. Our sexuality, in its fullest sense, is a tapestry woven into the fabric of relationships we have with friends, family, elders, and others.

Finally, as Christians, we believe that sexuality is connected to our spirituality. As strange as it may sound, this connection means that "sexual desire" is not the same thing as "desire for sex," although they may overlap. Our embodied createdness, as either "male" or "female" (but not both), initiates a desire to go beyond ourselves to find our fullness in relationships, especially with our Creator. This Christian belief is summed up in Saint Augustine's famous statement: "You have made us for yourself, and our heart is restless until it rests in you."[4]

In effect, our sexual desire is our most essential human longing as gendered, sexual beings. We are wired to find completion in our Creator and also in the intimate sexual and relational bond with another person. In this way, sexual intimacy can provide a window into another dimension of reality—what we call transcendence. It is also why sex and marriage were considered one and the same thing in the Old Testament; it was acknowledged that sexual intimacy was a bond that fused two people together, both symbolizing and effecting the sacred bond of marriage.

In summary, within a Christian vision of human identity, our sexuality is intrinsically good and essential to who we are—it is part of our intended createdness. It goes deeper than just our physical bodies or even overtly sexual experiences, and it can possess transcendent power.

All this begs the question: if our sexuality is so important, how do we steward it well as Christians? This is where we encounter the competing visions I described previously.

---

4 Augustine, *Confessions* 1.1, in *Oxford World's Classics*, trans. Henry Chadwick (Oxford: Oxford University Press, 2008), 3.

The Fallen Culture of Authenticity

One of the most important sexual trends of our times is what social philosophers call our "culture of authenticity."[5] This vision of personal identity tells us that the deepest and most important part of who we are consists of our strongest feelings and emotional intuitions. If we can tap into this inner core, then it will give us a reliable moral script to live by and will help us become who we truly are—our unique, authentic selves. Personal authenticity elevates intimate sexual relationships as central to our search for meaning because this is where we experience our feelings and true self most powerfully. So the key quest in life is to find our "soulmate": that person who is a perfect fit for us and will satisfy our emotional, psychological, and sexual needs. We sometimes call this mythical unicorn "The One."

There have been many midwives for this culture of sexual authenticity, but at its heart is Sigmund Freud's potent imagery of human sexuality being like a powerful internal spring that wells up within us. Freud believed that these internal forces are so powerful that if we do not freely express them sexually, then they will rupture in unhealthy ways (e.g., celibate priests and sexual abuse scandals). The most influential thing Freud did was to fuse the ideas of sexual expression and personal health together so that it is a cultural belief today that an active sex life is critical to human well-being. This belief has translated onto college campuses as the idea that an unsexed campus life is a sad and unusual existence that involves foregoing an essential part of our sexual maturing. But is that view really true?

This quest to find ourselves through romantic sexual relationships has triggered the two contradictory forces of fantasy and fatalism. Our romantic culture is still captivated by the idea that we will find salvation in a magical soulmate who will fulfill all our needs while not demanding the same from us. This endless search finds tangible expression in one of the key trends within modern relationships,

---

5 Charles Taylor, *A Secular Age* (Cambridge, MA: Belknap Press of Harvard University Press, 2007), 475.

"serial monogamy."[6] This social phenomenon involves a person entering into a series of consecutive relationships during their twenties and thirties while delaying the commitments of marriage and family until later stages of life. This new sexual ecology, combined with the freely available panacea of online pornography, is creating challenges for both men and women.

On the other side of the fantasy quest for a soulmate who will "save" us lurks modern fatalism about the longevity of relationships and the role of sex. A well-known author described her experience of talking to a group of US college students about the "mystery" of sexual intimacy.[7] During the lecture, a young man candidly explained that in a new relationship, he preferred to get sex out of the way quickly to get rid of the tension. When the author asked him if that didn't also get rid of the mystery of sex, he looked at her blankly and said, "Mystery? I don't know what you're talking about. Sex has no mystery." The church has often been accused of making too big a deal about sex, but I think the opposite is true. We've often made too big a deal about the rules about sex without describing why sexual intimacy really *is* a big deal.

So how does our secular culture of authenticity play out in the lives of young people on college campuses? According to a group of sociologists who undertook a massive survey of college students across the United States, among the students there were surprisingly consistent "sexual scripts."[8] These scripts added up to a set of unquestioned beliefs about sexuality, even though the sociologists observed that these beliefs were generally not true in reality. These "sexual scripts" were that

- long-term exclusivity in relationships is not possible.

- the introduction of sex is necessary to sustain a fledgling or struggling relationship.

---

6 Mark Regnerus and Jeremy Uecker, *Premarital Sex in America: How Young Americans Meet, Mate, and Marry in America* (New York: Oxford University Press, 2011), 23–24, 191–92.

7 Naomi Wolf, "The Porn Myth," *New York Magazine*, October 9, 2003, http://nymag.com/nymetro/news/trends/n_9437/.

8 Regnerus and Uecker, *Premarital Sex*, 143–45.

- men are slaves to their lower impulses and so cannot be expected to control themselves.

- it does not matter what other people do sexually; you are free to make your own decisions.

- pornography won't affect your relationships.

- everyone else is having more sex than you are.

- sex is fun and doesn't need to mean anything more.

- marriage can always wait.

- moving in together is a definite and positive step toward marriage.[9]

What is so tragic about these sexual scripts is not that they offend our religious beliefs but that they distort human identity and experience so profoundly. The Christian vision of life seeks to describe a way of being human that accurately reflects who we are as beings created in the image of God. Within this vision, sexual intimacy is not an end in itself (a god to be served) but a servant of the greater goal of human flourishing, which includes faithful and enduring relationships. The sad reality of these secular sexual scripts is that they are causing harm to a whole generation of young people because they present falsehoods as truth and fatalism as hope.

Understanding a Christian Vision of Sex and Relationships

If these scripts are the sexual ecology we live in, how do both we and our students resist it, and how do we steward our bodies well as Christians?

First, we need to understand and own what we believe about our sexuality. We can explore this through what makes us, as humans, different from other creatures. Whereas animals act out of instinctive

9 Regnerus and Uecker, 236–50.

reflexive desires like hunger, sex, and fear, we are hermeneutical creatures, which means we have desires about our desires.[10] We can decide whether the urges and appetites we have are the ones we want. We make these decisions all the time in different areas of our lives, whether it's foregoing a sudden sugar craving for the greater priority of being healthy or missing a party to study for an important test. As humans, we are constantly prioritizing and choosing between the different things we want. Put in theological terms, Christian moral vision is the idea that we can choose higher desires or "hypergoods," which then order everything else we want and do.[11]

As Christians, we also believe that Scripture is our "primary text" or ultimate source of truth, which helps us define these hypergoods so that we can interpret and align our lives with the unchanging truth we find in the Bible. In a sense, Scripture is a lighthouse, and we are ships at sea, finding our bearings from God's solid ground and his guiding light. But our secular culture of authenticity has reversed this dynamic. Its "sexual scripts" tell us that our personal feelings, desires, and appetites are our most reliable source of truth so that we, ourselves, are the primary text, and Scripture must be interpreted and harmonized with who we are.

So what is the Christian vision for sex found in Scripture? In summary, our sexuality has three dimensions—it is eschatological, metaphysical, and formational. These may sound like strange words for a chapter on sex, but let's take a closer look.

The Eschatological Dimension

Our biggest challenge today is to engage our Christian imaginations while living in a culture that believes there is nothing beyond the here and now. Through our secular cultural lens, there is no ultimate future to prepare for and there is no sacred canopy to live under that makes sense of who we are and what we should do. But the Christian vision of life could not be more different. Our defining belief is that

---

10 Charles Taylor, *Sources of the Self: The Making of the Modern Identity* (Cambridge, MA: Harvard University Press, 1992), 4, 20, 47.

11 Taylor, 63–73.

our lives, including our sexuality, are being swept up into a bigger story—authored by God—that gives significance, purpose, and hope to every decision we make, whether big or small. The picture we get of our ultimate future in the book of Revelation is of the eternal wedding feast of the lamb, when Jesus returns in Revelation 19:7–10. This passage is a picture of complete social intimacy when we will know Jesus and other people closer than any marital or sexual embrace. This future sets the horizon for our lives and gives them shape and purpose because if we are made for this social and relational destiny, then we're called to live now as prophetic citizens of that future age. Seeing into this future is why both Jesus and Paul could say that they lacked nothing despite being celibate; they could see all of life in light of that ultimate perspective.

Once we fix our eyes on this picture, we can see that all relational states, whether single or married, are different expressions of life that find their purpose in God's Kingdom and the church. Probably the most countercultural witness we have in our highly sexualized culture is the Christian idea that we can embrace this future story and live a healthy life through singleness and nonsexual friendships as well as through committed sexual relationships in marriage.

This reality was one of the radical sexual innovations introduced by the apostles and New Testament writers. They lived in a culture that was built on marriage and family as its fundamental unit, leaving unmarried citizens as outliers and misfits within this cultural system. And yet, the apostles were able to articulate a positive purpose for both marriage and singleness as twin sexual vocations for serving the unfolding Kingdom of God.[12] In the same way, we need to own our radical spiritual heritage because we, too, live in a culture that is obsessed with sex and romantic fantasies. The New Testament does not promote one form of life as better than the other (e.g., marriage versus singleness) because both relational states play a positive and important role in God's mission and the church.

---

12 For example, see 1 Corinthians 7 for Paul's discussion. In Matthew, Mark, and Luke, Jesus describes the passing away of marriage following the resurrection of the dead (see Matt. 22:30; Mark 12:25; and Luke 20:35).

We also need to face the challenge of stewarding our bodies in a secular world. In Galatians 5, through his imagery of the war between the Spirit and the flesh, the apostle Paul describes the cosmic crisis we experience today as living in between the times. Paul is using these terms in their eschatological sense.[13] This concept is not about our sinful bodies fighting against our pure souls, and Paul does not make that distinction—nor does it exist within Scripture. It is about the big-picture story. Paul is saying that we still live in the age of the flesh, which is the old age animated by human sin and brokenness. The good news is that the age of the Spirit, which is God's future rule, has already broken into our present existence through the life, death, and resurrection of Jesus. Paul urges the Galatians (and us) to acknowledge this crisis: that we are torn between these ages and need to live decisively in the present and future age of the Spirit.

Here is the significance of Paul's teaching for us. Our culture of authenticity says that we can simply make peace with our sexual desires by succumbing to them and even proudly owning them. In fact, this approach is how we become our true selves. In contrast, the Christian vision of human identity is that to become our true (authentic) selves, we first need to confront our fallen (inauthentic) desires with the truth, grace, and power of Jesus and to embrace the redeemed sexuality of our present and future identity in Christ. Richard Hays described the struggle of Christian bodily stewardship:

> Those who demand fulfilment now, as though it were a right or a guarantee, are living in a state of adolescent illusion. To be sure, the transforming power of the Spirit really is present in our midst; on the other hand, the "not yet" looms large; we live with the reality of temptation, the reality of the hard struggle to live faithfully. Consequently . . . some may find disciplined abstinence the only viable alternative to disordered sexuality. The art of eschatological moral discernment lies in working out how to live lives free from

13 Gordon D. Fee, *God's Empowering Presence: The Holy Spirit in the Letters of Paul* (Peabody, MA: Hendrickson, 1994), 817–19.

bondage to sin without presuming to be translated prematurely into a condition that is free from "the sufferings of this present time."[14]

In summary, the eschatological dimension of our sexuality describes the tension we live in as Christians. Given the power of this challenge, the church has often focused on what it's right to do rather than on what it's good to be, on defining the rules about sex rather than the nature of the good life in Christian terms. In the highly charged area of sex and relationships, we certainly need clear boundaries that protect us and others, but we also need a guiding vision of life that makes sense of those boundaries and gives them a motivating force.

The Metaphysical Dimension

The second dimension of Christian sexuality is the metaphysical dimension. We believe that there is a greater heavenly reality, which is a present and parallel dimension to ours and even more real than what we can see. This, again, is where our Christian imagination requires a bit of shock treatment. C. S. Lewis described this view through the idea of "transposition."[15] Using a musical analogy, he said that if there is a rich orchestral score playing in heaven right now that expresses the fullness of God's character and what his Kingdom looks like, then as followers of Jesus we can recognize and play these same musical themes in our current lives. We can join in with and witness to God's character and the reality of heaven in our present contexts on a college campus.

So how can we play these heavenly harmonies in our sexual lives? The Christian vision is that we can only find and express our true selves in faithful, committed relationships—whether sexual or

14 Richard B. Hays, *The Moral Vision of the New Testament: Community, Cross, New Creation, A Contemporary Introduction to New Testament Ethics* (San Francisco: HarperSanFrancisco, 1996), 393–94.
15 C. S. Lewis, "Transposition," in *The Weight of Glory and Other Addresses* (New York: HarperCollins, 2001), 91–115.

social—and we actually lose ourselves when we pursue our lower desires or appetites. We are made in the image of God (Gen. 1:26–27), and through Jesus, a sexual being just like us, we are called "to put on the new self, created to be like God in true righteousness and holiness" (Eph. 4:17–24). So if we are created to be "like God," what does Scripture reveal about God?

First and foremost, God lives in self-giving community with the Trinity—what theologians describe as a divine dance (*perichoresis* in Greek), whereby the generous sharing of love between the Father, Son, and Spirit blurs the boundaries between them as they intimately engage with one another. This relational model of radical self-giving is the template for our own identity because Jesus welcomes us into the relationships he shares with the Father and Spirit (John 14:15–21).

God is popularly characterized as a distant and detached figure, often angry and judgmental, but on the contrary, the image of him in Scripture is of an intimate, passionate, and loving Creator. In both the Old and New Testaments, God describes his relationship with his people as that between a bride and groom, even using graphic love poetry to express this bond in the Song of Songs. He is a faithful and committed lover.

The story recorded in Scripture is of God making a covenant with his people and then persevering in love despite their constant infidelity. This covenant commitment finds its final expression in the astonishing gift of Jesus himself. Our boldest claim as Christians is that, through Jesus, God has fully revealed himself to us and has identified with us by taking on our human existence, binding our destiny to his forever.

Nothing could be more reassuring as we seek to steward our sexuality within the powerful riptides of modern culture. Jesus was and remains a gendered being and he's known the challenges, frustrations, limitations, and temptations of being human. But he's not just a sympathetic friend; he's also our Savior. Jesus is the only person who has overcome death and is the first person of the new humanity (Rom. 8:29). In order to steward our sexuality well, we need to seize the truth that no part of our lives is beyond God's grace and healing;

nothing we do—no desires, temptations, or addictions—lies beyond the reach of his forgiveness and hope.

One of the most common problems I see as a pastor is people's reluctance to bring their failures and mistakes to God in order to receive his forgiveness and healing. Our sense of guilt or shame, especially when it comes to matters of sex, often drives a wedge between us and God. And yet nothing could be further from his intention or desire. Jesus is God's radically outstretched arm of grace toward us. His atoning death removes any distance between us and ushers us into friendship with him. We will struggle to steward our bodies confidently if we walk under the destructive shadow of shame and fail to grasp the heart of the gospel: that Jesus died for our sins and is our champion and friend. This friendship is not predicated on our faultless performance or perfect behavior; if it were, Jesus's circle of friends would be a very exclusive group! Jesus is not a remote or judgmental God; he is our gracious, ever-loving Savior. His radical act of love has offered us intimate friendship with the source of life and has breathed resurrection hope and healing into the challenge of human sexuality.

Furthermore, there is a common misperception in both the church and our culture that Christian sexuality involves fighting against our nature and stoically imposing an artificial way of living over and against who we really are. But the metaphysical claim of Christian sexuality is that the opposite is true. Although we still live in the age of the flesh, and our frailty and brokenness are still a challenging reality, we are seeking to tune into our created and redeemed identity. So if the eschatological dimension of our faith says that our sexuality is defined by, and will find its fulfillment in, God's ultimate future, then the metaphysical dimension gives our sexual lives present significance. Christian sexuality is not about grimly clinging on to a future hope; it's about pursuing a life of flourishing and fulfillment now because it describes sex as it really is, and it gives us contexts where genuine intimacy can be nurtured and protected.

These timeless principles, like gravity, are written into the universe by a loving Creator who longs for us to thrive. An example from the amazing world of neuroscience comes from the anthropologist

Helen Fisher, who described three different "brain systems," or stages of attachment, within intimate relationships:

- infatuation

- sexual intimacy

- deep emotional attachment[16]

Her team interviewed people at different stages of relationships while taking functional MRI brain scans. What they observed, as you'd expect, was that the most dramatic period of a relationship was the first phase, essentially strong infatuation. They found that "falling for someone" impacts the same brain centers with a similar intensity to cocaine. This area is the "motor" of the mind, associated with our basic drives like hunger, craving, and focus. Fisher described this first romantic phase as one of the most addictive substances in the human experience.

The second phase of attachment is sexual intimacy. Sex is a powerful bonding agent between people, and Fisher said that there is really no such thing as "casual sex" because the cocktail of hormones and neurotransmitters released during sex act as an indelible bonding agent between those involved. Fisher was not championing a traditional Christian understanding of sex. She is a Darwinian evolutionary sociologist, and yet her team's findings confirm the Christian conviction that there is more to sex than just sex.

Finally, the third key stage of a relationship is the quieter, deeper emotional bonding that occurs in warm, shared experiences like taking a walk on a beach or watching a movie together. Although less spectacular than the first two stages, the physiological dynamics here deepen the emotional bond.

There are a few important truths to take from these findings. First, they show that our embodied createdness—our divine design—is actually in tune with the biblical vision of intimacy. This realization

---

16 Helen Fisher, "Why We Love, Why We Cheat," filmed in September 2006 in Monterey, CA, TED video, 23:15, https://www.ted.com/talks/helen_fisher_why _we_love_why_we_cheat.

should give us confidence that when we guard and intentionally hold together these three relational dynamics or stages, they become like strands of a rope that progressively weave and entwine two people into "one flesh."

These findings also show the challenge of human sexuality and provide a stark warning. Our secular "culture of authenticity" has allowed, and even encouraged, these three forces to become detached from one another, and it has taught us to search for our true selves in our most powerful emotions and sexual desires. The problem, of course, is that those first two stages of a relationship will always feel the most powerful, and so a new crush or sexual attachment will inevitably feel more real than an existing one. As Fisher said, these three stages may coexist within us but be attached to different people at the same time so that we might feel love and warmth toward our spouse and yet long for someone else. You can then understand why Scripture warns to "guard your affections." Once we allow these powerful forces to engage at cross purposes within us, we discover the awful pain, confusion, and conflict that can take hold within the human heart. Our desires, when left unchecked, can become a tidal force that engulfs us.

Christian Sexuality Is Formational

By describing Christian sexuality as formational, I mean that we are seeking to resist our lower (inauthentic) sexual desires and to embrace our true (authentic) sexual desires as we conform ourselves to Jesus as our model and mentor. The most important form of support we have for this journey is our spiritual family, the church. We cannot steward our sexual lives alone. The hope of being Christian is that we surround ourselves with trusted friends, mentors, and counselors—brothers and sisters in Christ—whom we can honestly share our journey with and lean on when it counts.

As I conclude, I would encourage you to ask yourself and your students one practical question. Is there someone of the same sex that you speak honestly with about your life, including issues of sex, relationships, and temptation? If not, who would you trust to play that role in your life? Forming these relationships of mutual honesty, trust, and accountability will be the most important step you and your students take toward stewarding your sexuality well, while at college and in the future.

———————

For further reading on this topic, see my book *Divine Sex: A Compelling Vision for Christian Relationships in a Hypersexualized Age* (Brazos Press).

Part Two

From Fall to Redemption

Chapter 7
Fashion
Clothing Collegians in Christ

Robert Covolo

But we know that when Christ appears, we shall be like him, for we shall see him as he is.

—1 John 3:2

Clothing matters to collegians. For those working with young adults, this is a truism. While there is not a "one-size-fits-all" college student, the average collegian spends a good share of their disposable income on clothing.[1] This reality reflects a simple fact: campus is not only where college students read, write, and reside; it is also their runway. But why does clothing play such an important role for collegians, and what should we make of this phenomenon? Should we chalk up the focus college students put on dress to a benign or even a positive reflex? Or should this impulse give those working with collegians concern?

This chapter explores the role of fashion in the life of college students. Those working with collegians need to help their students engage their relationship to dressing distinctly as Christians. To do this, I will draw from two resources. Our first source

---

1 "Spending Habits in High School vs. in College," 1st Financial Bank, accessed June 11, 2022, https://students.1fbusa.com/college-life/spending-habits-in-high -school-vs-in-college.

is the considerable direction Scripture offers on the role of dress. As we shall see, the Bible has a lot to say about how everyday dress relates to being clothed in Christ (Rom. 13:14). Our second resource is the burgeoning field of fashion studies.[2] This young but exploding discipline is a rich resource for those seeking to understand how the use of fashion impacts the everyday lives of young adults. But before launching, it is important to get a handle on some key terms.

What Is Fashion?

Most people use the terms "fashion" and "clothing" somewhat interchangeably. But fashion theorists draw a distinction between the two.[3] Clothing is (typically) items of cloth designed to be worn to cover the body. This term is closely related to "apparel," which refers to items of clothing being sold in a store; to "adornment," which refers to items that we put on the body to enliven or decorate it; and to "dress," which is used to refer to putting things on the body so as to adorn, protect, or signify it, among other purposes.

In addition to these terms is the word "fashion." As it turns out, fashion is not as easy to define as the other terms.[4] While a hard-and-

2 The past half century has seen an explosion in the number of conferences and publications exploring the nature of fashion. A simple Amazon.com search will reveal a plethora of resources. In addition to degree programs offered at universities around the globe, "elite schools" focused on fashion studies include Parsons School of Design (New York), The Fashion Institute of Technology (New York), Central Saint Martins (London), London College of Fashion, Royal College of Art (London), Istituto Marangoni (Milan), Politecnico di Milano (Milan), École de la Chambre Syndicale de la Couture Parisienne (Paris), ESMOD (Paris), Antwerp Royal Academy of Fine Arts (Antwerp), and Bunka Fashion College (Japan).

3 For an example of someone who completely disassociated fashion and clothing, see sociologist George Simmel, *Simmel on Culture*, ed. David Frisby and Mike Featherstone (London: Sage, 1997), 190.

4 In fact, an entire discourse has arisen called "fashion theory" that studies the nature and impact of fashion. For an excellent primer on fashion theory, see Malcolm Barnard, *Fashion Theory: An Introduction* (New York: Routledge, 2014). For a more advanced discussion on the nature of fashion, see Agnés Rocamora and Anneke Smelik, eds., *Thinking through Fashion: A Guide to Key Theorists* (New York: I. B. Tauris, 2016).

fast definition of fashion might be elusive, there are some features that all fashion theorists acknowledge about fashion. One of these salient features of fashion is its inherent connection to change. In fact, the term "fashion" can be used to refer to any kind of regular replacement within a given sphere of culture where things move in and out of a cultural currency—be it ideas or automobiles.[5] Fashion can be applied to everything from theories in the academy to architectural styles, but in this chapter, the term will refer to the systematic, rapid interplay of items of dress and styles of personal adornment.

A second recognized feature of fashionable dress is its unique relationship to Western modernity.[6] There are a variety of factors in the modern West that have given rise to fashion—the emergence of capitalism, the industrial revolution, technological developments, democratic initiatives, social mobility, and so on. In what follows, we will see how this unique relationship of fashion to modern Western values shapes collegians. But one immediate implication of the close relationship of fashion to Western modernity is already apparent; namely, all Americans (college students included) participate in fashion.[7]

5 See Joan Entwistle, *The Fashioned Body: Fashion, Dress and Modern Social Theory*, 2nd ed. (Maiden, MA: Polity, 2015), 45.

6 For the special relationship between fashion and Western modernity, see Christopher Breward and Caroline Evans, eds., *Fashion and Modernity* (New York: Bloomsbury Academic, 2005); Giles Lipovetsky, *The Empire of Fashion: Dressing Modern Democracies* (Princeton: Princeton University Press, 1994), 15; Elizabeth Wilson, *Adorned in Dreams: Fashion and Modernity* (New Brunswick, NJ: Rutgers University Press, 2003), 16; Fred Davis, *Fashion, Culture, and Identity* (Chicago: University of Chicago Press, 1992), 26, 28; Ulrich Lehmann, *Tigersprung: Fashion in Modernity* (Cambridge, MA: MIT Press, 2002); and Chris Breward, "Style and Modernity," in *Fashion* (Oxford: Oxford University Press, 2003), 159–68.

7 As Anne Hollander stated, "Everybody has to get dressed in the morning and go about the day's business . . . what everybody wears to do this has taken different forms in the West for about seven hundred years and that is what fashion is." Anne Hollander, *Sex and Suits* (New York: Alfred A. Knopf, 1995), 11.

Stylizing Our Lives

If you ask the average college student what draws them to the clothing they wear, a likely answer is the clothes they chose "look cool" (or some similar slang). In other words, they find some clothing notable for the feelings and associations it evokes. Clothing is not the only thing that evokes "cool." And of course, the quest for "cool" is not limited to college students. Most Americans (Christians included) have come to take for granted that a thing's perceptible form and felt qualities (i.e., its "coolness") are connected to what is appreciable and meaningful in life. Said another way, for most Americans, "cool" is not just about the eye being drawn to shiny or stylish objects. Rather, "cool" is part of what it means to live life well.[8] This is decisively so because most Americans believe stylizing one's life (creating a compelling "lifestyle") is central to a life well lived.

Is this reality because Americans are hedonistic consumers? Consumerism is a real threat—to say nothing of the secular employment of style en route to a merely immanent life.[9] (I shall say more about this later.) But before writing off the stylization of our lives, we would do well to hear the words of Ecclesiastes 9:8. Confronted with the emptiness ("vanity") of life given death's obliterating power (Eccles. 9:1–3), the writer of Ecclesiastes points his readers to the inherent promise of life's daily gifts (vv. 4–10). It is here (while listing death-denying daily gifts) the writer of Ecclesiastes charges his readers, "Let your garments always be white" (v. 8 NRSVUE). In short, the writer claims the simple joy of fresh, delightful clothing can serve as a spiritual protest against death's (seeming) conquest.

What does this admonition have to do with advising college students regarding style? For starters, it means that the act of everyday adornment can be charged with hope. Indeed, playing with color and form is one way to engage in the joyful celebration of youthfulness—a

---

8 William Dyrness, *Poetic Theology* (Grand Rapids, MI: Eerdmans, 2011), 11.

9 Of course, the content of a given "cool lifestyle" shifts from person to person and period to period. For example, in the last decade, the lifestyle of "van life" has emerged. This neo-Romantic vision involves dropping out of the rat race, buying a van, and living a nomadic life in a converted van (or bus).

way to "remember your Creator," if you will (Eccles. 12:1). Particularly helpful in this regard is the work of Christian philosopher Calvin Seerveld.[10] In his "Joy, Style, and Aesthetic Imperatives with the Biblical Meaning of Clothes and Games in the Christian Life," Seerveld argued that "joy is the defining mark of full-fledged aesthetic obedience."[11] For Seerveld, joy is particularly at home (enters most easily and pervasively) in the daily styles we develop. Style may not make or break a person. But for Seerveld, "style is one of the good works for which we were created in Christ Jesus."[12]

Seerveld sees adorning one's body as an important daily ritual whereby people take time to move into an aesthetic registrar. Even more, attending to daily dress can serve as an excellent training ground for honoring God through what Seerveld called "aesthetic obedience"; that is, getting dressed can serve as a time to engage the aesthetic aspects of God's good creation as found in our own bodies, which are "fearfully and wonderfully made" (Ps. 139:14).

Clothing as an art form can elevate our lives and honor God. But of course, not all art elevates. As with other forms of art emerging in modernity, fashion can take on sub-Christian forms. For example, fashion can be used to draw a flat and perverse fixation on parts of the body. Alternatively, we can stylize our clothing so as to hide from others. We can dress like a poison dart frog—using obnoxious colors to signal social toxicity. Or again, we can dress in a way that signals deep irony, confusion, or incoherence. These examples remind us that not all style involves a playful engagement with the aesthetic registrar. For art not only creates; it communicates. This fact leads us to another important thread for clothing collegians in Christ: clothing as communication.

---

10 Calvin Seerveld, "Joy, Style, and Aesthetic Imperatives with the Biblical Meaning of Clothes and Games in the Christian Life," in *Normative Aesthetics*, ed. John H. Kok (Sioux City, IA: Dordt College Press, 2014), 81–95.
11 Seerveld, 82.
12 Seerveld, 87.

Clothing and Communication

Every college student knows their social world is shaped by their choice of clothing. (Many did, after all, survive the peer pressure of high school!) In other words, they know clothing communicates, and this communication impacts how people perceive and relate to them. The apostle James recognizes the power of dress to communicate when he warns his readers about disparate responses to two church visitors: "a man wearing a gold ring and fine clothing" and "a poor man in shabby clothing" (James 2:2–4 ESV). It is noteworthy that James does not chastise his readers for picking up the clear signals of the new attendee's dress. Rather, he confronts them for their prejudicial treatment. Said another way, James is not arguing for "class blindness" (they could clearly see one visitor was rich and one was poor by what they wore). Instead, he is calling the church to operate like a healthy family wherein everyone (regardless of class) is enthusiastically welcomed.

Take another example from Scripture revealing the power of clothing to communicate. Leviticus 19:19 tells us, "You shall not . . . wear a garment of cloth made of two kinds of material" (ESV). This odd command fits within a host of holiness codes in Leviticus that were designed to make the people of Israel stand out from their pagan neighbors. In this case, Israel was to be distinct precisely because of the textiles they wore. Again, this passage implicitly recognizes the power dress holds for communicating (and therefore creating and sustaining) a sense of community. Even today people dress to express not only individual distinction but also (and at the same time) social belonging. We dress to connect, and those seeking to nurture the spiritual lives of college students would do well to take seriously the emotional bids for connection that collegians wear on their sleeves.

Let's turn to a more controversial text revealing the power of clothing to communicate. Deuteronomy 22:5 charges, "A woman shall not wear a man's garment, nor shall a man put on a woman's cloak, for whoever does these things is an abomination to the LORD your

God" (ESV). Here—drawing from Genesis 1:27, which tells us God created people "male and female"—the author claims God has definite opinions about gender expression. While our cultural moment may view a bricolage of gender-bending clothing as nothing more than creative mashup and self-expression, this verse suggests otherwise. Of course, the subject of gender ushers us into a host of issues that we don't have time to address here. Even so, and as important as such issues may be, we can't miss Deuteronomy's implicit claim that dress is a form of communicating not only one's gender identity but one's views about gender.

The previously mentioned passages remind us that dress communicates both belonging and distinction. It simultaneously binds us to others (Lev. 19:19) and demarks us from others (Deut. 22:5).[13] In light of this power of dress, what guidance should we give college students under our care? One of the most interesting passages dealing with dress is Galatians 3:26–28. Here Paul writes, "For as many of you as were baptized into Christ have put on Christ. There is neither Jew nor Greek, there is neither slave nor free, there is no male and female, for you are all one in Christ Jesus." What is often missed here is these various (ethnic, class, gender) social identities were displayed in the distinct clothing people wore. This is why Paul leads this passage by reminding his readers they have "put on Christ." By doing so, Paul is reminding his Christian audience that their Christian identity trumps any other belongings or distinctions. But again, what might this mean for directing students? For starters, putting on Christ should undo divisions. It does this not by homogenizing dress and destroying distinct social identities (or blurring them, as the case may be) but by relativizing all identities in light of our shared identity in Christ.

---

13 Here I am indebted to the work of Lauren F. Winner. For a popular discussion with practical illustrations of how dress both draws together social groups and divides them at the same time, see Lauren F. Winner, *Wearing God: Clothing, Laughter, Fire, and Other Overlooked Ways of Meeting God* (New York: HarperCollins, 2014), 41–51.

In turn, another application of "putting on Christ" emerges. To dress as a Christian is to adorn ourselves with the same other-centered focus of Christ. In this regard, theologian Thomas Aquinas suggested virtuous dress entails dressing in such a way that the dignity and honor of others are recognized (Rom. 12:10).[14] So rather than dressing merely with an eye toward ourselves, Aquinas called Christians to dress in a way that elevates those around us—dress being a vehicle of hospitality by which people we meet during the day are elevated. (After all, they are the ones who have to look at us!) This idea of using dress as an act of hospitality by which we honor others, elevate social contexts, and ennoble human interaction is foreign to a generation growing up with the idea that dress is for self-expression. But if wearing Christ is about having the same attitude as the one who came to love and serve others (Phil. 2:5–8), we will want to ask ourselves (and the college students we serve) these questions: Are we dressing as an act of exclusion or embrace? Is there hospitality in the way we dress? Does our dress communicate honor and respect for others? Are we able to exude the warm welcome of Jesus in what we're wearing? Or is our outfit a logo-centric billboard designed to draw attention to ourselves?

Approaching dress as a way to communicate warmth, hospitality, respect, and honor is counterintuitive to those of us immersed in late-modern fashion. One reason for this reality is communication itself (via dress, words, or any other forms) has become "problematized" in late modernity. Here, the long history of semiotics—the science of how language communicates—with names like Roland Barthes (author of *The Language of Fashion*) and Jacques Derrida enters.[15] As with gender, the issues surrounding the semiotics of

---

14 For Aquinas on fashion, see Robert Covolo, *Fashion Theology* (Waco, TX: Baylor University Press, 2020), 14–19.

15 Roland Barthes's *The Language of Fashion* (London: Bloomsbury, 2013) sought to use fashion as an example of his structural semiotics, which Barthes would come to abandon later in life. Jacques Derrida's work on "deconstruction" is most associated with his book *Of Grammatology* (Baltimore: Johns Hopkins University Press, 1998).

fashion are beyond the scope of this chapter.[16] Yet a word should be said about how Derrida has found his way into all our closets. In the wake of critical theories, sign systems have been deemed "unstable," "undecidable," and "fluid." As a result, dressing in late modernity carries with it our culture's soft-relativism, as "there are no absolute values that exist outside the play of fashionable difference."[17] In turn, identity has become purely a constructed and performed project. Surface and veneer become the final words on reality. Meaning becomes the mere product of individual subjective expression. In short, there are no longer final meanings to our dress (or any other text for that matter). There is only the endless parade of random, stylistic allusions.

Such viewpoints are at odds with approaching the Bible as the unchanging word revealing the eternal Word made flesh, but less obvious is how postmodern fashion embodies ideas that are incommensurate with a Christian view of semiotics, identity, and reality. Therefore, it is helpful to ask some diagnostics about our dress Is the layering of irony, satire, and cynicism found in postmodern dress compatible with someone who believes in the resurrection of the body? How can one dress in heroin chic (a style that suggests a lifestyle of drug abuse) while seeking to bear the fruit of self-control? Can we reconcile an endless recycling of styles with the drama of redemption climaxing in the return of Christ? Can we be dressed to kill while praying for our enemies? I ask these questions to push at a simple truth: not all styles are fitting for those proclaiming the Christian message. The question is not one of "right" or "wrong" but whether something "fits" or harmonizes with following Christ. After all, dress is a visual metaphor. And like all metaphors, it is not either/or but one of resonance and dissonance to greater or lesser

16 Malcolm Barnard's *Fashion as Communication* (New York: Routledge, 2002) is the best dedicated monograph on fashion and communication. Barnard drew deeply from the Derrida school. By my lights, a more Christian reading of the semiotics of fashion would draw less from Jacques Derrida and more from Hans-George Gadamer and Paul Ricœur. For Gadamer and Ricœur the excess of meaning in a text is not a "flaw" that makes language "unstable" but the vehicle by which meaning is made possible.

17 Barnard, 166.

degrees. In short, if we are going to help collegians live a life that displays Christ, we shouldn't be afraid to ask them if they think their dress serves or detracts from that aim.

Dressed in Blood

John Calvin lived in Paris during the rise of early modern fashion. Recognizing the craze for clothing among his contemporaries, Calvin charged Christians to watch their spending on clothes, lest they inadvertently clothe themselves in "the blood of the poor."[18] Calvin's concern for the human cost of popular dress is as relevant as ever. Indeed, in the past two decades, several documentaries have exposed the unjust labor practices haunting the fashion industry.[19] As Elizabeth Klein famously put it, there is a shockingly high cost to cheap fashion.[20] This cost is no better evident than in the Rana Plaza factory collapse that killed over 1,100 garment workers. While some companies have responded since the collapse to improve the working conditions in countries like Bangladesh, the fashion industry has a long way to go. More recently, questions have emerged on what it means to hold companies accountable and if "bottom up" ethical consumption actually helps.[21] In short, protecting the world's real fashion victims is not as easy as we might hope.

These issues should be taken seriously by those seeking to guide collegians; after all, the Bible gives us numerous admonitions

---

18 John Calvin, "On Luxury," in *Calvin's Ecclesiastical Advice*, trans. Mary Beaty and Benjamin Farley (Louisville, KY: Westminster John Knox, 1991), 86. See also Covolo, *Fashion Theology*, 26.

19 Some films exposing the dark side of the fashion industry include *The True Cost*, directed by Andrew Morgan (Los Angeles: Life Is My Movie Entertainment, 2015), film; *Luxury: Behind the Mirror*, directed by Sandrine Rigaud (Paris: Premières Lignes, 2018), film; and *The Clothes We Wear*, directed by Detlef Flintz (Berlin: DW, 2020), film.

20 Elizabeth Klein, *Overdressed: The Shockingly High Cost of Cheap Fashion* (New York: Portfolio, 2013).

21 For an example of this challenge, see Elizabeth Klein, "The Twilight of the Ethical Consumer," *Atmos*, October 19, 2020, https://atmos.earth/ethical -consumerism/.

regarding our treatment of the poor (Prov. 11:26; 22:16, 22–23; Matt. 25:34–40; James 2:14–17; etc.). Again, as with other issues we've already touched on such as gender and semiotics, unjust labor and environmental sustainability move us beyond the scope of this chapter. That said, those nurturing the spiritual lives of collegians should point to the global realities behind our everyday fashion choices. For help, we can find direction from the numerous Christians who are leading the way in seeking to protect the poor and the environment while making thoughtful, elegant garments.[22]

Most collegians won't be directly involved in addressing how the fashion industry wreaks global havoc, but few will escape the strong pull of invasive market forces in their personal lives. Fashion theorists have long seen fashion as symbolic of consumerism.[23] Given the inordinate amount of money collegians spend on fashion, those seeking to help college students should have frank conversations about what it means to approach our finances as good stewards who forego a perfect wardrobe for the sake of others (Matt. 6.25).

This concern for others brings us back to Calvin. According to Calvin, we cannot "put on Christ" without self-denial. When collegians make concrete sacrifices for the sake of blessing others, they display the same glad self-giving of Christ himself, the one who laid aside the splendor and glory of heaven to be stripped and placed on a cross—all so that we might be dressed in his beautiful robes of righteousness (Isa. 61:10).

22 For a handy list of ethical Christian fashion brands, see the list produced by Gretchen Saffles, "Ethical Fashion," Well Watered Women Co., July 15, 2022, https://wellwateredwomen.com/ethical-fashion/.

23 Notable in this regard is Thorstein Veblen's famous *The Theory of the Leisure Class: An Economic Study of Institutions* (1899), wherein Veblen credited fashionable clothing as a primary way upper classes display their pecuniary strength. It was recently republished as Thorstein Veblen, *Theory of the Leisure Class* (Oxford: Oxford University Press, 2009).

Fashion, Narrative, and Self-Expression

Perhaps the most pernicious part of being a fashion slave is not the way it curtails our response to the less fortunate. Perhaps consumerism's most deadly venom is found in the way it inscribes us into seductive narratives that dominate our lives. This seduction is possible precisely because dress plays an important role in telling the stories of our lives.[24] Our daily dress provides the backdrop that gives our mundane actions meaning. When we dress, we project (often tacitly) how we would like our day to go: the groups we will associate with, the activities we will engage in, and the way people will perceive us. As psychologists of dress know all too well, the person often most influenced by what is worn is the person doing the wearing.[25] Our daily dress is much more powerful than we think, for it draws us into our narratives like actors in a play. It focuses our attention, bringing parts of who we are and what we seek into focus.[26] Our bodies bring with them their own ways of knowing[27]—all the more so when it comes to the dressed body. It follows that those desiring to nurture collegians spiritually should pay attention to the stories students are wearing. Long before a student opens their mouth, they share their story through what they wear.

Fashion is one of the key components used to construct and perform the stories of our lives. But fashion also relays the story of the (late) modern West. Said another way, fashion is not a neutral instrument that we use but a practice that carries its own ways of seeing. For example, it is often said that the point of fashion is to "express yourself." When we get dressed, it is assumed we do so by looking inside ourselves to bring something inside ourselves to the outside

---

24 See Julia Twigg, "Dress and the Narration of Life," in *Fashion and Age: Dress, the Body and Later Life* (London: Bloomsbury, 2013), 75–95.

25 Carolyn Mair, *The Psychology of Fashion* (London: Routledge, 2018), 91–110.

26 See John Harvey, "What Shall I Wear, Who Shall I Be," in *Clothes: The Art of Living* (Stocksfield, UK: Acumen, 2008), 35–47.

27 For the role dress plays in shaping our worldview and actions, see James K. A. Smith, *Imagining the Kingdom: How Worship Works* (Grand Rapids, MI: Baker Academic, 2013), 21.

for others to see, be it a mood, an aspect of our personality, or our way of viewing ourselves. This understanding of dressing draws from what has been called "expressive individualism."[28] Today in the West, people assume each person has a unique and inexhaustible inner domain from which they *can* and by which they *should* bring things to the foreground.[29] Expressive individualism believes self-expression is critical for a meaningful life, for to not be true to our inner reservoir of beliefs and feelings is to commit a grave injustice against ourselves.

It is not hard to see how expressive individualism is at odds with elements of the Christian faith. After all, as Christians, we are not only individuals but also complementary members of one another called to lay aside our preferences (Rom. 12:5; Phil. 2:7). Additionally, far from seeing ourselves as radically unique individuals, we are also alike in that we are all made in the image of God (Gen. 1:26). Moreover, true freedom is found not by defining ourselves but by having God call us his very own (1 John 3:1). I could go on, but even so, we must not throw out fashion. Fashion may be a carrier of expressive individualism, but we need not be infected. The solution is not to reject fashion's self-expression, but to put it in its proper place. After all, God created us as individuals. Recognizing our individuality, communicating it, expressing it, and celebrating it is part of recognizing the Creator who made us the unique selves we are.[30] The problem is not with expressing our individuality, per se, but expressive individualism

28 Robert Bellah, *Habits of the Heart* (New York: Harper & Row, 1985), 32–35. Also see Charles Taylor, *Sources of the Self* (Cambridge, MA: Harvard University Press, 1989), 389.

29 Charles Taylor defined expressive individualism as the philosophy that "each of us has his/her own way of realizing our humanity, and that it is important to find and live out one's own, as against surrendering to conformity with a model imposed on us from outside, by society, or the previous generation, or religious or political authority." Charles Taylor, *A Secular Age* (Cambridge, MA: Belknap Press of Harvard University Press, 2007), 475.

30 For a defense of the importance of recognizing the individual, see Richard J. Mouw, "On Being Fair to 'Individualism,'" in *The God Who Commands: A Study in Divine Command Ethics* (Notre Dame, IN: University of Notre Dame Press, 1990), 43–54.

(note the "-ism"). Here, I am talking about turning self-expression into an all-encompassing philosophy that gives us final reality (I am whatever I feel I am), a theory of knowledge (truth is what I feel truth is), and our deepest values (free expression of one's preferences is the highest good).

Putting on the Imperishable

Though I could go on, the previous section suffices to demonstrate the unique challenges collegians face in their daily dress. We've seen that—far from a superficial subject—to think deeply about daily fashion introduces complex issues surrounding gender, semiotics, and contemporary notions of the self. Seeking to help college students "put on Christ" in an age of late-modern fashion requires awareness of these issues. But we should not end there.

Putting on Christ is not ultimately about censuring fashion. Rather, it involves making fashion "obedient to Christ" (2 Cor. 10:5). Helping collegians bring fashion under Christ's reign starts by revealing the power fashion holds. And foremost among fashion's power is the hope it injects into our self-imagination. (People turn to retail therapy for a reason, after all!) When collegians dress, they often do so envisioning themselves as an attractive, mature, life-filled person who is noticed by others. In other words, behind so much of our dress is a longing to be creatures of glory, to "put on the imperishable" (1 Cor. 15:52–53 ESV). As C. S. Lewis said so well, on that final day when we stand before Christ, our great longing to be noticed will once and for all be satiated. We will stand before him who knows all and is present everywhere as glorious and welcomed. Our great fear of being "repelled, exiled, estranged, finally and unspeakably ignored" will be once and for all utterly dispelled.[31]

Until that time, we put on Christ and help those we lead to do the same. We do so by setting a vision for how dress—as with every other aspect of embodied existence—can become a vehicle for joy as we

---

31 C. S. Lewis, *The Weight of Glory and Other Addresses* (New York: Collier, 1949), 15.

style the aesthetic body. We do so by loving those in our daily lives, honoring them with how we dress the social body. And we do so by looking forward with great hope and joy to the day when our bodies will be glorious beyond recognition, when we will make supermodels look like hags—the day when "we shall be like him, for we shall see him as he is" (1 John 3:2).

Chapter 8
Your Body and Your Mind
Social Media

Felicia Wu Song

B ack in 2011, two hundred University of Maryland undergraduates went on a twenty-four-hour fast from digital media and
technology.[1] Afterward, when tasked to write about their experience, students consistently complained about three results: being
bored, feeling left behind on the latest news and events, and feeling
as if "going without media meant . . . going without their friends and
family." Students used terms like "jittery," "very anxious," "frantically
craving," "in withdrawal," "miserable," and "unbearable" to describe
their feelings on going without the digital for one day.

Going without digital media and technology as these students did
over ten years ago does not quite feel the same as how it does today.
This study was conducted long before the likes of today's TikTok,
Snapchat, and social media influencer landscape. To consider what
this study signals about the psychological impact of social and digital
media on young people is not even to address the types of anxieties
they feel when dealing with the acceleration of social dramas in their
personal lives or feeling inadequate and envious when comparing
one's bland life with the unattainable charm and allure of what they
see online.

---

1 Susan Moeller et al., "A Day without Media," International Center for Media
and the Public Agenda, 2010, https://withoutmedia.wordpress.com.

A recent Pew study reported that 48 percent of eighteen- to twenty-nine-year-old Americans report being constantly online.[2] Some scholars describe our digital existence as one in which we live in a deep state of permanent connectivity: always tethered twenty-four seven as email, social media, and messaging open us up to friends, family members, colleagues, news, and entertainment from the wider world. Permanent connectivity also means permanent availability and chronic vulnerability to whatever news, message, or happening is going to come our way. As such, we come to live in a state of being on call: like a doctor or residential director who never shuts off her cell phone. We have come to feel that being online is necessary to being a good employee, good friend, good colleague, good family member, or good leader.

As more and more of us struggle under the resulting pressures to keep up, we may be prone to direct our frustrations toward our smartphone, our social media, or that app or email in-box that has us wrapped around its finger. In this focus, it is easy for us to forget that tech companies create platforms and devices and run our digital services. It is also easy to overlook the ways our digital habits are not merely matters of willpower but corporeal in nature and that our bodies have become deeply trained by technologies and technological systems that often know us better than ourselves. Developing a clearer sense of how deeply our digital lives are structured to reward continuous use of our apps and devices—and structured to make any attempt to resist such use costly—we might better understand how to live well in our bodies with our technologies.

Addictive by Design

The basic brain science behind how we physiologically get "hooked" on digital stimulation has become more widely understood over the last few years. We've come to grasp that every time our smartphone

2 Andrew Perrin and Sara Atske, "About Three-in-Ten U.S. Adults Say They Are 'Almost Constantly' Online," Pew Research Center, 2021, https://www.pewresearch.org/fact-tank/2021/03/26/about-three-in-ten-u-s-adults-say-they-are-almost-constantly-online/.

pings with a notification, a dopamine release is activated in our brains, along with opiates and other "pleasure" neurochemicals that charge up the portion of our brains generally referred to as the "reward center." We experience a rush of satisfaction when we encounter something novel online, and we develop an appetite for more. Troublingly, this reaction is the same basic neurological mechanism found at work in years of research on drug, alcohol, and gambling addictions.[3]

While our world has always had compulsion-inducing activities, what makes our current digital media and technologies uniquely concerning is that they are mobile and therefore inescapably ubiquitous. Today, they are carried in our pockets and our bags or strapped on our wrists so that they seem to be living and breathing alongside us as we move throughout the day. Furthermore, our current digital media and services deliver content that is infinitely novel—there is always a now email, new post, new video, or new message to check. We have come to live in such a state of permanent connectivity that even when our devices are not in view or on our bodies, our consciousness has become sufficiently trained and thoroughly immersed in the habits of being formed by an unceasing awareness of how, as Dalton Conley has described, life is constantly being lived "elsewhere."[4] Our bodies are in one place, but our minds and consciousness dwell on the stuff of our screens.

These collective habits indicate that we are a people whose momentary ideas or desires can be pursued and gratified immediately.[5] Clinical cases of gaming or pornography addictions can develop with heavy digital use in large part because today's digital ecology offers unfettered access with no constraints of time or space. In

---

3 See Wilhelm Hofmann, Kathleen D. Vohs, and Roy F. Baumeister, "What People Desire, Feel Conflicted about, and Try to Resist in Everyday Life," *Psychology Science* 23, no. 6 (April 30, 2012), 582–88, https://doi.org/10.1177/0956797612437426; and David Greenfield, "The Addictive Properties of Internet Usage," in *Internet Addiction: A Handbook and Guide to Evaluation and Treatment*, ed. Kimberly S. Young and Cristiano Nabuco de Abreu (Hoboken, NJ: John Wiley, 2007).

4 Dalton Conley, *Elsewhere, U.S.A.* (New York: Vintage, 2010).

5 Greenfield, "Addictive Properties of Internet," 133–53.

particular, regarding desires and actions that are culturally discouraged or considered taboo, the anonymity that usually characterizes our digital usage allows for a new quality of psychological disinhibition that frees individuals from the typically regulatory pressures of social norms and emboldens them to pursue such desires with little accountability.

In addition to the addictive potential of the digital in our lives, the general impact of screen time and digital usage on the health and resilience of our brains has been of increasing concern. Some research shows that our brains fatigue considerably after heavy multitasking and are unable to reason or be creative at full capacity.[6] Other cognitive studies suggest that even the sheer anticipation of email or other digital stimulation is taking up working memory in our brains.[7] The possibilities that our brains may be overtaxed and overstimulated from multitasking with heavy digital use all point to the fact that we actually know very little about the long-term physiological effects of our permanent connectivity and, quite frankly, are prone to guessing wrong when we attempt to optimize our productivity with digital technologies.

Questions about contemporary surges in anxiety and depression found among high school and college students get inevitably linked to questions about the impact of the growing dependence on—and the earlier introduction of—digital devices in young people's lives. The hunch that there may be a correlation between heavy digital reliance and negative psychological outcomes is confirmed, in part, by researchers who recommend that when it comes to our physiological reactions to regular digital use, we need to be talking about not only dopamine and addiction but also cortisol and stress.

Psychologists and neuroendocrinologists are increasingly concerned that our chronic digital practices are causing our cortisol levels to rise more frequently. The mere sight of our phones nearby, or even the perception that we have heard a notification, has the

---

6 Matt Richtel, "Outdoors and Out of Reach: Studying the Brain," *New York Times*, August 16, 2010.
7 Richtel.

capacity to elevate our cortisol levels.[8] A 2018 report noted that constant exposure to social media, email, and news apps on smartphones is causing users to experience a "constant sense of obligation, generating unintended personal stress."[9] Because this stress creates discomfort, we often feel compelled to check our phones ever more in order to relieve the stress.[10] However, once we do check, we usually encounter something newly unexpected, which then causes our cortisol level to rise yet again, and we feel further compelled to resolve that anxiety by further pecking at our phones. This is how we slip into a cycle of experiencing stress, attempting to alleviate the anxiety, and then being struck by a new wave of stress—again and again. As the body's main stress hormone is activated when we perceive a threat, our bodies physiologically prepare for a fight-or-flight response that often outstrips what is needed. A rise in cortisol causes temporary spikes in our blood pressure, heart rate, and blood sugar, which increase one's risk of a whole gamut of serious health problems in the long term. This physiological reaction also impairs our brain's prefrontal cortex, having the effect of decreasing our ability to self-regulate and control our behaviors.[11]

This is what is happening to us as we become habituated to living daily in the chemical crosswinds of dopamine and cortisol. If we are honest, isn't it the case that on the occasions when nothing has actually changed on our phones since the last time we checked, we often feel restless (perhaps even disappointed) because we have failed to experience the hit of dopamine *or* cortisol we have come to anticipate? Grasping the breadth of these physiological effects of our contemporary digital practices is, in itself, sobering. It becomes upsetting to realize that tech companies have always known of these effects and have even gone so far as to employ this knowledge and expertise to

---

8 Catherine Price, "Put Down Your Phone. Live Longer," *New York Times*, April 30, 2019, D6.

9 Julie H. Aranda and Safia Baig, "Toward 'JOMO': The Joy of Missing Out and the Freedom of Disconnecting," *MobileHCI '18: Proceedings of the 20th International Conference on Human-Computer Interaction with Mobile Devices and Services* (September 2018), https://doi.org/10.1145/3229434.

10 Greenfield, "Addictive Properties of Internet."

11 Price, "Put Down Your Phone."

keep us hooked. Over the past few years, a critical mass of founding executives of major social media platforms has come to admit that they knew exactly what they were doing. When interviewed, Sean Parker, the first president of Facebook and founder of Napster, acknowledged,

> The thought process . . . was all about: "How do we consume as much of your time and conscious attention as possible?" . . . We need to . . . give you a little dopamine hit every once in a while, because someone liked or commented on a photo or a post or whatever. And that's going to get you to contribute more content, and that's going to get you . . . more likes and comments. . . . It's a social-validation feedback loop . . . exactly the kind of thing that a hacker like myself would come up with, because you're exploiting a vulnerability in human psychology. . . . The inventors, creators—it's me, it's Mark [Zuckerberg], it's Kevin Systrom on Instagram, it's all of these people—understood this consciously. . . . And we did it anyway.[12]

Much of contemporary digital media relies on the principles of behavioral psychology. B. F. Skinner famously demonstrated how a hungry rat could be trained to expect a food pellet when it pressed a lever. The unexpected discovery was in finding that a rat was actually more motivated to press the lever when the pellet was delivered intermittently rather than consistently with each press. This unpredictable form of reinforcement was what conditioned the rat to behave as Skinner intended. What became known as "the principle of variable rewards" was the key to hooking them.[13] And the eureka moment lies in realizing that it's exactly the same for us as human beings. As many have observed, social media's feedback mechanisms of "likes" and notifications essentially function like a Skinner box.

---

12 Mike Allen, "Sean Parker Unloads on Facebook: 'God Only Knows What It's Doing to Our Children's Brains,'" *Axios*, November 9, 2017, https://www.axios.com/2017/12/15/sean-parker-unloads-on-facebook-god-only-knows-what-its-doing-to-our-childrens-brains-1513306792.
13 Ian Leslie, "The Scientists Who Make Apps Addictive," *Economist*, October 20, 2016, 69.

Like Skinner's rats, we have been trained to check our apps repeatedly in hopes of landing on a piece of unpredictable stimuli. It turns out that the most effective triggers that prompt us to check our phones and apps are our friends. And social media platforms have ingeniously developed ways to use our friends as a means of keeping our attention tied to their sites. Many of us may presume that the apparently random rhythm of "likes" and posts that we see on our feeds is simply due to the fact that we don't get around to checking our devices and one another's posts at the same time. While this presumption may partially explain the asynchronous dynamic that characterizes how we collectively engage social media, what is largely driving the pattern of notifications and posts we receive is an algorithm that calculates when and what new content to promote and withhold, in such an intermittent and alluring manner that its strategic unpredictability will drive users to a sufficient degree of psychological insecurity that yields the most checking, most posting, and most commenting.

This intermittent patter of notifications is where the strategic brilliance of social media platforms shines. For it seems that the special sauce of the Instagrams, Snapchats, and Twitters of this world is a built-in feedback mechanism that preys on our human desire for quantifiable and repeated peer acknowledgment and affirmation. While the desire for social belonging is a fundamental feature of the human condition, what is unique about a social media platform is how it has become the sole proprietor of the social space where everyone we care about checks in and through which we continually chase our sense of security and affirmation.

In all, scholars have observed that our experiences in social media are not unlike what gamblers describe as being in "the machine zone"—a state of mind in which their attention is wholly locked on what's happening on the screen and the immediate world around them recedes to the background.[14] Media scholar Siva Vaidhyanathan described it this way: "Facebook is designed to keep you immersed,

---

14 See Adam Alter, *Irresistible: The Rise of Addictive Technology and the Business of Keeping Us Hooked* (New York: Penguin, 2018); and Natasha Dow Schüll, *Addiction by Design: Machine Gambling in Las Vegas* (Princeton: Princeton University Press, 2012).

to disconnect you just enough so you lose track of the duration and depth of your immersion in the experience, and to reward you just enough that you often return, even when you have more edifying, rewarding, or pleasurable options for your time and effort within your reach. This is not an accident."[15]

So what can we do as people living in this digital age? It is one thing to limit our tech usage and to employ apps that block those platforms that are most tempting to us. But a life that is not driven by the pulsing digital flow of notifications is not one that can be exclusively achieved through acts of negation. We need a paradigm that helps us down a journey of actually *becoming* a different kind of person than who we are now. Those of us who identify with the Christian faith, in particular, can move toward a more thoughtful technological practice by drawing on historical Christianity's resources of theology and spiritual practices that situate our embodiment as central to our humanity.

Digital Practice as Liturgy

A helpful place to begin imagining what a faith-informed technological life might look like is to name what our working theological anthropology is or, more simply, what we think it means to be human in relation to God. In *Desiring the Kingdom*, philosopher James K. A. Smith explained that many Christians live as if human beings are primarily thinkers.[16] We think that if we have the right beliefs, our lives will follow suit and be transformed accordingly. But he argues that human beings are not primarily shaped by our mind's thoughts and beliefs; rather, it is our *love*—what churns in our guts and is evident in what we do with our bodies—that ultimately motivates the outcomes of our lives.

By anchoring our personhood in the visceral and bodily rather than the cerebral, Smith proposed a theological anthropology that is

15 Siva Vaidhyanathan, *Antisocial Media: How Facebook Disconnects Us and Undermines Democracy* (New York: Oxford University Press, 2018), 37.
16 James K. A. Smith, *Desiring the Kingdom: Worship, Worldview, and Cultural Formation* (Ada, MI: Baker Books, 2009), 41.

especially helpful for understanding our relationship with our digital technologies. He wrote, "The way our . . . desire gets aimed in specific directions . . . is through practices that shape, mold, and direct our love. . . . Habits are formed by practices: routines that inscribe particular ongoing habits into our character, such that they become secondary nature to us. . . . Some of the habits and practices that we are regularly immersed in are actually thick formative practices that over time embed in us desires for a particular version of the good life."[17] Therefore, when we are left to our own devices and are unreflective about our practices and simply follow the taken-for-granted norms in our society, we inevitably find ourselves engaging in what Smith termed "secular liturgies." These liturgies are personal and cultural habits that we routinely perform with our bodies, which have the effect of *mis*forming our desires. They ultimately misdirect our desires toward those things that falsely claim to fulfill our longings and that manage to draw us away from the very communion with God for which we were created. Whether it is manifested through how we seek out some inchoate satisfaction when we go shopping, how we absentmindedly eat prepackaged meals in front of a screen, or how we daily feel discontented about our self-worth when we step on the bathroom scale, these secular liturgies routinely encourage us to bow down to the culturally endorsed gods of our society rather than the Creator God, who loves and seeks to make us and all creation whole.

When it comes to our technologically saturated lives, social psychologist Sherry Turkle wonders out loud in her book *Alone Together* about the meaning of her daily ritual of waking up and going to sleep by checking her email on her phone while still in bed.[18] In light of Smith's notion of secular liturgies, if we see how checking our phones has replaced the practices of Scripture reading and prayer that Christians have historically engaged during the early morning and late evening, this mundane ritual becomes rather sobering. Indeed, what soul formation (or misformation) is taking place when we go to sleep

---

17 Smith, 80–83.

18 Sherry Turkle, *Alone Together: Why We Expect More from Technology and Less from Each Other* (New York: Basic Books, 2012), 154.

and arise with our emails and social media feeds bookending our bodily rest?

After accounting for the secular liturgies that form us, Smith called on Christians to engage in counterliturgies that push back against these misformations of the heart. Instead of only focusing on what misforming habits to remove or submit to prayer and reflection, what life-giving practices can we take on? In response to our secular liturgies—checking our phones whenever we are bored, texting that friend with whom we seek to avoid having the awkward conversation, our daily wind down of thirty minutes with Candy Crush—we can start asking ourselves questions: What are our counterliturgies to these secular liturgies? How can these new practices begin to turn our faces toward the Kingdom of God rather than regularly burying them into our screens?

A fertile place to start exploring ideas for counterliturgies is within the Christian heritage of spiritual disciplines. The disciplines of solitude, silence, Scriptural reading, prayer, and fasting can all be practiced in their traditional forms or adapted to the digital context (such as fasting from particular apps or devices). They can be seen anew as counterliturgies that push back against the subtle but real misformations of the heart that occur when our lives are chronically framed by the dictates of the digital.

Another approach to counterliturgies is to conduct experiments that encourage us to step out of our comfort zones and develop a taste for something new that, though uncomfortable at first, might actually become a precious source of life and vitality. One simple experiment is monotasking. Over and against our secular liturgies of digital multitasking, what if we engaged in counterliturgies of monotasking (when we drive, only driving; when we wait in line, just waiting)? What happens to my brain if I stop filling it with content, noise, and agenda? Do I become more aware of the *place* where I am? Do I become aware of the *people* around me? What do I hear in my soul, or from God, when there is quiet and stillness in me?

Yet another approach to counterliturgies is to identify and guard what is precious and sacred in one's life. Recognizing our embodied nature in space and time, we can consider what it could look like to protect sacred places and sacred times in our day. Are there places like dinner tables or bedrooms that we can seek to protect for communion or rest? Are there times like waking up or going to bed that are precious and deserving of the freedom to be alone with one's own waking thoughts, seeing the morning light, or being unplugged in the evening so one can return to oneself in rest?

To realize how our digital routines serve as secular liturgies and how bodily counterliturgies gradually retrain our loves toward the Kingdom of God is to privilege praxis and body in ways that may feel foreign to many contemporary Christians whose basic sense of spirituality and faith is primarily rendered as a matter of the "heart" or "mind." Because spirituality and the material body have often been framed historically as binary opposites, and bodily matters have been perceived as being "of the flesh" and therefore something we ought to manage primarily through the regulatory lens of moral purity, many Christians pay little attention to what the rest of our visceral senses and corporeal body are doing. While Christian conversations about the body are often preoccupied with the virtues and vices related to what we smoke (or not), what we drink (or not), who we marry (or not), who we sleep with (or not), how we reproduce (or not), and what we read or watch (or not), we are curiously unconcerned about many *other* practices we engage with our bodies on a pretty regular basis. Arguably, it is these mundane bodily practices that may shape us even more profoundly than the ones the church conventionally vexes over.[19]

Admittedly, if we take a step back and consider how our imaginations about Christian formation often lack consideration of our corporeal reality, it is a rather peculiar state of affairs. For a people whose message of good news is centrally located in the bodily presence of Jesus, who lived out his divine calling in our historical midst—needing sleep, food, and drink as we do; being jostled by crowds as we are; navigating all the social expectations that came with the gender, class, and ethnicity that he carried in his physical body—and who

---

19 This same critique can be made of the general lack of attention paid to how we spend our money, how we engage with our work lives, and whom we fraternize with (and with whom we don't).

specifically gave his followers an act to perform (a meal to share instead of a creed to recite),[20] we are oddly ignorant of, and even alienated from, how our embodied selves and corporeal experiences might be fundamental parts of our spiritual journeys.

Certainly, in Scripture, there is much evidence of a high view of human embodiment. The opening account in Genesis deemed physical creation and human beings good. The incarnation of the divine in the person of Jesus Christ was the ultimate act of self-identification with both our human frailty and our image-of-God-ness. Jesus's ministry is notable because it not only involved teachings but also powerfully featured a willingness to commune with the physically sick and disabled—those who were considered ritually unclean and socially marginalized. Jesus chose to care for people through the physicality of intervention, knowing that their bodily healing would enable them to be communally restored, establishing them with full social status—perhaps for the first time—and bringing great rejoicing in the hearts of so many people. Jesus's own corporeal death and resurrection signal how bodies play a meaningful role in our humanity *and* a central role in God's redemption of all creation. As these examples demonstrate, in contrast to the dominant gnostic tendencies to disregard the body as a burden that the spirit or soul seeks to shed, the significance and glory of embodiment actually run through much of Christian Scripture and theology. It is up to our communities of faith to live actively into Jesus's incarnation by taking seriously how our human embodiment matters when we invest in contemporary Christian formation. As Tish Harrison Warren warned, "If the church does not teach us what our bodies are for, our culture certainly will. If we don't learn to live the Christian life as embodied beings . . . we will learn a false gospel, an alternative liturgy of the body."[21]

---

20 Observation made by N. T. Wright as noted by Tish Harrison Warren, *Liturgy of the Ordinary: Sacred Practices in Everyday Life* (Downers Grove, IL: InterVarsity, 2016), 64.
21 Warren, 44.

The Modern Disregard of Presence

The ironic dynamic at work in our contemporary digital lives is that, even though our body's physiology and psychology are being exploited for commercial ends, the design of our sociotechnological practices for friendship and community are often bent on minimizing the importance of our embodiment. As social theorist Eva Illouz insightfully observed, "It is not so much that Internet technology impoverishes personal and emotional life, but rather that it creates unprecedented possibilities for sociability and relationship but empties them of the emotional and bodily resources which have until now helped them carry on."[22] The normalization of messaging, social media, and email as means of social interaction reflects a modern disregard for the roles that physical presence and the accompanying package of verbal and nonverbal cues play in how we come to interact with one another, how we come to love and belong to others, and how we become our very selves. While we have developed a full lexicon of emojis, GIFs, and digital norms to carry on our relationships, we lean so much on these digital resources that it is easy to neglect, and even avoid, the resources of our physicality that have historically oriented our understanding and experience of the world and one another.

Scholars like Sherry Turkle have suggested that young people prefer texting and messaging over and above face-to-face or voice-based interactions because these devices and practices give us the ability to control and "dial down" other people's access to us.[23] The unpredictable variables in vocal or face-to-face contexts include the risks of awkward silences, the uncertainty read on the faces of our interlocutors, the delicate negotiating of dull conversations, and the fumbling for right words. Instead of working to better meet these less appealing aspects of shared presence, it is much more convenient to simply hide, flatten out, and edit away our discomforts with a few well-chosen acronyms or memes. In comparison to the narrow bandwidth of communication that messaging affords,

---

22 Eva Illouz, *Cold Intimacies: The Making of Emotional Capitalism* (Cambridge: Polity, 2007), 111.
23 Turkle, *Alone Together*, 15.

face-to-face conversations—rich in nonverbal cues—and even phone conversations now feel comparatively overwhelming: far too taxing and requiring too much energy.

Admittedly, raising these sorts of concerns about social ties and interactions maintained online opens up complicated terrain. After all, these platforms that can afford us more dialed-down versions of one another are the very same platforms that brilliantly open up new possibilities and avenues of sociability that are profoundly impactful, and even essential, to so many who are marginalized or isolated in their proximate everyday lives. For many who are minoritized, these platforms can be lifelines to networks and communities that sustain a sense of self and mental well-being. Undoubtedly, the uses of these platforms are incredibly varied. And yet, it is possible to say that while individuals may in fact use social media to develop very thick and robust ties, they are also easily used to grant us distance from one another and permission to become accustomed to relationships of limited liability. Not wanting to ask too much of one another, and not wanting to be beholden to others, texting can grant us distance, control, and convenience. We can come to neglect the reality of our embodiment or ignore our proximate surroundings, for it is far easier to let one another publicly signal absence and unavailability with our device use than risk encountering one another and having to negotiate the delicate but deeply existential act of acknowledging or rejecting someone's presence.

In this way, whether we are at home on the couch with family, housemates, or neighbors in proximity or if we are sitting in a waiting room surrounded by strangers, our digital devices often detach us from the reality of how our embodied presence is a part of our personhood and how we carry "the weight of glory" in our very beings through our presence. C. S. Lewis famously preached a sermon with that title, saying,

> It is a serious thing to live in a society of possible gods and goddesses, to remember that the dullest and most uninteresting person you can talk to may one day be a creature which, if you saw it now, you would be strongly tempted to worship, or else a

horror and a corruption such as you now meet, if at all, only in a nightmare. . . . There are no ordinary people. You have never talked to a mere mortal. . . . Next to the Blessed Sacrament itself, your neighbour is the holiest object presented to your senses. . . . It is in the light of these overwhelming possibilities, it is with the awe and the circumspection proper to them, that we should conduct all our dealings with one another, all friendships, all loves, all play, all politics.[24]

If in our daily haste our hearts are chastened to remember with whom we are actually interacting, perhaps we would think twice before hiding behind our technologies to avoid that dull and uninteresting person or putting on our headphones to excuse ourselves from exercising "the awe and circumspection" appropriately due to our holy neighbors.

If our contemporary digital practices make it easy for us to overlook the glowing holiness in other people and to ignore the significance of our embodied presence in one another's lives, then we need to reconsider the place of technology in our lives today. To do so is to grapple with not only the realities of our corporeal bodies in our spiritual formation but also an opportunity for people of faith to recognize and reinvest in our Lord Jesus Christ's radical invitation to live into his very real presence, which brings healing and life into the world.

A growing number of college students today have an acute awareness of how their digital habits are impoverishing their lives but feel overwhelmed when navigating the digital demands on their lives. A first step might simply be helping students understand that modest adjustments like using a stand-alone alarm clock or spending the first fifteen minutes of their morning tech free can actually make a substantive difference in replenishing their mindset and spirit. Next steps might involve inviting students to counterliturgical occasions when they can experience the goodness and beauty

---

24 C. S. Lewis, *The Weight of Glory and Other Addresses* (New York: Macmillan, 1980), 45–46.

that is possible when hiking, watching a sunset, or having coffee together without devices on hand. In the end, we need to shift our focus from merely thinking about how to *limit* our technology and start being more serious about practicing our humanity—recovering our sense of presence and place in the fullness of our sacred bodies and relationships.

Chapter 9
Beyond Anxiousness

Stephen T. Beers and Lea D. Hart

"I don't know what I will do if this doesn't work out," she anxiously commented as we noticed the green digits of the dashboard's clock flip past midnight in the university's van. She was a sophomore pre-med major taking molecular biology, and her reasoning went something like this: "If I get a C on my test, and a B in this course, and my GPA falls below what I need to be competitive for med school—or worse yet, I end up losing my academic scholarship—then, I won't finish college or get into med school and become a doctor. Which means I won't be able to become a medical missionary, and I will miss my calling from God." For her, each exam in her course of study was another opportunity to lose it all. This conclusion may be understandable, but how she (and virtually every other college student) manages these anxious moments will set in motion her ability to grow stronger (increasing her resilience) or, if handled poorly, will reduce her ability to navigate a host of life's typical developmental challenges.

College has always been a time for discovering oneself, acknowledging one's strengths and weaknesses, and distinguishing between interests and passions. The maturation process is never linear; therefore, along the way, students will experience failures and successes, suffering and joy. Student development theorists include the process of moving through crisis, suffering, and pain as a significant part of the typical maturation journey into the healthy ownership of one's identity, establishing healthy relationships, managing emotions, and finding purpose.[1]

The past decade of national data suggests that college students' mental health struggles are uniquely concerning. These struggles were exacerbated by the pervasive impact of COVID-19, which disrupted students' schedules, limited direct services, and negated support structures. Illustrating this dramatic shift, Baylor University's CARE Team reported a 110 percent increase in counseling cases over the pandemic.[2] Similarly, a fall 2020 national survey found that "unsurprisingly, mental health has worsened over the course of the pandemic. Almost 75 percent of respondents reported their mental health has worsened, worsened somewhat, or worsened significantly since the beginning of the pandemic. High percentages of respondents have experienced stress or anxiety (87.03%), disappointment or sadness (78.06%), or felt lonely or isolated (77.47%) during the pandemic. For many respondents, stress (84.25%), anxiety (82.35%), sadness (73.23%), and depression (60.7%) have all increased since the beginning of the pandemic."[3] Student mental health challenges on college campuses have included rises in both clinical generalized anxiety disorder and nonclinical anxiety. Anxiety tops the most frequent list of students' presenting problems.[4]

This chapter will focus on how university professionals might work to support students in managing their nonclinical anxiety, but these insights will also enable faculty and staff to support all students facing anxious moments. We will start by defining relevant terms. Next, we will provide insight into how culture has influenced this generation's ability to manage stressors. Finally, the chapter will conclude

1 Arthur W. Chickering and Linda Reisser, *Education and Identity* (San Francisco: Jossey-Bass, 1993).

2 Helen Huiskes, "It Takes a Campus: Pandemic Expands Mental Health Resources at Christian Colleges," *Christianity Today*, December 17, 2021, https://www.christianitytoday.com/news/2021/december/christian-college -mental-health-counseling-pandemic-demand.htm.

3 "Student Mental Health Survey (September 2020)," Active Minds, https://www .activeminds.org/wp-content/uploads/2020/10/Student-Mental-Health-Data -Sheet-Fall-2020-1.pdf.

4 "Student Mental Health Survey."

with a review of tools to assist students in managing these anxious moments. Our goal is to enable faculty and staff to assist students in developing personal wellness, or well-being, leading to resilience.

Clarifying the Term "Anxiety"

In our society, "anxiety" is commonly used when referring to nonclinical distress. Clinical anxiety, known as generalized anxiety disorder (GAD) in the *DSM-5*, is different from the colloquial anxiety referenced here and is not the subject of this chapter. Following is a brief outline of GAD symptoms and how they compare with nonclinical anxiety.

Common symptoms of GAD include, but are not limited to,

- difficulty controlling excessive anxiety and worry about a number of events for at least six months.

- evidence of three (or more) of the following six symptoms: restlessness or feeling keyed up or on edge, being easily fatigued, difficulty concentrating or mind going blank, irritability, muscle tension, and sleep disturbance.

- clinically significant distress or impairment in social, occupational, or other areas of functioning not attributable to the physiological effects of a substance, another medical condition, or mental disorder.

The primary focus in evaluating for GAD is to make note of the duration, severity, and impairment of the disturbance.[5]

In a study of late adolescents, the literature suggests a subthreshold concept of GAD, which is not considered a diagnosis in the *DSM-5*.[6]

[5] American Psychiatric Association, *Diagnostic and Statistical Manual of Mental Disorders: DSM-5* (Arlington, VA: American Psychiatric Association, 2013), 222.

[6] M. Burstein et al., "Threshold and Subthreshold Generalized Anxiety Disorder among US Adolescents: Prevalence, Sociodemographic, and Clinical Characteristics," *Psychological Medicine* 44, no. 11 (August 2014): 2351–62, https://doi.org/10.1017/S0033291713002997.

This subthreshold concept requires the duration of symptoms to last three months instead of six, excludes the controllability criterion noted in the *DSM-5*, and requires one of the six symptoms.[7] This type of subthreshold GAD certainly exists in the undergraduate population.

In contrast, the common symptoms of nonclinical anxiety or distress include poor sleep quality, fatigue, low-grade fevers, and an increase in headaches.[8] Symptoms can also include chest pain, high blood pressure, digestive issues, and body aches.[9] The presentation of this type of emotional stress can mimic similar symptoms of GAD; however, the distinction lies in the severity and impairment of the disturbance.

Leading Cultural Influences Generating Anxiousness

In 2017 and 2018, a group of seven Council for Christian Colleges and Universities (CCCU) senior student affairs officers met to research this topic. Their published work in 2019 outlined the cultural and developmental influences that generated much of the current situation.[10] Since this report was published, students' struggles have only been exacerbated by the impact of the COVID-19 pandemic.[11] This section will summarize their findings that have persisted.

---

7 Burstein et al., 2351–62.

8 Muhammad Faris Fauzi et al., "Stress, Anxiety and Depression among a Cohort of Health Sciences Undergraduate Students: The Prevalence and Risk Factors," *International Journal of Environmental Research and Public Health* 18, no. 6 (2021): 3269, https://doi.org/10.3390/ijerph18063269.

9 "How Stress Affects Your Body and Behavior," Mayo Clinic, accessed May 10, 2022, https://www.mayoclinic.org/healthy-lifestyle/stress-management/in-depth/stress-symptoms/art-20050987.

10 Stephen Beers et al., "A Praxis Briefing: Mental Health on the Campus: Defining Challenges and Opportunities," *Growth: Journal of the Association for Christians in Student Development* 18, no. 18 (2019): 6–24, https://pillars.taylor.edu/acsd_growth/vol18/iss18/1/.

11 Aleksandar Kecojevic et al., "The Impact of the COVID-19 Epidemic on Mental Health of Undergraduate Students in New Jersey, Cross-Sectional Study," *PLoS ONE* 15, no. 9 (2020): 1–16, https://doi.org/10.1371/journal.pone.0239696; Jungmin Lee, Hyun Ju Jeong, and Sujin Kim, "Stress, Anxiety, and Depression among Undergraduate Students during the COVID-19 Pandemic and Their Use of Mental Health Services," *Innovative Higher Education* 46 (2021): 1–20, https://doi.org/10.1007/s10755-021-09552-y.

Increased Threats and Unhealthy Sense of Threats

The American Psychological Association's 2018 report on stress in America suggests that Gen-Z individuals are more likely to report their mental health as fair or poor.[12] Coupling this with a culture of constant news reporting regarding "crises," one can appreciate one of the challenges that this generation has experienced—a landscape saturated by the highlighting of stressors. The world seems much more dangerous, but just as important, some of these threats are sadly relevant to our students' experiences.[13] Child-abuse prevention experts categorize these as adverse childhood experiences, or ACEs. Examples include experiencing violence, living with family members who abuse substances, or having parents separate through divorce or incarceration. Our previous report noted, "Sixty two percent of U.S. adults surveyed reported experiencing at least one adversity during childhood . . . with 1 in 6 adults having experienced 4 or more types of ACEs."[14] These traumatic experiences will continue to influence a student's ability to manage everyday stressors. Our empathy and support will go a long way in starting the necessary healing.

Overpressuring and Overprotecting Parenting Styles

There is not much staff can do with this category other than acknowledging that students come to college after spending eighteen-plus years under various external influences. Parents may have unintentionally overprotected their children from acceptable and necessary life challenges that allow them to learn when the stakes are low. "Snowplow" parents have cleared an easier pathway for their children and, in the short run, facilitated what looked like developmental gains. An emerging concern is that this "clearing a pathway" may

---

12 American Psychological Association, "Stress in America: Generation Z. Stress in America™ Survey," press release, October 2018, 4, https://www.apa.org/news/press/releases/stress/2018/stress-gen-z.pdf.

13 Beers et al., "Praxis Briefing."

14 "Adverse Childhood Experiences," Prevent Child Abuse America, December 2021, 2, https://preventchildabuse.org/wp-content/uploads/2021/12/PCA-Aces-One-Pager-2021-10202021.pdf.

contribute to the lack of students' resilience, thus hampering their ability to navigate traditional challenges, setbacks, and failures.

Parents may have also placed an undue amount of personal pressure on their children. Unreasonable expectations around achievements, illustrated by parents developing a child's resume in early elementary in order to get into special school programs or pushing a "you can change the world" mindset, increase student anxiety. These parenting styles may be more descriptive of a majority-culture family's experiences; therefore, sensitivity should be used when applying this data to the diverse student populations at your campus.

Excessive Technology

In June of 2007, the iPhone was introduced to the world, revolutionizing the mobile phone industry and ushering in the era of personalized screen use. This generation of college students is the first to grow up in this technologically expanded world. In her book *iGen*, Jean Twenge reported on the challenges this hyperconnected world has created for this generation. She found a negative inverse relationship between significant screen use and good mental health.[15] Not least among the problems is the increased access to social threats. Namely, these threats have escalated to twenty-four-seven cyberbullying and the constant opportunity for unguided social comparison. Unhealthy screen time reduces face-to-face socializing and increases sleep deprivation. The COVID-19 pandemic has only exacerbated the impact of this type of distress and mobile phone addiction.[16]

Underdeveloped Coping Skills

Illustrated in the opening story of the pre-med student, stunted development of healthy coping skills creates situations where students

15 Jean M. Twenge, *iGen: Why Today's Super-Connected Kids Are Growing Up Less Rebellious, More Tolerant, Less Happy—and Completely Unprepared for Adulthood (and What That Means for the Rest of Us)* (New York: Atria, 2017).

16 Yu Peng et al., "Perceived Stress and Mobile Phone Addiction among College Students during the 2019 Coronavirus Disease: The Mediating Roles of Rumination and the Moderating Role of Self-Control," *Personality and Individual Differences* 185 (February 1, 2022): 1–7, https://doi.org/10.1016/j.paid.2021.111222.

"pathologize" difficult but natural developmental challenges. Carol Dweck reported that a lack of coping skills can lead to a "fixed" mindset, where students struggle to navigate everyday challenges. Alternatively, a "growth" mindset provides pliability and a healthy pathway for the student to manage and mature from life's trials.[17] Furthermore, the loss of simple yet profound coping skills—like healthy habits of eating, exercise, and sleep or adopting spiritual disciplines— limits a student's ability to successfully navigate life's stressors.

Decreased Social Skills and Social Support

Primary to the traditional-aged college student's growth is the further development of interpersonal relationships and mature healthy interdependence.[18] Healthy friendships and community connections can provide mental health support throughout one's lifetime. The college student's reflex is to look down at their phone, isolating themselves— "When I get to class, everyone stares at their phone until the professors starts to lecture." We may be losing some simple social-skill sets around making friends, expressing empathy, using civil dialogue, and applying appropriate assertiveness that leads to healthy connectivity and social support. Some claim that a culture of self-absorption and entitlement are emerging concerns for this generation. This claim may or may not be true, but the segregating and self-focused aspects of technology and the emerging social messages of fierce individualism may be leading to a fracturing social structure.

Cultural Shift Away from a Biblical Metanarrative

Culture has and will continue to shift with the generations. Currently, the Western world is moving away from a Judeo-Christian–based metanarrative (post-Christian) and toward the deconstructed posture of postmodernity. In this shift, defining "truth" is a function of self-authorship. Explicitly, in this postmodern, hyperindividualistic world, there is a drift from an external locus of what is "True" (biblical

---

17 Carol S. Dweck, *Mindset: The New Psychology of Success* (New York: Random House, 2006).
18 Chickering and Reisser, *Education and Identity*.

revelation) toward an internal locus of truth or an epistemological self-authorship.[19]

This shift from external truth to individually created truth can generate dissonance in how students see and experience the world. Does this shift generate unreasonable work for the student in having to define what is true and good for every situation (i.e., defining sexuality, social justice, human purpose)? Secondarily, this deconstruction may present itself as freeing the individual for flourishing, but does it also open the individual toward narcissism? Furthermore, conflicts inevitably arise in navigating two individuals' competing pursuits of flourishing. Who arbitrates this impasse? In moving from a foundational Christian epistemological perspective to a postmodern, post-Christian posture, the process of a preeminent self-authorship will dilute life-giving and life-directing theological constructs like sin, self-sacrifice, and healthy suffering.

Moving Past Anxiousness into Christ-Enlivened Well-Being

Helping students move past anxiousness begins with an institutional response that is in sync with students' responsibilities of embracing and deploying personal, Christ-enlivened wellness and well-being practices. Leaders in higher education should influence systematic shifts in campus culture and initiate program offerings for all students. Andrew Mendoza wrote, "Student well-being must be promoted at every level of the institution, from the classroom and residence halls to libraries and athletic facilities."[20] Institutions can start by ensuring that direct support is available for students in crisis. Similarly, appropriate and diverse student mental health counseling services should be accessible. Furthermore, institutions should leverage resources and deploy an array of wellness programming. This programming

---

19 James E. White, *Serious Times: Making Your Life Matter in an Urgent Day* (Downers Grove, IL: InterVarsity, 2004).

20 Andrew Mendoza, "Well-Being across the Campus," in *Overwhelmed: The Real Campus Mental-Health Crisis and New Models for Well-Being*, ed. Sarah Brown (Washington, DC: Chronicle of Higher Education, 2020), 30.

should include resilience focus and mental health campaigns, and it may also include appropriately managed prescreening to identify higher-risk students.[21] The unique needs and resources of each campus will guide what can be successfully deployed and sustained. Organized in the following sections are some recommended illustrative practices. These are organized into five themes: Transformed Thinking (both Thinking Biblically and Thinking Differently), Curating Inputs, Skill Building, Belonging, and Being Human. Student anxiety is as diverse as the students who make up each campus population; therefore, it is important to provide a varied offering of wellness and well-being programming.

Thinking Biblically: Reconstructing a Biblical Narrative That Directs Our Lives

"I didn't get the job," one student reported to me as we stood in my garage. I (Steve) would eventually respond, "It will be amazing to see how the Lord will use this disappointment and redirection in your life." Moving past anxiety into Christ enlivened well-being starts in the mind. One's assumptions about this world change how we see and experience trials. In a 2021 study, "Moralistic Therapeutic Deism" (MTD) emerged as the most popular worldview in the United States.[22] The term was introduced by sociologist Christian Smith in 2005. Smith summarized what he heard from the youth in America about God. He described those students' theological construct as MTD, which entails the following: God remains distant, people are supposed to be good, the universal purpose in life is to be happy and feel good about oneself, there are no absolutes, good people go to heaven, and God has limited

---

21 Andrew Downs et al., "Using the WHO-5 Well-Being Index to Identify College Students at Risk for Mental Health Problems," *Journal of College Student Development* 58, no. 1 (2017): 113–17; Wei How Darryl Ang et al., "Effectiveness of Resilience Interventions for Higher Education Students: A Meta-analysis and Metaregression," *Journal of Educational Psychology* (2022): 1–25, http://dx.doi.org/10.1037/edu0000719.

22 George Barna, "Introducing America's Most Popular Worldview—Moralistic Therapeutic Deism," George Barna, April 30, 2021, https://www.georgebarna.com/research/388722_introducing-america%E2%80%99s-most-popular-worldview%E2%80%94moralistic-therapeutic-deism.

demands upon people.[23] If this thinking is still a dominant force in a college student's mindset, then there is significant work to be done in reconstructing a Christian metanarrative. Specifically, if we are to assist students to navigate anxious moments, then helping them have an accurate understanding of the world they live in and how to pilot through it will enable them to move toward well-being.

On the surface, one may not immediately see the challenge of this theological drift, but let's look at two simple examples of how one's theological assumptions make handling anxiety difficult. First, if the universal purpose in life, as stated in MTD, is to be happy and feel good about oneself, a few questions immediately arise when we face challenges. What is happiness, and who gets to define how to get there? Furthermore, because there are no absolutes (as MTD suggests), conflicting pursuits of happiness can cause us to derail one another's quests. So if our chief end in life is our personal happiness, and God has ordained this, what are we to assume when trials and tribulations (loss of a job opportunity) come our way, especially when we have no control over those outcomes? In contrast, if our primary purpose is "to glorify God, and to enjoy him forever,"[24] then trials are no longer in conflict with our ultimate purpose in life. A trial may be difficult, but in the Christian theological construct, God is not surprised by it; he has allowed/ordained it and is committed to being with us. This theological posture reorders our thinking around managing difficult situations. The decade-old hymn "Great Is Thy Faithfulness" summarizes Christ-enlivened thinking: "All I have needed Thy hand hath provided, Great is Thy faithfulness, Lord unto me." The writer is reminding us that God is in control, he is faithful, and he provides all that we need.

A second example highlights the experiential difference between an MTD belief that God remains distant compared with the God

---

23 Christian Smith and Melinda Lundquist Denton, *Soul Searching: The Religious and Spiritual Lives of American Teenagers* (Oxford: Oxford University Press, 2005).

24 The Presbytery of the United States, *The Westminster Shorter Catechism* (1647; republished, 2020), accessed October 28, 2022, https://www.westminsterconfession.org/resources/confessional-standards/the-westminster-shorter-catechism/.

described in the Old and New Testaments who pursues us and wants to be with us even through the difficult times. Christian theology states that God is present in this world and actively working for the good of humanity and his people. On the surface, an MTD God who is distant with limited demands may sound appealing, as it suggests ultimate individual freedom. But in contrast, when a person can have a personal relationship with the loving God of all creation, everything changes. This is the God who, the psalmist wrote, "knit me together in my mother's womb" (Ps. 139:13b). Scriptures describe the incarnate Christ as a shepherd who pursues the one lost sheep. To be sure, the Christian God has expectations, but they are in concert with how he has created us. The loss of a job opportunity can now be seen within the purview of God's active will for our lives or his guiding presence highlighting when we are out of sync with his ways. But either way, the trials don't define us as alone or unworthy (as the many psalms of lament reveal). In Christ we belong—we are adopted, secure, and chosen. We are called into purposeful and meaningful. colaboring roles. We are not alone as we face trials. In fact, God has given us his Spirit to seal, guide, and be ever present. A Christ-enlivened biblical narrative changes every part of our thinking and directs our actions. It shifts our understanding of our purposes both here and for eternity.

Thinking Differently: Finding Well-Being through New Thinking Patterns

"I am so sorry to tell you," the doctor started, "but these torn ligaments have finished your season and probably your athletic career." No student athlete wants to hear this news, but how she mentally navigates this difficult experience can build resilience and bring about well-being. In simple terms, this athlete's "thinking" about her injury can free her for a life journey with new opportunities. This learned resilience posture can then be applied in all areas of her life. "Once we truly know that life is difficult—once we truly understand and accept it—then life is no longer difficult," postulated M. Scott Peck.[25]

---

25 M. Scott Peck, *The Road Less Traveled: A New Psychology of Love, Traditional Values, and Spiritual Growth* (New York: Touchstone, 2003), 15.

Cognitive behavioral therapy (CBT) is a type of counseling therapy that is effective when working with individuals suffering from anxiety disorders. Its core principles include the following: (1) psychological problems are based in part on faulty or unhelpful ways of thinking and (2) in part on learned patterns of unhelpful behavior, and (3) people suffering from psychological problems can learn better ways of coping with them, thereby relieving their symptoms and becoming more effective in their lives.

CBT treatment usually involves changing thinking patterns. These strategies might include learning to recognize one's distortions in thinking that are creating problems and then to reevaluate them in light of reality, gaining a better understanding of the behavior and motivation of others, using problem-solving skills to cope with difficult situations, and developing a greater sense of confidence in one's own abilities.[26]

Nontrained individuals should not attempt to provide CBT, but we all can utilize these principles. This echoes what the apostle Paul wrote in a letter to the Romans: "Let God transform you into a new person by changing the way you think" (Rom. 12:2a). Similarly, the work of Dweck suggests a healthy person has a "growth" mindset because they believe they have agency in managing challenges. In a growth mindset, one does not see life's unanticipated detours or failures as a personal descriptor but instead as an opportunity for growth.[27] Student developmental researchers have embedded in their theories a process where "challenge" is the hinge point for growth.

Curating Inputs: Managing Technological Influence

Arguably, most people in the world today live with access to abundance. Our modern world is blessed with access to more than we need to sustain life and flourish. Therefore, what has emerged in this

---

26 American Psychological Association, "What Is Cognitive Behavioral Therapy?," *Clinical Practice Guideline for the Treatment of Posttraumatic Stress Disorder*, 2017, https://www.apa.org/ptsd-guideline/patients-and-families/cognitive-behavioral.

27 Dweck, *Mindset.*

world of abundance is the need to curate our consumption in order to avoid unhealthy indulgence and gluttony that can increase anxiety. These management principles apply to a range of consumables from food to the use of technology. In the previous chapter, Dr. Song provided insight into the current impact of technology on students and society. But it bears repeating that to reduce anxiety and establish personal well-being, one must curate the technological inputs available today. Author Andy Crouch reminds us that it is the patterns of choices we make that are most powerful in shaping our lives. He recommended taking a Sabbath from the influences of technology, "not just one day every week, but also one hour (or more) every day and one week (or more) every year."[28] Establishing a discipline of curating all that we intake, particularly technology, will increase our wellness and well-being.

Skill Building: Learning Coping Skills for Stress and Anxiety

As noted previously, the patterns we establish shape our lives. So in managing stress and anxiety, there are several coping-skill patterns that can be learned. The few shared here are illustrative. These positive coping skills help the individual navigate the moment of anxiousness and can also enable the individual to avoid making additional mistakes, compounding the problem. For example, avoid "verbally abusing" others while being appropriately angry. Interestingly, the brain's amygdala assists in managing our emotional responses to threats, commonly known as part of our fight, flight, or freeze response. This physiological response enables us to react quickly to a natural danger. Yet in most modern-day situations where we are not in physical danger, we need to utilize what experts call the "rational brain" to override our physiological prompts. Gary Oliver, at the Center for Healthy Relationships, proposed we develop our use of the rational brain in slowing down our initial fight, flight, or freeze response enabling us to rationally respond in healthy ways

---

28 Andy Crouch, *The Tech-Wise Family: Everyday Steps for Putting Technology in Its Proper Place* (Grand Rapids, MI: Baker Books, 2017), 98.

that resolve the situation and reduce the probability of saying things we will regret.[29]

A second illustration is to intentionally take time to focus our thoughts on gratitude (e.g., Eph. 5:4). A daily counting of one's "blessings" goes a long way in reposturing our mental state toward a healthy mindset. In a 2021 *Harvard Medical School* publication, the researchers stated, "Gratitude helps people feel more positive emotions, relish good experiences, improve their health, deal with adversity and build strong relationships."[30] Whether using the rational brain, focusing our minds on gratitude, embracing spiritual disciplines (Chapter Eleven), or Sabbath keeping (Chapter Four), we can utilize healthy stress-management practices around virtually every challenge. In summary, the acquisition and deployment of a host of healthy coping skills assist students in managing stress and anxiety in real time.

Belonging: Leaning into a Supportive Community

"I have come to believe that the antidote to trauma is a relationship," Tim Clinton, president of the American Association of Christian Counselors (AACC), poignantly stated.[31] Belonging to and being supported by a community is an important aspect of successfully managing stress and anxiety. Solomon, the ancient Hebrew king, reminds us why two people are better than one: "If either of them falls down, one can help the other up" (Eccles. 4:10a). As one student communicated, describing important components of a healthy classroom community, "The setting is the key, one marked by both safety and belonging . . . in which I felt nurtured and valued, by both the professor and my fellow students."[32] Institutions cannot require relationships nor force

---

29 Gary Oliver, *Winning @ Work . . . and at Home: Emotional & Relational Intelligence Skills for Personal and Professional Success* (Siloam Springs, AR: John Brown University Center for Healthy Relationships, 2019).

30 Harvard Medical School, "Giving Thanks Can Make You Happier," Harvard Health, August 14, 2021, https://www.health.harvard.edu/healthbeat/giving -thanks-can-make-you-happier.

31 Tim Clinton, "The Power of One Another," *Christian Counseling Today* 24, no. 3 (2021): 8.

32 Alexander C. Kafka, *Building Students' Resilience: Strategies to Support Their Mental Health* (Washington, DC: Chronicle of Higher Education, 2021), 49.

friendships, but institutional leaders and students themselves can provide opportunities for all members to find belonging.

The New Testament has a number of "one another–ing" passages that direct individuals on how to live and function as a healthy community. To greet, accept, serve, honor, encourage, carry burdens for, forgive, and love one another are part of a larger list of attributes of a healthy social structure. When these characteristics are intentionally modeled and deployed in residence halls, commuter lounges, choir programs, sports teams, and classrooms, each of these emerging communities will provide critical support to assist students in navigating stress and anxiety. Additionally, campuses can provide programming regarding "friend making" or may establish life-coaching, student-mentoring, and peer-counseling programs. All these initiatives have a place in providing direct student support. The key is to find ways to invite students to belong.

Being Human: Living within the Limits of Our Humanity

"Two all-nighters in a row. I'm a mess," another student confessed. Understanding, accepting, and managing our lives within normal human limitations is justifiably difficult. Stress and anxiety are sure to follow when individuals attempt to live outside of their human capacity. The National Wellness Institute's "wellness wheel" lists six aspects of our humanness: physical, social, intellectual, spiritual, emotional, and occupational.[33]

As described in previous chapters, healthy patterns of sleep, nutrition, and exercise are baseline components of living within our human finiteness, impacting our ability to manage anxiety. Providing program ideas for each of the wellness wheel categories is beyond the scope of this chapter, but a focused illustration around exercise may be helpful. In an unpublished study done by students at a CCCU institution, the researchers found a "correlation between intramural participation and mental wellbeing." Participants reported that they "benefitted socially from actively participating in intramural sports."

[33] "The Six Dimensions of Wellness," National Wellness Institute, accessed August 16, 2022, https://nationalwellness.org/resources/six-dimensions-of-wellness/.

The students also stated that "participating in intramural sports provided them with stress relief."[34] The monograph *Building Students' Resilience* reported, "Stress produces a surge of cortisol, which activates the fight or flight response. It concentrates in the frontal cortex and that interferes with focus, concentration and decision-making. So, when you go for a run, this burns cortisol 'clearing your head.'"[35] The benefits of exercise are undeniable. The real challenge is embracing the concept of living within our human limits and organizing our lives to do so.

Conclusion

The goal of this chapter has been to provide clear and documented descriptions of significant contributors that have increased college student anxiety. Cultural influences such as increased threats, parenting styles, and technology each play their part in creating challenges for healthy student mental health. The statistics are sobering, and many of the debilitating cultural influences leave their mark well before the freshman year and, more importantly, well outside of college faculty and staff's control. Yet coping skills and life-giving habits can be learned and mastered. Unhelpful input can be limited. Cycles of poor and disruptive thinking can be altered, giving fresh perspective to the challenges that are faced in life. This chapter is intended to give us hope—a hope grounded in research and revelation that can be acted upon.

---

34 McKenna Bender, Jordyn Buckland, and Ashton Howe, "Impact of Intramurals on College Students' Mental Well-Being" (n.p.: John Brown University, 2018).
35 Kafka, *Building Students' Resilience*, 38.

Chapter 10

Depression

The Role of Student Affairs Leaders in Supporting Struggling Students and Helping Them Build Resilience

Connie Horton

Deep down inside, nothing changes. I'm still alone and unhappy. I feel like the biggest failure in the world. I try talking to God. I pour out my heart, I cry, I pray. I can't concentrate on prayer long. They are scattered and mixed up. It seems as if God was just a band-aid taught by those attempting to deal with life. It doesn't work. He doesn't do anything when you really hurt. When you feel so bad you just want to stab yourself and watch the worthless blood seep out. I'm crying out. He's not here. He left me. All the time, no one is there. No one can help me sort out what is going on. I can't figure myself out. I haven't known which way is up for months. Everyone thinks I'm smart and have it all together. They are so wrong. I'm broken in billions of pieces. Let me die please.

—Excerpt from a student story, shared on
Messiah University's "Stories of Hope" webpage[1]

---

1 "Our Stories of Hope," Messiah University, accessed July 7, 2022, https://www.messiah.edu/info/20902/self_help_resources/1436/our_stories_of_hope_depression.

The fallenness of our world and our bodies produces deep and sometimes agonizing spiritual questions for our students. How do we, as student life professionals, help students steward them in the midst of their moments of personal brokenness? We must start by recognizing the depth and breadth of psychological brokenness on campuses today.

College student mental health concerns, including depression, have been the focus of much popular and professional press in recent years. Secular and faith-based professional organizations such as the National Association of Student Personnel Administrators (NASPA), the American College Health Association, the American Psychological Association (APA), the Council for Christian Colleges and Universities, and the Association of Christians in Student Development have frequently featured these topics at their annual conferences. National and student newspaper headlines have highlighted stories of overwhelmed counseling centers and tragedies such as student suicides. Collaborative efforts such as the Center for Collegiate Mental Health and a mental health task force group of chief student affairs officers at Christian universities and nonprofits such as the Jed Foundation have been formed to help understand and address the needs.

There is good reason for this increased attention. University counseling centers report dramatically increased numbers of students accessing their services. Between 2009 and 2015, for example, the number of students seeking services at their campus counseling centers grew by an average of 30–40 percent while enrollment only grew by an average of 5 percent.[2] Christian institutions are not exempt and have rates of depression similar to other universities.[3]

2 "2020 Annual Report," Center for Collegiate Mental Health, January 2021, https://ccmh.psu.edu/assets/docs/2020%20CCMH%20Annual%20Report.pdf.

3 Helen Huiskes, "It Takes a Campus: Pandemic Expands Mental Health Resources at Christian Colleges," *Christianity Today*, December 17, 2021, https://www.christianitytoday.com/news/2021/december/christian-college-mental-health-counseling-pandemic-demand.html; Julia Klausli and Carrie Caudill, "Depression for College Students in a Traditional Christian Culture Context: The Role of Attachment, Spirituality and Social Support," *Mental Health, Religion & Culture* 21, no. 1 (2018): 105–15, https://doi.org/10.1080/13674676.2018.1458083.

Some speculate this increase in counseling center visits is simply due to decreased stigma and greater openness to receiving mental health services or that it is temporary due to the global pandemic. However, pre-COVID surveys beyond counseling centers to larger student bodies of colleges and universities demonstrate that these factors definitely do not explain the whole story. For example, on the National College Health Assessment Survey II in 2011, 31 percent of undergraduates reported that at least sometime during the last year they felt "so depressed it was difficult to function."[4] Numbers continued to increase over the years, and by 2019, 45 percent of students reported that experience.[5] That same year, 55 percent of students reported feeling hopeless, and 13 percent seriously considered suicide. Data from UCLA's Higher Education Research Institute observe similar trends.[6] Students' self-reported quality of mental health has continued to decrease.[7] Likewise, the APA's Stress in America Study found that people from Generation Z are the most upset about many national concerns (e.g., school shootings, the rise in suicide rates) and the least likely generation to report their mental health to be very good or excellent.[8] Again, there is evidence that students at Christian institutions are following the national trends.

4 American College Health Association—National College Health Assessment II, *Reference Group Executive Summary Spring 2011* (Hanover, MD: American College Health Association, 2011), https://www.acha.org/documents/ncha/ACHA-NCHA-II_ReferenceGroup_ExecutiveSummary_Spring2011.pdf.

5 American College Health Association—National College Health Assessment II, *Reference Group Executive Summary Spring 2019* (Silver Spring, MD: American College Health Association, 2019), https://www.acha.org/documents/ncha/NCHA-II_SPRING_2019_US_REFERENCE_GROUP_EXECUTIVE_SUMMARY.pdf.

6 Kevin Eagan et al., *The American Freshman: Fifty-Year Trends 1966–2015* (Los Angeles: Higher Education Research Institute, 2016).

7 Ellen Stolzenberg, "The Mental and Physical Well-Being of Incoming Freshmen: Three Decades of Research," *Higher Education Today*, September 6, 2018, https://www.higheredtoday.org/2018/09/06/mental-physical-well-incoming-freshmen-three-decades-research/.

8 American Psychological Association, "Stress in America: Generation Z. Stress in America™ Survey," press release, October 2018, https://www.apa.org/news/press/releases/stress/2018/stress-gen-z.pdf.

Unfortunately, colleges and universities can expect that they will continue to experience an influx of students entering their campuses who already have significant struggles with their psychological health in the coming years. The Surgeon General, Vivek Murthy, noted that "Mental health challenges in children, adolescents, and young adults are *real and widespread.* Even before the pandemic, an alarming number of young people struggled with feelings of helplessness, depression, and thoughts of suicide—and rates have increased over the past decade."[9] These mental health concerns, self-injury, and even deaths by suicide have increased dramatically among child and adolescent populations to the point that organizations such as the American Academy of Pediatrics, the American Academy of Child and Adolescent Psychiatry, and the Children's Hospital Association recently declared a "National Emergency in Child and Adolescent Mental Health."[10]

Just considering trends can be overwhelming. Practically, student affairs leaders (SALs) have lived this reality and know well that it is not just the counseling centers that are experiencing increased demands. Residence life, student activities, campus safety, and virtually all student-facing areas are dealing with this "new normal" of escalating depression, suicidality, and other mental health emergencies.

Once we recognize the depth and breadth of this problem, how can we offer meaningful support and healing to students who struggle with depression and create experiences and encourage practices that will help students be resilient? An understanding of definitions and dynamics of depression, components of treatment and

---

9 "U.S. Surgeon General Issues Advisory on Youth Mental Health Crisis Further Exposed by COVID-19 Pandemic," US Department of Health and Human Services, December 7, 2021, https://www.hhs.gov/about/news/2021/12/07/ us-surgeon-general-issues-advisory-on-youth-mental-health-crisis-further -exposed-by-covid-19-pandemic.html, emphasis added.

10 "AAP, AACAP, CHA Declaration of a National Emergency in Child and Adolescent Mental Health," American Academy of Pediatrics, 2021, https://www .aap.org/en/advocacy/child-and-adolescent-healthy-mental-development/ aap-aacap-cha-declaration-of-a-national-emergency-in-child-and-adolescent -mental-health/.

healing, and practical resilience skills will help the SALs at a faith-based institution be an important part of a healthy response.

Gaining Empathy: Understanding Symptoms and Dynamics of Depression

A general understanding of what depression is and some of the dynamics of the phenomena can help an SAL gain empathy for depressed students and be most effective in offering compassionate support. Most SALs are not mental health professionals and therefore need not be experts in diagnostic details or distinguishing between types of depressive disorders. However, understanding typical symptoms is important in having a sense of what a depressed student may experience.

Different from just having a sad moment or experiencing a period of grief after a recent loss, students who are depressed typically have an ongoing feeling of sadness or a depressed mood. They might tell you they "have no reason to be sad" and that what they used to experience as pleasurable is no longer enjoyable. Students experiencing depression may also experience physical symptoms such as increased or decreased appetite or weight, sleep disturbances, and fatigue. Cognitive symptoms of depression can include thoughts of worthlessness or excessive guilt and difficulty concentrating or making decisions.[11]

Symptoms can range in severity and duration and may cause significant distress or impairment in functioning. For students, this may include interference with their social lives, student employment, or academic performance. In the fall of 2021, 22 percent of undergraduates surveyed reported depression interfered with their academic performance.[12] Perhaps most concerning is that depressive symptoms can include hopelessness and suicidality.

---

11 American Psychiatric Association, *Diagnostic and Statistical Manual of Mental Disorders: DSM-5* (Arlington, VA: American Psychiatric Association, 2013).

12 American College Health Association—National College Health Assessment III, *Reference Group Executive Summary Fall 2021* (Silver Spring, MD: American

Depressed Christian students, of course, experience these same, difficult symptoms but may have an overlay of additional faith-based complications. They may feel guilty for feeling depressed, thinking that if they had enough faith or were a "good enough" Christian, they would not have this experience. These students may be ashamed and embarrassed to be around their Christian friends whose faith seems to give them a more positive outlook. Alternatively, their depression may lead to doubts about their faith as they wonder why a loving God would allow them to continue to suffer despite their prayer and efforts. Of course, faith can be a powerful resource and will be discussed later, but it is important to empathize with how Christian students may use faith "against themselves."

Depressive symptoms tend to build on one another, often referred to as a downward spiral. A student, for example, who has a depressed mood and low energy might stop exercising and decline social invitations. This tendency may lead to a more depressed mood, which might lead to further isolation. After this pattern continues for a while, thoughts of worthlessness may develop. The student might forget that they were invited but declined the invitations and start thinking others do not want to be around them. This could lead to more social withdrawal and a further depressed mood. The withdrawal pattern might expand to include skipping chapel and classes. It may be especially likely if the student begins experiencing fatigue and difficulty concentrating, which makes walking to class and paying attention more difficult. This downward spiral continues to create a worsening situation.

Help for the Hurting: Treatment and Healing

Students who have been experiencing significant depressive symptoms for some time should be referred to your college or university's counseling center. Counselors work through a variety of theoretical approaches. Many will use some variation of the cognitive behavioral

---

College Health Association, 2022), https://www.acha.org/documents/ncha/NCHA-III_FALL_2021_REFERENCE_GROUP_EXECUTIVE_SUMMARY.pdf.

therapy (CBT) approach, as this has been shown to be among the most effective in treating depression. Cognitive behavioral therapy addresses cognitive distortions and encourages healthy behavioral patterns that help turn around the downward spiral. With coaching, a student may learn to challenge thoughts of worthlessness, take a chance on a social engagement, and begin feeling able to exercise. Some CBT therapists explicitly integrate Christian concepts such as religious imagery and biblical ideas into the rationale, homework, or approach to challenging irrational thoughts.[13] For a subset of students, medications may be an adjunct to treatment, as their depressive symptoms—such as disrupted concentration and fatigue—are so severe that it is difficult to fully engage in treatment.

Professional mental health treatment is not the whole solution. Students navigating minor, brief periods of depressed moods may not need to see a psychologist or psychiatrist, and students who are seeing those professionals will also benefit from broader support. Professionals across student affairs can have a significant role. Staff in residence life, student activities, spiritual life, intercultural affairs, campus recreation, career services, and other departments who provide student programming and mentoring can make a positive difference. In supporting students who are dealing with depression, wisdom and discernment are important. Following are three considerations that may be helpful in navigating a path.

Don't Assume You Know Why a Student Is Experiencing Depression

When an SAL learns that a student is depressed, they should resist the urge to prescribe a solution based on presumed reasons for the student's depression. The causes of depression are variable and sometimes multilayered, and reductionist explanations should be avoided.

Much has been written in recent years about what factors may be contributing to increased levels of depression among college

---

13 Michelle Pearce, *Cognitive Behavioral Therapy for Christians with Depression: A Practical Tool-Based Primer* (West Conshohocken, PA: Templeton, 2016).

students. Certainly, the role of technology, and particularly social media, is one factor that has received significant attention. Researchers such as Jean Twenge have found a strong correlation between social media use and depression in teens.[14] The use of technology increases factors that lead to depression such as social comparisons, bullying, fear of missing out (FOMO), and sleep deprivation. As the APA's Gen-Z study confirmed, attention to so much negative news can be distressing.[15] Through their phones and computers, college students are regularly exposed to numerous threats in the world such as terrorism, war, school shootings, global pandemics, political divisiveness, bleak economic forecasts, and climate change. Thus, there are broad stimuli impacting most college students, at least to some degree. Beyond these factors, however, there is infinite individual variability.

Depression may also be caused by *biological* factors. For some college students, there is a genetic basis for being more vulnerable to depression or depressed moods.[16] Other students have medical conditions or medications that may also impact their mood.[17] Sustained stress, which many students experience, and was exacerbated during COVID, can also create brain chemistry changes that lead to depression.[18] Finally, sleep deprivation and alcohol abuse can also contribute to depression.[19]

14 Jean M. Twenge, *iGen: Why Today's Super-Connected Kids Are Growing Up Less Rebellious, More Tolerant, Less Happy—and Completely Unprepared for Adulthood (and What That Means for the Rest of Us)* (New York: Atria, 2017).

15 American Psychological Association, "Stress in America."

16 "The Biology of Depression," Psychology Today, accessed July 7, 2022, https://www.psychologytoday.com/us/basics/depression/the-biology-depression.

17 Christopher Celano et al., "Depressogenic Effects of Medications: A Review," *Dialogues in Clinical Neuroscience* 13, no. 1 (2011): 109–25, https://doi.org/10.31887/DCNS.2011.13.1/ccelano.

18 Jacob Schachter, Alex A. Ajayi, and Phuong Linh Nguyen, "The Moderating and Mediating Roles of Mindfulness and Rumination on COVID-19 Stress and Depression: A Longitudinal Study of Young Adults," *Journal of Counseling Psychology* 69, no. 5 (2022): 732–44, https://doi.org/10.1037/cou0000626.

19 R. Kathryn McHugh and Roger D. Weiss, "Alcohol Use Disorder and Depressive Disorders," *Alcohol Research: Current Reviews* 40, no. 1 (2019): 3–10, https://doi.org/10.35946/arcr.v40.1.01; Anna Wirz-Justice and Rutger H. Van den Hoofdakker, "Sleep Deprivation in Depression: What Do We Know, Where

Psychological factors such as thoughts, view of self, and coping skills can also make a person more or less likely to struggle with depression.[20] Studies found, for example, that students who have negative self-concepts, are hypersensitive to rejection, or have a tendency to ruminate are more likely to have depression.[21]

A person's *social* life, past and present, can make a significant difference in mood. Negative social experiences such as abuse, poverty, racism or other discrimination, and loneliness contribute to depression.[22] For college students, unpredictable and unsupportive family life have been shown to be associated with depression.[23]

Spiritual factors can also be significant. Some students may feel depressed when going through what has been referred to as a "dark night of the soul," a difficult but important spiritual experience. While spiritual wrestling may ultimately lead to spiritual growth, it is initially a difficult process. Distorted religious teaching may also contribute to excessive guilt and feelings of worthlessness, leading to depressive symptoms.[24]

Do We Go?," *Biological Psychiatry* 46, no. 15 (1999): 445–53, https://doi.org/10.1016/S0006-3223(99)00125-0.

20 Yuxiao Zhao et al., "The Psychological Factors Mediating/Moderating the Association between Childhood Adversity and Depression: A Systematic Review," *Neuroscience and Biobehavioral Reviews* 137 (2022): 1–16, https://doi.org/10.1016/j.neubiorev.2022.104663.

21 Olivia Remes, João F. Mendes, and Peter Templeton, "Biological, Psychological, and Social Determinants of Depression: A Review of Recent Literature," *Brain Sciences* 11, no. 12 (2021): 1–33, https://doi.org/10.3390/brainsci11121633.

22 Deborah Belle and Joanne Doucet, "Poverty, Inequality, and Discrimination as Sources of Depression among US Women," *Psychology of Women Quarterly* 27, no. 2 (2003): 101–13, https://doi.org/10.1111/1471-6402.00090; Julia C. Poole, Keith S. Dobson, and Dennis Pusch, "Childhood Adversity and Adult Depression: The Protective Role of Psychological Resilience," *Child Abuse & Neglect* 64 (2017): 89–100, https://doi.org/10.1016/j.chiabu.2016.12.012.

23 Caitlyn O. Hood, Lisa Thomson Ross, and Nathan Wills, "Family Factors and Depressive Symptoms among College Students: Understanding the Role of Self-Compassion," *Journal of American College Health* 68, no. 7 (2020): 683–87, https://doi.org/10.1080/07448481.2019.1596920.

24 Christopher M. Faiver, Eugene M. O'Brien, and R. Elliott Ingersoll, "Religion, Guilt, and Mental Health," *Journal of Counseling & Development* 78, no. 2 (2020): 155–61, https://doi.org/10.1002/j.1556-6676.2000.tb02573.x.

Clearly, there are many causal pathways to depression. A biopsychosocial-spiritual perspective can be helpful in making sense of these phenomena.[25] This more comprehensive model recognizes there may be multiple factors contributing to depression and that these factors are likely interacting with one another.

Help Students Draw on Their Spiritual Resources

SALs at Christian institutions typically view their work as ministry and desire to support students, helping them mature personally and spiritually. Listening well, providing a nonanxious presence, empathizing, and helping bear the burdens of depressed students by patiently walking with them in their dark times is a sacred, albeit sometimes difficult, ministry that requires great wisdom. Rather than seeing these students as somehow "other," SALs will do well to relate to these persons as fellow travelers, recognizing that all of us experience depressive feelings as part of the human condition. At the same time, it is important to understand that some students have a much more difficult journey than most. They may be experiencing a severe acute episode of depression or bear the difficult burden of chronic depressive feelings.

Professionals aware of depressed students' tendency to feel discouraged, worthless, and guilty should be cautious they are not sending messages such as "All you need is Jesus" or "If you just prayed more or were a better Christian, you would be healed." Certainly, an SAL in the right role and relationship with a student may pray with the student, and prayer should be encouraged. Given that the severity and duration of depression can vary, SALs should, without minimizing the power of God, avoid promising that depression will lift immediately. Some students may have brief periods of depression, which will lift quickly with support, prayer, good sleep, and other new habits. Other students, even with those same resources and extended professional psychotherapy and medication,

---

25 Andrew R. Hatala, "Towards a Biopsychosocial-Spiritual Approach in Health Psychology: Exploring Theoretical Orientations and Future Directions," *Journal of Spirituality in Mental Health* 15, no. 4 (2013): 256–76, https://doi.org/10.1080/19349637.2013.776448.

may continue to experience depression as their "thorn in the flesh" for many years.

Pastoral conversations, emphasizing "God with me" (e.g., Deut. 31:6) and passages that reinforce the concept through images of God such as "shepherd" (Ps. 23) and "hiding place" (Ps. 119), could offer meaningful comfort to a depressed student. Oppositely, negative religious coping, such as viewing God as hostile, has been shown to contribute to depressive symptoms.[26] Helping students consider psalms of lament and praise will give them words for their experiences and help them recognize the reality that both difficult feelings of depression *and* the reality of the love of God can be true at the same time. Biblical stories (e.g., Elijah and Job) of those who experienced depression may lessen a student's guilt and give hope.

Without using a guilt-inducing style, SALs can invite students to consider involvement in a healthy faith community. In a church family, they may find encouragement in their relationship with God, social support, and service opportunities—all of which can help with depression. Other spiritual practices that have been shown to help with depression should also be encouraged. Depressed students, who are prone to overly attend to the negative aspects of their life, may find a gratitude journal a way to focus on blessings even in the midst of their challenges.

Don't Do This Work Alone: Refer, Refer, Refer

Although SALs have a powerful role, they need to make sure they never do this work alone, never "keep secrets," and receive supervision along the way. Referrals to both pastoral counselors and mental health professionals are crucial. SALs should ask depressed students directly about the severity and duration of their feelings and if they have thoughts of self-harm or killing themselves. Students who have depressive feelings that are severe or long lasting and those who have thoughts of self-harm should always be referred to

---

26 Joshua J. Ahles, Amy H. Mezulis, and Melissa R. Hudson, "Religious Coping as a Moderator of the Relationship between Stress and Depressive Symptoms," *Psychology of Religion and Spirituality* 8, no. 3 (2016): 228–34, https://doi.org/10.1037/rel0000039.

the counseling center. If there is an immediate life-safety concern, of course, campus safety or 911 should be contacted. Many students have prior experience with mental health professionals, but other students may be wary about counseling. Seeking help for mental health struggles should be normalized, and the SAL can make clear they will stay connected through affirmations such as "Just like you would go to the doctor for an infection, going to a psychologist for feelings like you're having can be helpful. Can I walk you there? I'll check in with you afterward."

SALs should also encourage students who are struggling with depression to consider how the resources offered by other university departments may be helpful.[27] Campus recreation, for example, might be a powerful referral, as exercise has been well documented to lift mood.[28] Fitness classes and intramurals could also add an important social element. Chaplains or campus ministers could provide additional spiritual counsel and point the student to a faith community. The volunteer or service center could assist the student in beginning to serve others, a practice that has been shown to have positive effects on mood. Student activities can help a student find clubs or organizations, as cultivating connection with peers is key.[29]

Resilience Skills and Practice

An important reality for SALs to remember is that for all students, life will inevitably be difficult at times. Jesus never promised otherwise and, in fact, spoke to the reality that "in this world you will have trouble" (John 16:33). Thus, the whole student body will benefit from the development and practice of resilience skills. Hearty resilience skills, grounded in faith, can help prevent depression for some students and help others who do struggle with depression be more equipped to

27 Stephen Beers et al., "A Praxis Briefing: Mental Health on the Campus: Defining Challenges and Opportunities," *Growth: Journal of the Association for Christians in Student Development* 18, no. 18 (2019): 6–24, https://pillars.taylor.edu/acsd_growth/vol18/iss18/1/.

28 Jacob D. Meyer et al., "Influence of Exercise Intensity for Improving Depressed Mood in Depression: A Dose-Response Study," *Behavior Therapy* 47, no. 4 (2016): 527–37, https://doi.org/10.1016/j.beth.2016.04.003.

29 Beers et al., "Praxis Briefing."

navigate difficult times and stay safe even during the worst periods. Christian SALs should seek to develop resilient students who can, like Paul, have experiences in which they are "hard pressed on every side, but not crushed; perplexed, but not in despair; persecuted, but not abandoned; struck down, but not destroyed" (2 Cor. 4:8–9). Like the old hymn proclaims, we believe it can "be well with [their] soul," even when "sorrows like sea billows roll."[30]

After years of escalating student mental health concerns and crises, the Resilience-Informed Skills Education (RISE) program was developed at Pepperdine University.[31] We were glad that distressed students were availing themselves to counseling, case management, and pastoral care services and grateful for the collaborative work of many departments in managing crises to help support students' safety in their worst moments. But we wanted to do more proactively. We believed a Christian university should have a unique approach to equipping students to navigate the challenges of life and helping them develop needed resilience skills. Thus, RISE was developed, including six biblically sound, research-based dimensions.

The Physical Dimension. Scriptures regarding the body as a temple (e.g., 1 Cor. 6:19) are often referenced when speaking to adolescents and college students regarding sexual decision-making. While that is certainly important, teaching about body stewardship should be broader. Taking care of one's body is an important way of honoring God and increasing the probability that one will continue to have the physical and mental health to serve as called. Numerous studies have demonstrated the link between physical care of the body

30 Horatio Gates Spafford, "It Is Well with My Soul," part 1, box 1, folder 11, American Colony in Jerusalem, http://hdl.loc.gov/loc.mss/mamcol.016.

31 Brad Dudley et al., "Resilience Informed Skills Education: Find Your Way Upstream" (presentation, NASPA Strategies Conference, Boston, MA, January 13–15, 2022); Connie Horton, La Shonda Coleman, and Brad Dudley, "Teaching Students Resilience Skills: The RISE Program at Pepperdine" (presentation, ACSD Annual Conference, Marion, IN, June 8, 2022); Connie Horton and Pepperdine University, *Resilience Roadmap* (Malibu, CA: Pepperdine University Press, 2021), https://issuu.com/pepperdine/docs/pepperdine_20university_20rise_20roadmap?fr=sZmU2ODgwOTUxOQ.

and mood.[32] The RISE program teaches students the importance of taking care of their bodies by getting good sleep, eating a nutritious diet, and exercising. Students who are sleep deprived, eat a diet that is mostly junk food, or are sedentary are not being good stewards of their bodies and are much more likely to struggle with depression. By giving practical information and tips, students can be informed as they consider ways of being good stewards of their bodies. This will help prevent or reduce the severity of depressive moods.

The Social Dimension. Many biblical passages, including the over fifty "one another" passages (e.g., Gal. 6:2; Col. 3:13), make it clear that we were created to be in relationships. God intended us to live in community and have the support of others as we navigate life's challenges. Not surprisingly, research confirms the value of relationships. Social support is an important resilience factor and one that is particularly salient for students who are depressed.[33] Students may struggle with developing relationships because they are socially anxious, are distracted by technology, feel "too busy" for relationships, or simply do not have the social skills to enjoy true friendships. Depression can also interfere significantly with social relationships, and then a lack of social connection may exacerbate the depression. RISE encourages students to value and make time for relationships, teaches specific social skills, and helps them develop empathy.

The Cognitive Dimension. Scripture encourages us to intentionally "set [our] minds on things above" (Col. 3:2) and teaches that we are changed by the "renewing of [our] mind[s]" (Rom. 12:2). Research verifies the importance of thoughts. Those with healthy thinking patterns are more likely to be resilient and less likely to be depressed. The RISE cognitive dimension first teaches students to have realistic

32 Brittany Yates, Maru DeLetter, and Evelyn Parrish, "Prescribed Exercise for the Treatment of Depression in a College Population: An Interprofessional Approach," *Perspectives in Psychiatric Care* 56, no. 4 (2020): 894–99, https://doi.org/10.1111/ppc.12508.

33 Steven M. Southwick et al., "Why Are Some Individuals More Resilient Than Others: The Role of Social Support," *World Psychiatry* 15, no. 1 (2016): 77–79, https://doi.org/10.1002/wps.20282.

expectations, to recognize that "in this world you will have trouble" (John 16:33). Students are encouraged to consider that when they accept that there will be disappointments, hurts, and heartaches in life, those moments are still difficult, but they may be viewed as less catastrophic or overwhelming and will be less likely to result in safety emergencies. The cognitive dimension also teaches the importance of developing a growth mindset.[34] Many biblical passages encourage us to grow, learn, and mature. Proverbs 1:5, for example, urges the "wise" to "listen and add to their learning" and the "discerning" to "get guidance." Consistent with that teaching, RISE helps students avoid a fixed mindset, one that views deficits as permanent. Students are encouraged to change attitudes such as "I'm horrible at math" or "I'm just hot-headed" to "I will need to work at this math class and maybe engage tutors" or "I need to work on my anger-management skills and might benefit from seeing a counselor or spiritual mentor." A willingness to grow rather than give up will help students be more resilient, less depressed, and more successful. Finally, RISE teaches students to renew their minds (Rom. 12:2) by countering their own irrational and unbiblical thoughts. These destructive thoughts may be perfectionistic, they may be catastrophizing, or they may involve negative future forecasting. Using rational and biblical thinking to replace these thoughts (e.g., "My value as a person is based on being created and loved by God, not based on my performance on one exam or pleasing everyone"; or the wisdom from Jesus in Matt. 6:34: "Therefore do not worry about tomorrow, for tomorrow will worry about itself. Each day has enough trouble of its own"), students' lives are changed. Thinking in healthy ways will lead to less depression.

The Spiritual Dimension. Although, clearly, a Christian-faith perspective is woven into the other dimensions of RISE, the spiritual dimension adds some important components of how authentically connecting faith to life can help a student be more resilient. First,

---

34 Carol S. Dweck, *Mindset: The New Psychology of Success* (New York: Random House, 2006).

there is a discussion about seeing life through a faith perspective (e.g., having an awareness of a loving God with them and for them, understanding life from an eternal perspective, focusing on gratitude for blessings) can help them navigate challenging times. The importance of a faith community is also highlighted. Students, many of whom may not see the value of being committed to a particular church family (preferring to "shop around" or watch online), are encouraged to note that deeper involvement in a faith community can make a difference in resilience. RISE teaches that being in a faith community will regularly remind them of God's truths and can provide additional social support and opportunities to serve—all factors that will help resilience. Finally, students are encouraged to see the value of engaging in spiritual practices that can also help them navigate depression and become resilient.

The Service Dimension. A Christian worldview calls us to a life of service (e.g., Gal. 5:13) and to care for the "least of these" (Matt. 25). Some may recognize service is clearly a worthy calling but be surprised to see service addressed in a resilience program. Likewise, stressed or depressed students may feel they cannot possibly engage in service when they are so distressed. Research, however, verifies the counterintuitive reality that service is good not only for those being served but for the person doing the service.[35] Service helps broaden focus, give perspective, and minimize depression risks. Students are encouraged to consider macro service opportunities (e.g., serving regularly with a ministry or nonprofit) but also micro, day-to-day opportunities such as bringing soup to a sick roommate or writing a note of appreciation to a faculty member.

The Life-Skills Dimension. The Bible is full of practical life admonitions such as encouraging us to "[make] the best use of [our] time" (Col. 4:5 ESV); to avoid a "love of money" and be "content with what [we] have" (Heb. 13:5); and to "be very careful, then, how [we]

---

35 Jerf W. K. Yeung, Zhunoi Zhang, and Tae Yeun Kim, "Volunteering and Health Benefits in General Adults: Cumulative Effects and Forms," *BMC Public Health* 18, no. 1 (July 11, 2017): 1–8, https://doi.org/10.1186/s12889 017-4561-8.

live—not as unwise but as wise" (Eph. 5:15). Unfortunately, students are not always so intentional. While the cognitive dimension of RISE recognizes that life will have its inevitable challenges, in the life-skills dimension, RISE cautions students against making life unnecessarily *more* difficult. Students learn they add to their stressors when they make choices such as procrastinating, borrowing more than they need, or becoming "addicted" to social media. Those who get into difficulty in these areas will be less resilient and more prone to depression. These specific topics and others are addressed in the time-management, financial-management, and technology-discernment building blocks of the life-skills dimension. By learning to be intentional and wise in these areas, students will add to their resilience by avoiding unnecessary stressors that can be depressing.

Pepperdine's RISE program teaches these critical dimensions in numerous ways. A key component is a small-group program for all first-year students that is part of their required spiritual life programming. Each of the six sessions addresses one of the components of RISE and includes reflection on a relevant Bible passage, prayer, practical instruction, and discussion. Other RISE offerings include individual and small-group resilience coaching sessions, a residential resilience interest community, special events, and partnerships with faculty teaching liaisons who learn to integrate RISE material into academic courses. There are certainly numerous ways these concepts could be taught on other campuses to help students develop resilience skills and prevent, minimize, or cope with depression. SALs should consider how their campus programming is already addressing or could address these important topics on their campus. SALs who have a good understanding of these dimensions will also be well equipped to naturally include them in one-on-one conversations with students, including with student leaders, helping encourage faithful wise living, promoting resilience, and preventing or minimizing depression.

Summary

Depression is a very real experience for many students at our faith-based institutions. SALs can be an important part of the supportive response to students who are having minor and major depressive struggles. By understanding depression, being wise and discerning in walking with depressed students, and referring students to other resources, they will help students heal. Christian SALs can walk in confidence knowing they have a unique and valuable perspective to offer, one that recognizes the God-given infinite worth and value of each student and includes hope in Christ to share with those who are feeling hopeless. When Jesus spoke of the reality that "in this world you will have trouble," he also reminded us that we can have peace, as he has "overcome the world" (John 16:33). By teaching practical resilience skills that are animated by our Christian theology, SALs help prevent or reduce the suffering involved and help students navigate life's challenges during their college years and beyond. A final reflection captures this hope:

> After all this, I can't tell you how to fix depression. It's different for everyone. I do want you to see that it will go away. It may take time and patience and a lot of discomfort, but you will be free. All I can say is to keep trying different things. For me, it was breaking out of my old lifestyle long enough to see that I could do it. The medication and counseling helped me get through the most difficult times. Now, the skills I learned are what are going to keep me going.
>
> —Excerpt from a student story, shared on Messiah University's "Stories of Hope" webpage[36]

36 Messiah University, "Our Stories of Hope."

Chapter 11
Mental Health and Spiritual Disciplines

Steve Conn

---

f you have read this far into our monograph, you have already seen the evidence that there is a growing mental health pandemic in the United States and in higher education. Data from a special report released from the *Chronicle of Higher Education* indicate that 36 percent of students report struggling with major or moderate depression, 31 percent struggle with an anxiety disorder, and 40 percent of students have sought help from their school counseling centers.[1]

In student affairs, we are uniquely positioned and charged to speak to this issue. At the most utilitarian level, we are asked to keep students emotionally stable enough to attend class. Mental health is now a major persistence concern student affairs is being asked to manage. The most recent report issued by the National Alliance on Mental Illness found nearly two-thirds of students who dropped out of college cited mental health reasons as the primary motivation for withdrawal.[2]

---

1 Sarah Brown, *Overwhelmed: The Real Campus Mental-Health Crisis and New Models for Well-Being* (Washington, DC: Chronicle of Higher Education, 2020), https://www.aucccd.org/assets/documents/StatementsPressReleases/MentalHealth_v6_Interactive.pdf.
2 Darcy Gruttadaro and Dama Crudo, *College Students Speak: A Survey Report on Mental Health* (Arlington, VA: National Alliance on Mental Illness, 2012), https://www.nami.org/Support-Education/Publications-Reports/Survey-Reports/College-Students-Speak_A-Survey-Report-on-Mental-H.

More importantly, caring for others within our sphere of influence should be important to us because an honest engagement with our faith demands it. I am reminded of a previous ACSD monograph that encouraged Christian practitioners to view our role in caring for students as a sacred calling.[3] We are also exhorted throughout Scripture to love one another (John 13:34), to bear one another's burdens (Gal. 6:2), to be compassionate (Col. 3:12), and to seek the good of our neighbor (1 Cor. 10:24). If we are to love and pray for even our enemies, how much more so are we to love the very students we are hired to serve and support? It is therefore clearly our calling, responsibility, and privilege to help these students heal and grow emotionally just as much as it has always been our responsibility to support them academically.

University counseling centers are a great resource for addressing mental health concerns and should be used. Many students experience mental health challenges that need to be clinically addressed by professional health care providers. But we in student affairs should continue to contribute to student mental health in ways that are appropriate to our station. For the purposes of this chapter, I will focus narrowly on an area that is appropriate for nonclinically trained student affairs practitioners at a Christian campus: How can we encourage our students to engage with their faith in ways that promote mental health?

Religion and spirituality have often been cited as protective factors when it comes to mental health because people who exhibit higher levels of religiosity or spirituality are often in community, have a source of hope, and are more capable of coping with stressors.[4] Beyond that, of what value is Christianity to our students in terms of how they engage with mental health? Unfortunately, I have heard many well-meaning and caring individuals give unhelpful and

---

3 Timothy W. Herrmann and Kirsten D. Riedel, eds., *A Calling to Care: Nurturing College Students toward Wholeness* (Abilene, TX: Abilene Christian University Press, 2018).

4 Alexander Moreira-Almeida, Bruno Mosqueiro, and Dinesh Bhugra, eds., *Spirituality and Mental Health across Cultures* (Oxford: Oxford University Press, 2021).

sometimes discouraging advice wrapped in the form of Christian platitudes. It is true the Bible does tell us to "not be anxious about anything" (Phil. 4:6–7), but this reminder is of little use to someone who suffers from panic attacks. And no one I have ever spoken to has told me that their internal struggles were instantly solved when a friend reminded them to "let go and let God."

I believe our faith offers better than this. There is much excellent work being done by Christians in the counseling profession and by counselors who intentionally integrate Scripture into their practice. Additionally, there is much that could be said about the effective integration of Christianity and modern psychology, and many good books on the topic are worth reading (see, e.g., *Psychology, Theology, and Spirituality in Christian Counseling*[5] by Mark McMinn; *Christian Counseling*[6] by Gary Collins; or *God and Soul Care: The Therapeutic Resources of the Christian Faith*[7] by Eric Johnson). However, the aim of this chapter is not to explore a better integration of faith and formal counseling practices. The goal is to find better ways to encourage students to engage in spiritual disciplines as a form of self-care.

Spiritual Disciplines as an Approach to Mental Health

John Ortberg provided a simple definition for spiritual disciplines that I find accessible and useful when working with students. He defined spiritual disciplines as "any activity that can help [us] gain power to live life as Jesus taught and modeled it."[8] Ortberg explained that there are many things in the Christian life we would like to do or be but for which we currently lack the capacity. Disciplines are the activities that help train us and develop such capacity.

---

5 Mark McMinn, *Psychology, Theology, and Spirituality in Christian Counseling* (Carol Stream, IL: Tyndale House, 2011).

6 Gary Collins, *Christian Counseling*, 3rd ed. (Wheaton, IL: Tyndale House, 2007).

7 Eric Johnson, *God and Soul Care: The Therapeutic Resources of the Christian Faith* (Downers Grove, IL: IVP Academic, 2017).

8 John Ortberg, *The Life You've Always Wanted: Spiritual Disciplines for Ordinary People* (Grand Rapids, MI: Zondervan, 2002), 48.

I do believe those who have put their hope in the Lord should ideally be able to experience peace instead of anxiety and joy instead of depression. But I also believe this cannot happen through sheer effort or force of willpower any more than a person can instantly become kind, good, faithful, gentle, or self-controlled. In most facets of our spiritual life, we accept that change is a process that unfolds over time. Traditionally, Christians have turned to spiritual disciplines of cultivating the attitudes and character that produce the fruits of a Christian life. I think it logical that we stop telling students to effectively "stop being anxious or depressed" and instead invite them to practice the cultivation of peace and joy. To do so, I suggest we reexamine some common spiritual disciplines and consider how students may use them as a part of their training.

My goal for this brief chapter is to help us reconsider the role of spiritual practices in the lives of our students and how to encourage them to embrace these disciplines with renewed vigor and purpose. I will choose a few simple examples of common practices and briefly consider them as contributors to emotional health. Additionally, for each discipline, I will give a brief introduction to how the discipline is featured in the Bible, some examples of mental health benefits found in psychological literature, and some recommendations for student practice.

Celebration and Gratitude

Scripture exhorts us on many occasions to be grateful and to thank God. This comes naturally when we experience blessings. David gave thanks to God after defeating the Philistines (2 Sam. 22), Hannah thanked God when she found out she was to bear a son (1 Sam. 2), and Jesus gave thanks to God before feeding the five thousand (John 6:11).

Such conditional gratitude comes naturally. But a more intentional form of gratitude is expected of believers because of God's inherent goodness. Despite our life circumstances, God's goodness, grace, and constant love deserve thanksgiving and praise at all times. We are to give thanks always (Eph. 5:20), in all circumstances (Thess. 5:18), and because God is good and righteous (Pss. 118:24; 107:1; 7:17; 1 Chr. 16:34). Countless other examples throughout Scripture describe gratitude as both a posture we should take toward God and a specific practice we should perform on a regular basis.

The field of positive psychology has also recognized the benefits of gratitude in our everyday lives.[9] Various studies have demonstrated that a posture of gratitude can help individuals interpret their circumstances differently and improve their mood,[10] relationships,[11] self-esteem,[12] and overall happiness.[13] Considering the struggles college students face specifically, it is good to note that gratitude is also negatively correlated with feelings of helplessness, depression, and suicidality.[14]

An often-cited study by Robert Emmons and Michael McCullough established that gratitude was a malleable characteristic that could be affected by daily or weekly habits of journaling or reflecting on blessings.[15] This finding served as the basis of numerous gratitude

9 Lillian Jans-Beken et al., "Gratitude and Health: An Updated Review," *Journal of Positive Psychology* 15, no. 6 (2019): 705–15, https://doi.org/10.1080/17439760.2019.1651888.

10 Rhonda Swickert et al., "The Mediational Roles of Gratitude and Perceived Support in Explaining the Relationship between Mindfulness and Mood," *Journal of Happiness Studies* 20, no. 1 (March 2018): 815–28, https://doi.org/10.1007/s10902-017-9952-0.

11 Sara B. Algoe, Jonathan Haidt, and Shelly L. Gable, "Beyond Reciprocity: Gratitude and Relationships in Everyday Life," *Emotion* 8, no. 3 (June 2008): 425–29, https://doi.org/10.1037/1528-3542.8.3.425.

12 Chi Lin, "The Effect of Higher-Order Gratitude on Mental Well-Being: Beyond Personality and Unifactoral Gratitude," *Current Psychology* 36, no. 1 (2017): 127–35, https://doi.org/10.1007/s12144-015-9392-0.

13 Martin E. P. Seligman et al., "Positive Psychology Progress: Empirical Validation of Interventions," *American Psychologist* 60, no. 5 (2005): 410–21, https://doi.org/10.1037/0003-066X.60.5.410.

14 Andrea R. Kaniuka et al., "Gratitude and Suicide Risk among College Students: Substantiating the Protective Benefits of Being Thankful," *Journal of American College Health* 69, no. 6 (2020): 660–67, https://doi.org/10.1080/07448481.2019.1705838.

15 Robert Emmons and Michael McCullough, "Counting Blessings versus Burdens: An Experimental Investigation of Gratitude and Subjective Well-Being in Daily Life," *Journal of Personality and Social Psychology* 84, no. 2 (2002): 377–89, https://doi.org/10.1037/0022-3514.84.2.377.

intervention studies that have demonstrated effectiveness in improving mood and well-being.[16]

RECOMMENDED PRACTICES FOR STUDENTS

- **Thank-you notes.** Write a thank-you note or letter (or email or text) to a person you are grateful for but have not thanked yet.

- **Counting blessings.** Make a habit of closing each day by writing down things you are thankful for or feel blessed by.

- **Sharing praise.** Make a point each day to share with another person a reason to praise God.

- **Worship.** Take time to participate in worship corporately and privately. Praying over a psalm or listening to a contemporary worship song praising God can serve as a gratitude meditation.

Gathering Together

In our highly individualistic society, it is often a temptation for students to approach their faith as something they can do alone. But Scripture paints a very different picture. One of the most famous examples of community for Christians is the early church. In the book of Acts, Luke described the church members as being devoted to "the apostles' teaching and to fellowship, to the breaking of bread and to prayer" (Acts 2:42). The author of Hebrews reminded readers not to neglect their duty to meet together (Heb. 10:25), and Jesus told his disciples that where two or three are together, he would be there with them (Matt. 18:20). Additionally, believers are charged to be in one another's lives in a variety of personal ways such as loving one another (John 13:14), being devoted to one another (Rom. 12:10), bearing with one another (Eph. 4:2), carrying one another's burdens

---

16 David R. Cregg and Jennifer S. Cheavens, "Gratitude Interventions: Effective Self-Help? A Meta-analysis of the Impact on Symptoms of Depression and Anxiety," *Journal of Happiness Studies* 22, no. 1 (2020): 413–45, https://doi .org/10.1007/s10902-020-00236-6.

(Gal. 6:2), confessing sins to one another (James 5:16), and encouraging one another (Heb. 10:25).

On Christian campuses, we often preach the virtues of close community and relationships based on these biblical ideas. A desire for community is why many of us require students to live in residence halls and have a meal plan. Our hope is that students' close proximity will help them develop relationships and a close connection with the institution and thereby persist to graduation. We also offer a wide array of student activities and organizations to give students the opportunity to get involved.

Additionally, students should consider how they can intentionally exercise the discipline of community for the purpose of their health and well-being. Studies show that social support can be negatively correlated with loneliness and depression[17] and positively related to physical health.[18] Perceived social support can also have a mediating influence, enhancing the effectiveness of standard treatment approaches to anxiety and depression. Close relationships between individuals can help people process stress in more beneficial ways[19] and view the world in a more positive, less threatening way.[20] People who are close to us also have an opportunity to help shape our healthy habits such as sleep, exercise, and diet.[21] Although I don't recommend students create diets for one another, I can see how the presence of friends inviting floormates to join them for dinner helps prevent them from too many nights of eating Pop-Tarts alone in their rooms.

17 Christopher M. Masi et al., "A Meta-analysis of Interventions to Reduce Loneliness," *Personality and Social Psychology Review* 15, no. 3 (2010): 219–66, https://doi.org/10.1177%2F1088868310377394.

18 Bert N. Uchino, "Understanding the Links between Social Support and Physical Health: A Life-Span Perspective with Emphasis on the Separability of Perceived and Received Support," *Perspectives on Psychological Science* 4, no. 3 (2009): 236–55, https://doi.org/10.1111/j.1745-6924.2009.01122.x.

19 Uchino, 236–55.

20 Brooke C. Feeney and Nancy L. Collins, "A New Look at Social Support," *Personality and Social Psychology Review* 19, no. 2 (2014): 113–47, https://doi.org/10.1177/1088868314544222.

21 Paula R. Pietromonaco and Nancy L. Collins, "Interpersonal Mechanisms Linking Close Relationships to Health," *American Psychologist* 72, no. 6 (2017): 531–42, https://doi.org/10.1037/amp0000129; Uchino, "Understanding the Links," 236–55.

We were created for community. Many of our practices as a university are designed around this truth, and we have numerous programs to promote community. But are students challenged to take advantage of these opportunities and to make their own efforts to develop close relationships as a discipline for their own growth and well-being?

RECOMMENDED PRACTICES FOR STUDENTS

- **Never eat alone.** Meal times are necessary, so take full advantage of them. Make an intentional effort to eat with others, if at all possible. This practice is easier for students who live on campus and have a meal plan. But even students who prepare their own food can make an effort to share their meal with a roommate or friend.

- **Join (and attend) at least one group.** You will undoubtedly have a number of group offerings to choose from. Although there are benefits to joining any form of social group, I recommend considering some form of a Bible study, small group, or accountability group, where other members are likely to be more involved in your life, engage in personal dialogue, and reach out to you if you are missing.

- **Intentional time.** College students are surrounded by peers. For many students, finding the opportunity for privacy is more of a challenge than finding a friend. However, it is easy to satisfy yourself with superficial interactions without taking the time to develop deep and meaningful relationships. Make the effort to spend an hour with a friend once a week to engage in uninterrupted conversation.

- **Confession.** If you do feel that you have a strong relationship with another individual or group, consider exploring the discipline of confession together. Jesus's followers have been given the authority to hear confessions and forgive in Jesus's name (John 20:23), yet this is a privilege we rarely take advantage of in Protestant circles. Author and psychiatrist Kurt Thompson recommended the practice of confessional communities as a means of living out God's calling, building community, and healing from the wounds of shame.[22]

Study and Reflection on Scripture

One of the most common practices we learn as young Christians is the study of Scripture. This can be considered broadly as something as simple as reading the Bible or as in-depth as a rigorous word study in the original Hebrew. Deuteronomy 11:18–23 encouraged the Israelites to store God's Word in their hearts, to write them on their doorposts, to think about them in the morning and evening, and even to wear them on their person. God's people are told to meditate on the book of the law, day and night (Josh. 1:8). The author of Psalm 119 said that he had "stored up" God's Word in his heart (v. 11 ESV), and Psalm 1 tells us that the man who meditates daily on the law of the Lord is like "a tree planted by streams of water" (v. 3). Jesus himself demonstrated an intimate knowledge of Scripture and had large portions of Scripture memorized, as was customary at the time.

The purpose and benefits of studying Scripture extend far beyond the emotional well-being of the reader. But for the purposes of this chapter, I suggest that we consider how being rooted in God's truth can be helpful to those who are struggling with negative thoughts and feelings perpetuated by the lies of this world. A very popular and clinically proven therapeutic approach to treating both anxiety and depression is cognitive behavioral therapy (CBT). One of the core principles of CBT is that many psychological problems are caused in part by negative or faulty patterns of thinking. Treatment therefore involves identifying negative or untrue thoughts, challenging them, and replacing them with thoughts that are true.[23]

---

22 Kurt Thompson, *The Soul of Desire: Discovering the Neuroscience of Longing, Beauty, and Community* (Downers Grove, IL: InterVarsity, 2021).

23 "What Is Cognitive Behavioral Therapy?," American Psychological Association, accessed June 16, 2022, https://www.apa.org/ptsd-guideline/patients-and-families/cognitive-behavioral.

People struggling with anxiety and depression may be battling common negative thoughts about themselves such as the ideas that they are worthless, deficient, or unlovable or that they need to perform to have value. Psychiatrist David Burns called these thoughts "self-defeating beliefs" and suggested that our conscious or unconscious adherence to these falsehoods can be at the root of many of our problems.[24] What better place for a believer to find a truth that refutes these lies than the words of God? The Bible tells us we are made in the image of God (Gen. 1:27), wonderfully made (Ps. 139:14), bought with a price (1 Cor. 7:23), and made children of God (John 1:12). We are told that God loves us so thoroughly that, although he knew we were still sinners, Christ chose to die for us (Rom. 5:8). These are just a few examples of instances in which the Bible authoritatively declares truth over who we are and what our value is. The Bible is also our source of truth for understanding God, love, morality, and many things about the nature of reality. These truths can be a powerful counter to the lies we often believe about ourselves and can be a great tool for those who are struggling with emotional difficulties based on these lies.

I do not believe that this oversimplification accurately describes the robust and nuanced therapeutic approach that is CBT. Nor do I believe that telling struggling students to read their Bibles more will be received as helpful advice unless it is couched in a broader context. What I *do* believe is that the discipline of focusing our attention on God's truth consistently and in targeted ways can be of great benefit, as it provides a rationale for challenging troubling thoughts.

RECOMMENDED PRACTICES FOR STUDENTS

- **Memorize Scripture.** Find some passages in Scripture that are meaningful and comforting to you, and memorize them. Practice writing them out over and over to help reinforce the message in your mind. The time spent memorizing will be of value as well as the ability to recall the passage in times of trouble.

---

24 David D. Burns, *When Panic Attacks: The New, Drug-Free Anxiety Therapy That Can Change Your Life* (New York: Harmony, 2007).

- **Challenge your thoughts.** Identify thoughts you struggle with, and see if the Bible directly addresses any of your negative thoughts or feelings. You may not find anything that speaks directly to your situation, and there is no need to force it, but perhaps this process of searching will help you find passages that comfort you in a different way.

- **Challenge your beliefs.** Consider any self-defeating beliefs you may have and evaluate them in the light of the Bible. Do you truly believe these statements to be true? What does the Bible have to say about them? You may have trouble identifying your self-defeating beliefs on your own. A simple online search for "common self-defeating beliefs" will provide you with examples to help get you started.

Prayer and Meditation

Prayer is a fundamental ritual that many of us have practiced since the beginning of our faith journey. It is modeled consistently throughout Scripture through the narrative of the Old Testament and the Gospels. We are also instructed by Jesus and the apostles to continue to pray consistently, joyfully, and with confidence (Rom. 12:12; James 1:5; Luke 21:36; Phil. 4:6; 1 Thess. 5:17).

There are many types of prayer modeled in Scripture. Some are prayers of worship or thanksgiving, such as the "sacrifice of praise" described in Hebrews 13:15 and exemplified by much of the Psalms. There are also prayers of confession (Ps. 51), prayers of intercession (1 Thess. 1:2), prayers of petition (Eph. 1:15), and more. Prayer is such a common part of the Christian life that it is easy to lose sight of what a miracle it is. It is nothing less than communing with the Creator God of the universe! Students may experience the benefits of prayer for their mental health as a result of divine intervention because they felt comforted by God or because they simply got their minds off their problems temporarily. All these positive outcomes are valid, and there are innumerable other theological and practical reasons to pray. In addition to these benefits, I would draw attention to another that has significant implications for this chapter: prayer can change our brains.

Frequent and extensive prayer has been associated with a thickening of the frontal lobes and the thalamus, which in turn is associated with lower levels of anxiety and depression.[25] Neuroimaging has also found prayer to activate the prefrontal cortex and the parietal lobe and to activate neurotransmitter systems that lessen the experience of anxiety and depressive symptoms.[26] Recent studies using fMRI imaging have found there is a statistically significant increase in a broad range of brain activity after participating in a guided prayer retreat.[27] In short, even students who were already convinced of the importance of prayer for theological reasons will likely be encouraged to know that the very act of praying can strengthen their brain as well as their spirit.

Prayer and meditation are similar in concept and may on occasion refer to the same thing. Whether this is true depends on the operational definition one is using for each term. Because there are many different approaches to both prayer and meditation, I think it best to treat them as two separate concepts that share some overlapping features.

Although neurological research on Christian prayer is scant, the research on meditation is prolific. A type of meditation practice known as mindfulness is currently gaining popularity in the United States. Mindfulness practices are evidence-based techniques that have been demonstrated to be beneficial for reducing anxiety, depression, and stress as well as improving attention[28] I theorize that additional

25 Andrew B. Newberg and Mark Robert Waldman, *How God Changes Your Brain: Breakthrough Findings from a Leading Neuroscientist* (New York: Harmony, 2010).

26 E. Mohandas, "Neurobiology of Spirituality," *Mens Sana Monographs* 6, no. 1 (2008): 63–80.

27 Nancy A. Wintering et al., "Effect of a One-Week Spiritual Retreat on Brain Functional Connectivity: A Preliminary Study," *Religions* 12, no. 23 (2020): 1–13, https://doi.org/10.3390/rel12010023.

28 For a robust meta-analysis of the benefits of mindfulness, see Simon Yat Ho Li and Daniel Bressington, "The Effects of Mindfulness-Based Stress Reduction on Depression, Anxiety, and Stress in Older Adults: A Systematic Review and Meta-analysis," *International Journal of Mental Health Nursing* 28, no. 3 (2019): 635–56, https://doi.org/10.1111/inm.12568.

research would show that most (if not all) of the benefits seen in the mindfulness literature would also appear in research about some types of Christian prayer. Although much of the mindfulness movement has roots in the Buddhist tradition, its origin does not mean all meditation must be considered from a Buddhist perspective. Jon Kabat-Zinn has developed a mindfulness-based stress reduction treatment without religious affiliation that is now used in various forms of modern therapy.[29] More importantly, meditation has been practiced by Christians for centuries. I recommend that those interested in developing a fully Christian meditation practice read *Christian Mindfulness*[30] for a historical look at meditation practices of the early church and the desert fathers as well as *Christ Centered Mindfulness*[31] for a contemporary look at how a modern Christian can wisely understand and apply mindfulness.

Conclusion

The church has a rich tradition with spiritual disciplines, and thoughtful and detailed explorations of these disciplines are abundant. As student affairs practitioners, I recommend we engage students with resources that provide an accessible overview of spiritual disciplines without overwhelming them. I have found *The Life You've Always Wanted* by John Ortberg,[32] *Celebration of Discipline* by Richard Foster,[33] and *The Spiritual Disciplines Handbook* by Adele Calhound[34] to be useful resources.

---

29 Jon Kabat-Zinn, *Full Catastrophe Living: Using the Wisdom of Your Body and Mind to Face Stress, Pain, and Illness*, revised and updated ed. (New York: Bantam, 2013).

30 Peter Tyler, *Christian Mindfulness: Theology and Practice* (London: SCM Press, 2018).

31 Katherine Thompson, *Christ Centered Mindfulness: Connection to Self and God* (Sydney: Acorn, 2018).

32 Ortberg, *Life You've Always Wanted*.

33 Richard J. Foster, *Celebration of Discipline: The Path to Spiritual Growth*, special anniversary ed. (San Francisco: HarperOne, 2018).

34 Adele Calhound, *Spiritual Disciplines Handbook: Practices That Transform Us* (Downers Grove, IL: InterVarsity, 2005).

I'd like to conclude this chapter with disclaimers. I do not recommend that the suggestions in this chapter replace conventional therapy for anyone who needs it. These recommendations are guidelines for healthy living and should not be confused with a treatment plan. The second qualification is that spiritual disciplines were not created as a tool for feeling good or for eliminating stress or negative emotions. They are designed for transforming ourselves to become the people God created us to be and bringing us to a place to commune with him more deeply. I propose only considering the "added benefit" of mental health when engaging in spiritual disciplines. It is my hope that recognizing this benefit may invite students to explore and engage with disciplines in new ways that will benefit them emotionally, spiritually, and holistically.

Chapter 12

Sex with a Person's Mediated Body

Pornography

John D. Foubert

I n a Christian book about stewarding the body, perhaps one of the most delicate topics to deal with is sexual stewardship. This chapter falls under that mantle, given that we will be talking about the complex issue of pornography, alternatively known as sex with a person's mediated body. By mediated body, I mean that another person's body is depicted in pictures or videos or described in print. By pornography, the definition I will use is from Michael Lastoria: "Any kind of material aimed at creating or enhancing sexual feelings or thoughts in the recipient and at the same time containing explicit exposure and/or descriptions of the genitals and/or sexual acts."[1] Given that pornography use often involves masturbation, particularly with male users,[2] using the words "sex" or "erotic" seems appropriate.

---

[1] Michael Lastoria, *Sexuality, Religiosity, Behaviors, Attitudes: A Look at Religiosity, Sexual Attitudes and Sexual Behaviors of Christian College Students: A Survey Study* (Houghton, NY: ACSD, Houghton College, 2011), 49.

[2] John D. Foubert, *Protecting Your Children from Internet Pornography: Understanding the Science, Risks, and Ways to Protect Your Kids* (Chicago: Northfield, 2022).

Unfortunately, a significant percentage of Christian student affairs staff are not confident regarding how to manage pornography. A recent survey of Christian student life staff across the nation found that only 31 percent agreed or strongly agreed with the statement "Our staff is adequately trained to handle pornography issues with students."[3] Another 30 percent slightly agreed, but 40 percent either slightly disagreed, disagreed, or strongly disagreed. Clearly, more education and training need to be done in this area.

This chapter briefly summarizes a biblical perspective toward pornography, reviews some of the social-scientific research on the effects of pornography, explores what redemption from pornography involves, and then provides practical advice for student affairs staff dealing with the issue of pornography on their campuses.

A Biblical Perspective

As the first chapter of this volume makes clear, we must first understand our bodies in light of creation. Psalm 139:13–14 states, "For you formed my inward parts; you knitted me together in my mother's womb. I praise you, for I am fearfully and wonderfully made." Thus, God creates everyone's body and does so in a wonderful fashion. Furthermore, the Bible emphasizes that the body is a gift from God, which as Chapter One mentioned, means that both female and male bodies are gifts from God. In addition, by creating us male and female, God shares with us and our bodies the power of creation through biological reproduction.[4] Thus, when a married couple has sex, it is in keeping with God's design. Sex binds two into one flesh.

Likewise, the New Testament makes clear that the Christian's body is a temple of the Holy Spirit, not one's own but rather bought with a price by Christ. Therefore, we should glorify God with our bodies (1 Cor. 6:19–20). These verses recall to us that our bodies are

---

3 Perry L. Glanzer et al., *Christ-Enlivened Student Affairs: A Guide to Christian Thinking and Practice in the Field* (Abilene, TX: Abilene Christian University Press, 2020), 188.

4 Timothy C. Tennent, *For the Body: Recovering a Theology of Gender, Sexuality, and the Human Body* (Grand Rapids, MI: Zondervan, 2020).

both sacred and ransomed—that we should place the highest value on honoring the Lord with them. The uniting of our body with the Spirit of God clearly demonstrates the body's goodness.

As a result, Christians can praise the depiction of the created human body in literature, sculpture, painting, film, or any humanly created medium that promotes aesthetic appreciation of God's creation versus erotic stimulation. Indeed, some of the greatest art in human civilization is meant to capture this celebration of the human body created by God.

Unfortunately, we also use the human body for fallen ends. Immediately before the same passage from 1 Corinthians, Paul contrasts the glorification of the body for God and God's purposes with the use of the body for fallen ends: "Flee from sexual immorality [Greek—*porneian*]. All other sins a person commits are outside the body, but whoever sins sexually, sins against their own body" (1 Cor. 6:18). As one can see, the Greek word for sexual immorality, *porneian*, is the basis for the English words "porn" and "pornography." *Porneian* takes that which is fearfully and wonderfully made and grossly misuses it.

The misuse takes two forms. First, the creators of pornography are like creators of counterfeit money. They hope to stimulate a person erotically for their own ends—usually to make money. In his recent book about the body, Timothy Tennent noted that "in biblical terms, whenever we reject God's image in us and replace it with a lesser image, that lesser image is known as an 'idol' or a 'false image.'"[5] Pornography is a counterfeit image of sex as created by God in that it is sex with an idol. However, Tennent argued that it is a mistake to refer to pornographic images as "dirty" because they depict bodies made in the image of God, and as such, the bodies depicted are not dirty. The first evil comes from the creator of pornography, who seeks to use their good body for counterfeit sex to achieve evil desires.

The second evil comes when others consume pornography. They desire to use the image of a person made in God's image for their own sexual pleasure. The vice of lust involves seeking to own or

---

5 Tennent, 14.

possess someone as an object and thus turns an image bearer into an object. This is why viewing pornographic images constitutes idolatry: because an image bearer is used as a means to satisfy selfishly sinful passions.

Because pornography incites lust, and the Bible defines lust as idolatry, to view pornography is to commit idolatry. Such idolatry redirects our love from Christ to a lustful attraction for an object. Tennent noted that "our sinful impulse is to satisfy what we want rather than die to self. Satisfying selfish desires can destroy our relationship with Christ just as it has destroyed many marriages and Christian ministries."[6] Pornography helps drive a wedge between people regarding an act God created to bring unity to a marriage, and it distorts this act into a lonely facilitator for self-pleasuring. In fact, research shows that using pornography results in loneliness in a way that is mutually reinforcing: pornography leads to loneliness, which leads to more use of pornography, and the vicious cycle continues.[7] Tennent concluded that "pornography is a 'disincarnation' turning the body into an icon of lust and sinful idolatry rather than of Christ."[8]

Similarly, in his book *Wonderfully Made*, John W. Kleinig argued that the idolatry of pornography leads people to devalue God's approval and lack fear in his disapproval. In a stinging rebuke, he summarized what its misdirected worship does to us spiritually: "[Pornography users] do not love God but love unnatural sexual stimulation more than him; they do not trust in him to provide comfort and enjoyment in marriage or part from it but rely on imaginative self-stimulation for sexual comfort and enjoyment. Our fascination with pornography therefore masks a deeper issue, our suicidal rebellion against God and our service of his creature rather than our life-receiving service of him."[9] Despite (or perhaps because of) his stinging rebuke, Kleinig recommended pastors encourage their flock to confess their

---

6 Tennent, 123.
7 Foubert, *Protecting Your Children*.
8 Tennent, *For the Body*, 124.
9 John W. Kleinig, *Wonderfully Made: A Protestant Theology of the Body* (Bellingham, WA: Lexham, 2021), 173.

pornographic sins, cleanse their guilty conscience, and cover themselves with Christ's purity to be assured of God's approval.

Similarly, since pornography use is counterfeit sex and union, biblical marriage and pornography use are in obvious, direct conflict. Marriage is self-giving, exclusive, and is a sign of our unity with Christ. Pornography, by contrast, is self-serving, promotes as much access to itself as possible, and is a sign of our separation from the Creator and the body of Christ.

Overall, as Sam Allberry observed, *porneian* is "not just a misuse of someone else's body and your body but a violation of your whole self. No wonder Paul tells us not just to avoid it but to flee it. The repercussions of engaging in it are enormous. It does something deep to who we are."[10] What those repercussions are for both ourselves and others we can learn through social science.

The Consequences of Pornography

One of the insidious things about pornography is that it not only is degrading to the performers but also harms participants and innocent bystanders. To begin, as Allberry noted, it harms one's whole being, including one's soul. For example, the more that young people use pornography, the less frequently they attend religious services, the less important their faith is to them, the less frequently they pray and feel close to God, and the more religious doubts they have.[11]

Of course, it also harms one's sexual life. In his book *Wonderfully Made*, Kleinig noted how pornography reprograms the brain, especially of young people. Tragically, he pointed out, pornography use leads to an inability to be sexually stimulated by a body, leaving the user requiring the artificial stimulation of pornography to create sexual desire. He continued,

10 Sam Allberry, *What God Has to Say about Our Bodies: How the Gospel Is Good News for Our Physical Selves* (Wheaton, IL: Crossway, 2021), 53.

11 Krystallenia Alexandraki et al., "Adolescent Pornography Use: A Systematic Literature Review of Research Trends 2000–2017," *Current Psychiatry Reviews* 14, no. 47 (2018): 47–58, https://doi.org/10.2174/2211556007666180606073617.

Like a drug that delivers a short high to its user that is followed by an emotional slump, it delivers a charge that does not last but requires ever-increasing indulgence to maintain its diminishing intensity and ward off the ever-increasing severity of its consequent low. The chemical transformation in a porn-addicted brain impairs normal sexual arousal and the natural, physical sexual response to another person. So, oddly, indulgence in pornography does not actually awaken normal sexual desire—it switches it off. Instead of increasing healthy sexual enjoyment, it decreases it. It does not enrich the sexual imagination but actually impoverishes it by its narrow focus on the physical mechanics of sex. In short, it peddles fake sex.[12]

Not surprisingly, he concluded that this counterfeit sex is never satisfying because it is "not explicit enough . . . because it shows so little of what actually happens when a married couple makes love with each other."[13]

In addition, a substantial amount of harm to others is done to a marriage through pornography use. Indeed, married men who use pornography are more likely than others to sleep with prostitutes. Couples who use pornography are more likely to believe that their marriage is in trouble, are more likely to discuss ending the marriage, are more likely to repeatedly break up, are less likely to view their relationship as good or strong, are less likely to feel like a team with their spouse, are less likely to believe their marriage is nearly perfect, and overall are less satisfied with their marriage.[14] In short, while marriage can be rightly thought of as an act of service toward

---

12 Kleinig, *Wonderfully Made*, 173.
13 Kleinig, 173.
14 Sam Perry and Kyle Longest, "Pornography Use and Marriage Entry during Early Adulthood: Findings from a Panel Study of Young Americans," *SocArXiv Papers* (2018): 1–35, https://doi.org/10.31235/osf.io/xry3z; Sam Perry, "Pornography and Relationship Quality: Establishing the Dominant Pattern by Examining Pornography Use and 31 Measures of Relationship Quality in 30 National Surveys," *Archives of Sexual Behavior* 49, no. 4 (2020): 1199–213, https://doi.org/10.1007/s10508-019-01616-7; Sam Perry, "From Bad to Worse? Pornography Consumption, Spousal Religiosity, Gender, and Marital Quality," *Sociological Forum* 31, no. 2 (2016): 441–64.

another, pornography encourages the dissolution of relationships and, in fact, is associated with less satisfaction with marriage.[15]

To pornography viewers over time, it rewrites their sexual script to favor objectifying and violent, not loving, behavior. In fact, research supports the objectifying nature of pornography. In a neurological study, men were shown pornography while they got an MRI to record what parts of their brains lit up when viewing pornography. The part of the brain that was activated when men viewed pornography was the part that references objects, not people. The objectifying nature of pornography is particularly insidious because the more you make someone out to be an object, the easier it is to commit violence against them. In fact, since the late 1990s, violence in pornography increased so much that it often depicted scenes where women vomit and are shown with men's bodily fluids on their faces. Indeed, my own studies have found that the more people use violent pornography, the less willing they are to intervene in a real-life situation where someone might be harmed sexually. Thus, pornography encourages a callous disregard for one's neighbor.[16]

Salvation and Redemption from Pornography

The most effective way to fight against this kind of idolatry is to start with recognizing that there should be no other gods before God, that we belong to him (body and soul). Salvation from pornography, like salvation as a whole, must always begin with confession. In addition, we must recognize that the most powerful force we can use to fight pornography is the power within us as temples of the Holy Spirit.

That being said, we must also recognize that pornography addiction influences our brain in important ways, and therefore, we must do all that we can to help those ensnared by it leave it behind. This is much easier said than done. Sadly, the state of social-science research at this time tells us nothing about how to deal with pornography addiction. The research today shows that pornography is a huge problem

---

15 Foubert, *Protecting Your Children.*
16 For more information, see Foubert, *Protecting Your Children.*

and that it is addictive; however, there is no research documenting how to get someone to overcome a pornography habit. That will begin to change soon. Currently, I am analyzing data from a study of men at two colleges, comparing those who went through a commercially available antipornography program with an untreated control group. It is my sincere hope that in the near future, I will be able to publicly share the results of this study and show at least one way to significantly reduce pornography use. In addition, I have other studies in the planning stages, such as a study of a commercially available online program that also seeks to reduce the pornography use of its users. The results of that study too should shed some light on this area in much need of research.

Practical Steps for Student Life Staff

Recently, a host of Christian books about a biblical perspective toward the body have been written such as *What God Has to Say about Our Bodies: How the Gospel Is Good News for Our Physical Selves*; *For the Body: Recovering a Theology of Gender, Sexuality, and the Human Body*; *Embodied: Living as Whole People in a Fractured World*; *Wonderfully Made: A Protestant Theology of the Body*; and *Love Thy Body: Answering Hard Questions about Life and Sexuality.*[17] These books would be excellent resources for student affairs leaders hoping to gain a deeper biblical understanding of the body. In addition, each of these books addresses pornography within the context of the larger biblical story.

In my book *Protecting Your Children from Internet Pornography: Understanding the Science, Risks, and Ways to Protect Your Kids*, I offer practical advice for how parents can interact with their children to hopefully deter them from viewing pornography and to help them process the experience as they do. The ideas can also be applied

---

17 Allberry, *What God Has to Say*; Tennent, *For the Body*; Greg Allison, *Embodied: Living as Whole People in a Fractured World* (Grand Rapids, MI: Baker Books, 2021); Kleinig, *Wonderfully Made*; Nancy Pearcy, *Love Thy Body: Answering Hard Questions about Life and Sexuality* (Grand Rapids, MI: Baker Books, 2018).

to the efforts of student affairs staff who wish to speak with college students about their own use of pornography. For example, just as I recommend that parents not freak out if they find that their children are watching pornography, I also recommend that student affairs staff take a measured approach to talking with students about their pornography use. By this, I certainly don't mean that we should excuse it or think it is no big deal. However, overreacting can undermine the honest dialogue we cultivate with students through the strength of our relationships with them. Thus, I encourage that student affairs staff have a calm conversation with students based on the facts of what pornography does to them, as partly enumerated in this chapter.

Fostering relationships with students where they come to feel like they can speak with you about anything can truly open the floodgates to talking about their pornography use, identifying the student's reasons for viewing it, and diagnosing their triggers to avoid its use in everyday life. In my view, it is important for student affairs staff to encourage porn-using students to use filtering and accountability software on their phones and, if necessary, consider purchasing a phone that does not transmit pictures. I also recommend that students go through the online program *The Freedom Fight* in order to fight the battle of internet pornography use. Finding an accountability partner is another helpful technique where people can apply James 5:16: "Therefore confess your sins to each other and pray for each other so that you may be healed. The prayer of a righteous person is powerful and effective."

Conclusion

This chapter has explored a theology of the human body through the lens of how pornography detracts from God's intent for our bodies. Pornography, at its root, is idolatry and is thus sinful. There are numerous practical ways we can work with college students to help them rid themselves of the cancer of pornography on their souls. Doing so is a critical factor in promoting the mental thriving of today's college students.

Chapter 13

Stewarding Diverse Sexual and Gender Identities

Mark A. Yarhouse, Stephen P. Stratton, and
Janet B. Dean

n this chapter, we combine a line of research we have conducted
with our clinical experience and the extant literature to offer a
vision of what stewardship looks like when extended to sexual and
gender identities. By sexual and gender identities, we are referring
to minority identities such as sexual minority statuses (e.g., lesbian,
gay, bisexual) and gender minority statuses (e.g., transgender and
nonbinary). We hope to explore how one might steward a human
body whose identity-based experience is that of a sexual or gender
minority during the young adult years. What helps and hinders self-
development for persons who are navigating these experiences as
Christians?

Sexual and Gender Identity

Sexual identity or sexual orientation identity refers to private and
public labels people use to think about themselves (a self-defining
attribution) or to convey their identity to others. Common sexual identity labels include gay, lesbian, bisexual, queer, and heterosexual or
straight. Depending on people's circumstances and developmental
journey, their private and public labels may or may not correspond
with one another.

Gender identity refers to a person's experience of themselves as a boy or a girl, a man or a woman, or a different gender identity than those (e.g., transgender, gender nonbinary). Most children are aware of themselves as a boy or a girl between the ages of two and four. However, in some instances, their awareness or experiences of themselves do not line up with their natal sex. This apparent discordant gender identity may lead to symptoms of gender dysphoria or distress associated with discordant identity and/or a transgender or other gender identity.

Developmental Considerations in Identity Formation

We recently published a book[1] that has continued with empirical data analysis related to sexual[2] and gender-diverse college students.[3] We have documented sexual identity formation as a developmental process through various milestones by which sexual minorities of faith navigate their experience of same-sex sexuality. These experiences include first awareness of one's same-sex sexuality, initial attributions about what their experiences mean to them, first disclosure of one's same-sex sexuality to another, adopting a private identity or making a self-defining attribution (e.g., gay, lesbian, bisexual), adopting a public sexual identity label (e.g., gay, lesbian, bisexual) that may or may not reflect affiliation with aspects of the lesbian, gay, bisexual, transgender, queer, and other LGBTQ+ community as a culture, and so on. Gender identity is not studied with reference to the same kinds of milestones as sexual identity; rather, we tend to think of early- (prior

1 Mark A. Yarhouse et al., *Listening to Sexual Minorities: A Study of Faith and Sexual Identity on Christian College Campuses* (Downers Grove, IL: InterVarsity, 2018).

2 Janet B. Dean, Stephen P. Stratton, and Mark A. Yarhouse, "The Mediating Role of Self-Acceptance in the Psychological Distress of Sexual Minority Students on Christian College Campuses," *Spirituality in Clinical Practice* 8, no. 2 (2021): 132–48, https://doi.org/10.1037/scp0000253.

3 Mark A. Yarhouse et al., "Listening to Transgender and Gender Diverse Students on Christian College Campuses," *Journal of Religion and Health* 60, no. 6 (2021): 4480–99, https://doi.org/10.1007/s10943-021-01425-0.

to puberty) or late-onset (at or following puberty) experiences of discordant gender identity.

In navigating their developmental journeys, Christian sexual minorities may be at risk for confusion and shame, the emotional experiences in which one believes one is responsible for an important shortcoming or deficit. This shame-based perception can lead a person to keep others at a distance and can foster self-rejection.[4] We believe that a shame-related pattern extended over time puts a person at risk of their attractions coming out in less healthy ways. Based on "hearing the voices" of many Christians within this developmental crucible,[5] we want those navigating same-sex sexuality, gender, and faith to find or create "scaffolding" around identity that allows them to steward their experience and to receive support as they navigate questions of faith, gender expression, potential future sexual behavior and relationships, the formation of a relational ethic, and so on. We have written elsewhere[6] that the most conducive "scaffolding" will be intentionally relational, intentionally formational, intentionally securing, and intentionally trinitarian. Taken together, we describe this faith-conscious environment as the communal structure for stewardship of one's sexual or gender identity. This environmental and contextual "scaffolding" appears to improve conditions for overall psychological well-being and growth.[7]

4 June Price Tangney and Rhonda L. Dearing, *Shame and Guilt* (New York: Guilford, 2002).

5 Stephen P. Stratton et al., "Sexual Minorities in Faith-Based Higher Education: A National Survey of Attitudes, Milestones, Identity, and Religiosity," *Journal of Psychology and Theology* 41, no. 1 (2013): 3–23, https://doi.org/10.1177/009164711304100101; Yarhouse et al., *Listening to Sexual Minorities*; Mark A. Yarhouse et al., "Listening to Sexual Minorities on Christian College Campuses," *Journal of Psychology and Theology* 37, no. 2 (July 2009): 96–113, https://doi.org/10.1177/009164710903700202.

6 Yarhouse et al., *Listening to Sexual Minorities*, 271–312; Janet B. Dean, Stephen P. Stratton, and Mark A. Yarhouse, "Becoming an Intentional Church Community: Relationships, Security, and Discipleship in Sexual Identity and Faith Development," *Christian Education Journal* 18, no. 2 (2021): 232–51.

7 Dean, Stratton, and Yarhouse, "Becoming an Intentional Church"; Michael R. Woodford et al., "Contemporary Heterosexism on Campus and Psychological Distress among LGBQ Students: The Mediating Role of Self-Acceptance," *American Journal of Orthopsychiatry* 84, no. 5 (2014): 519–29, https://doi.org/10.1037/ort0000015.

Identity development in any area of life is too significant and complex to imagine it can be accomplished alone. Self-development needs an embedding community; even one partner in the journey can make a difference.[8] Having a community of some sort is even better. Students have taught us that self-acceptance and healthy social support along with the safe haven of intrinsic religiosity (i.e., a deep faith that directs their lives) create the most formative environment for identity development—one with reduced psychological distress.

"Self-acceptance" is a complicated term within many faith-based communities, especially when used in reference to behaviors that might contradict doctrinal or scriptural expectations. Yet growing evidence indicates how self-acceptance significantly influences psychological distress[9] by enhancing the way social support and intrinsic religiosity impact the college and university experience of sexual minorities.[10] It is a necessary ingredient if one wishes to look at life realistically.

We propose that self-acceptance is not capitulation to personal experience or desire as the primary ingredient for self-development or religious or spiritual direction. Self-acceptance means that the whole self is accepted as having created worth, no matter what personal reality may look like. From a Christian perspective, self-acceptance brings unquestioned value to evaluation of the self. It might be said more pastorally that all persons can be confident in God's deeply graceful love. We believe that acceptance of this sort lays a reflective foundation for observing and contemplating who one is, who one has been, and who one wants to be. As Carl Rogers[11] noted, acceptance does not necessarily mean approval. It is our conclusion that self-acceptance can occur when there are aspects of self that are affirmed and other aspects that are not.[12]

---

8 Yarhouse et al., *Listening to Sexual Minorities*.
9 Dean, Stratton, and Yarhouse, "Becoming an Intentional Church"; Woodford et al., "Contemporary Heterosexism."
10 Dean, Stratton, and Yarhouse, "Mediating Role."
11 Everett L. Shostrom, dir., *Three Approaches to Psychotherapy* (Psychological Films, 1965), 106 min.
12 Dean, Stratton, and Yarhouse, "Mediating Role."

One can see oneself without automatically either approving or rejecting. Self-acceptance is reflective space that tends to resist impulsive polarization, steering away from viewing self from an either/or perspective. Although there is often a tendency toward embodied (i.e., cognitive, affective, and behavioral) reactivity, especially when facing self-judgment, acceptance creates the opportunity for nonreactive space where reality can be observed and considered. This approach resists the temptation to demonize some parts of self or sanctify others. Self-acceptance means those intersecting aspects of self are seen as who one is in the moment so the person one wants to be can grow and develop. This type of realistic self-awareness is the foundation for informed self-development and mature stewardship of self.

Stewardship based in self-acceptance allows for the experience of guilt rather than shame. Shame is a strong negative emotional state characterized by global devaluation of self or aspects of self, usually connected with a humiliating sense of being deeply flawed, morally defective, or worthless.[13] Guilt, alternatively, is a strong negative emotional state but less evaluative of self in general and more focused on specific behavioral errors or identifiable wrongs. Guilt tends to be less about a sense of humiliation and more about feeling humbled by regretted actions that inevitably arise in the course of self-formation. Guilt does not lead to psychological distress but can be adaptive, both personally and socially.[14] In contrast, shame splits the self into separate evaluating and evaluated parts, while guilt tends to create unified and accepting space for considering oneself in the midst of life experiences.

Appropriate self-acceptance creates graceful space where persons do not react automatically to censor or admonish themselves; they can observe, they can contemplate, they can choose how to be a steward of their experience. They can pay attention to those aspects of self and related specific behaviors without humiliation while being realistically humbled by behaviors that don't live up to their expectations or

---

13 Tangney and Dearing, *Shame and Guilt*.
14 Tangney and Dearing.

values. We suggest by living in this self-conscious reality, enhanced through self-acceptance, one finds space for intentional formation and identity development. Living without the ability to observe and then accept one's present reality makes self-formation more complicated and fragmented.

Without acceptance of one's various self-aspects, individuals may try to avoid fragmentation by taking an overly simplified approach—that is, allowing one self-aspect to define one's full identity. For example, a person might claim, "My sexual identity is who I am," or "The only thing about me that matters about me is my faith." This error of reductionism is often pushed by Western society and identity politics, yet stewarding oneself in this way truncates the comprehensiveness, complexity, and beauty of what it means to be fully human. As we listen to persons who are navigating sexuality and gender experiences in the context of their faith, we hear a different approach. Some students voiced a view of self-acceptance that strives to appreciate the messiness that exists within all human beings. They resisted surrendering to an approach that creates less-than-human caricatures based on one highly valued aspect of self or another. Students can like or dislike different aspects of self while still respecting the valued creation that they are.

Because of the impact of the minority experience on the formation of a self, the journey for persons navigating sexual and gender identity self-development is unique and at times precarious. We believe two intersecting concepts must be considered in any meaningful conversation about stewardship of sexual and gender identities in this context: self-cohesion and grace for self. These two seem best formed in the reciprocal matrix of self-acceptance in relational context. Stewardship of self grows when persons learn how to hold themselves within the experience of being held by others.

Self-Cohesion

We have been looking at how self-acceptance plays a role in the way psychological distress is experienced and managed in Christian settings.[15] Self-acceptance may be better understood as a core aspect of self-cohesion: the feeling that one's many qualities and experiences reside within a valued and integrated self,[16] the opposite of fragmentation. Although we have been referencing work based primarily on sexual minorities, we believe the idea of enhancing self-cohesion can be tentatively extended to gender minority students of faith. We have come to view self-acceptance as a foundational part of self-cohesion, along with a sense of self-worth, coherence, resilience, and self-regulation.

Self-cohesion holds together different parts of self, so individuals develop a greater sense of self-complexity. Those with limited self-complexity find their whole selves reinforced by positive experiences and threatened by negative ones, even when only one aspect of self is activated.[17] In contrast, those with greater self-cohesion tend to show more resilience. They develop the capacity to cope more efficiently with challenges or desires related to any part or parts of self. These persons may not experience significant mood swings or changes in self-evaluation when one or a few self-aspects are affected by life experiences. We speculate they may have greater stability in who they are, knowing that any one part does not fully define them, and thus they are better able to compartmentalize these events.

The alternative to this movement toward self-cohesion is self-division—a self-protective and often defensive strategy for maintaining felt security by hiding aspects of self that are unwanted or undesirable. Describing this process, Bland reported, "The contradictory states of self-expression and energy spent on concealing objectionable parts of self regularly lead to frustration and stagnation of self-development and spiritual formation."[18] Early in identity development, this immature tendency to split parts of self and aspects

---

15 Dean, Stratton, and Yarhouse, "Mediating Role."

16 Mario Mikulincer and Phillip R. Shaver, *Attachment in Adulthood: Structure, Dynamics, and Change*, 2nd ed. (New York: Guilford, 2017), 149.

17 Mikulincer and Shaver, 149.

18 Earl D. Bland, "The Divided Self: Courage and Grace as Agents of Change," *Journal of Psychology and Christianity* 28, no. 4 (December 2009): 326–37, 326.

of experience typically precedes the more mature capacity that holds together seemingly incompatible aspects of self.[19] In fact, splitting might be considered a precursor of the developmental advance that is necessary to hold that which is deemed good and bad. Persons develop optimally toward a mature identity without reliance on self-protective patterns that ignore parts of self or aspects of experience. We posit that a lack of awareness of perceived needs, whether unobserved or rejected, prevents intentional stewardship of an embodied human experience and hinders identity development and spiritual formation. Self-affirmation and self-denial cannot occur in a healthy way without adequate self-development.

Grace for Self

Intentional stewardship of one's sexual or gender identity may be best supported by processes that not only value self-cohesion but also are characterized by grace for self in complex developmental moments. Grace is not some simplistic approval-based process but a more complex acceptance-based engagement with self and others. It is exemplified and activated by the work of God to redeem and transform human persons and the rest of creation. In qualitative research[20] with Quakers in the Pacific northwest, grace was described as "an unearned, refining, relational experience"[21] marked by "a state of embodied, nonjudgmental, all-encompassing acceptance."[22] The authors found a connection between acceptance and grace for their interviewees. Although we have not formally studied this relationship in Christian sexual or gender minorities, the items of the self-acceptance scale[23]

---

19 Sheldon Cashdan, *Object Relations Therapy: Using the Relationship* (New York: Norton, 1988).

20 Kyle T. Webster et al., "Experiences of Divine Grace among Christian Friends," *Journal of Psychology and Theology* 50, no. 2 (2021): 192–209.

21 Webster et al., 203.

22 Webster et al., 205.

23 Carol D. Ryff, "Happiness Is Everything, or Is It? Explorations on the Meaning of Psychological Well-Being," *Journal of Personality and Social Psychology* 57, no. 6 (1989): 1069–81, https://doi.org/10.1037/0022-3514.57.6.1069; Carol D. Ryff and Corey Lee M. Keyes "The Structure of Psychological Well-Being

that we used have many similarities to those measuring "Grace to Self."[24] Might self-acceptance and grace track together for sexual and gender minorities who are attempting to steward sexuality, gender, and faith as an embodied relational experience?

Grace is a broad, multifaceted concept that finds its grounding in religious and spiritual traditions, but it can also be recognized in secular contexts as well. Robert Emmons and colleagues referred to grace as "a necessary prerequisite for human flourishing"[25] and then further as "the gift of acceptance given unconditionally and voluntarily to an undeserving person by an unobligated giver."[26] Notice the relational nature of the way grace is explained. The described grace is most often embedded in explicit or implicit relations with God, but it is also recognized in human relationships as well.[27] The gift of acceptance can be given interpersonally from one person, divine or human, to another human person. As we talk about different parts of self, it is not hard to conceive how grace might also be given intrapersonally. Grace researcher Rodger Bufford and colleagues affirmed that one could indeed apply the concept of grace to the way persons manage themselves.[28] As such, the implementation of grace may be viewed as an aspect of stewardship of self that relates to acceptance-based processes with God, others, and self. From a Christian perspective, it is God's grace to us that motivates us to show grace to others. God's grace to us also motivates us to grow in our capacity to show grace to ourselves.

Revisited," *Journal of Personality and Social Psychology* 69, no. 4 (1995): 719–27, https://doi.org/10.1037/0022-3514.69.4.719.

24 Rodger K. Bufford, Timothy A. Sisemore, and Amanda M. Blackburn, "Dimensions of Grace: Factor Analysis of Three Grace Scales," *Psychology of Religion and Spirituality* 9, no. 1 (2017): 56–69, https://doi.org/10.1037/rel0000064.

25 Robert A. Emmons et al., "Psychological and Theological Reflections on Grace and Its Relevance for Science and Practice," *Psychology of Religion and Spirituality* 9, no. 3 (2017): 276.

26 Emmons et al., 277.

27 Adam S. Hodge et al., "Experiencing Grace: A Review of the Empirical Literature," *Journal of Positive Psychology* 17, no. 3 (2022): 375–88, https://doi.org/10.1080/17439760.2020.1858943.

28 Bufford, Sisemore, and Blackburn, "Dimensions of Grace."

Grace related to God, others, and self creates the conditions for healthy embodied outcomes, such as lower personal distress, increased inner stability, and enhanced religious commitment. In reviewing previous studies, Adam Hodge et al. found a lack of grace tended to correspond with more depression and shame in addition to various other negative mental health outcomes.[29] Fewer empirical studies have investigated specifically the relationship between grace and intrapersonal functioning, yet grace was found to be positively related to the inside-self variables of "internal state of awareness" and "inner support,"[30] which may hypothetically share qualities with what we are calling self-cohesion. Finally, for our purposes, a clear positive relationship between grace and intrinsic religiosity was found across many of the studies. Although these are but a few of the findings related to the new and growing research on grace, it does appear that grace improves how persons engage self-related experiences, potentially affecting stewardship.

Although we've been discussing a broad understanding of grace, we want to emphasize what Bufford, Sisemore, and Blackburn[31] identified as "Grace to Self." This was one among five specific factors—including experiencing God's grace, costly grace, grace to others, and grace from others—that emerged from three prominent grace instruments.[32] Grace to Self is a trait that looks at the way people make space for grace in relation to their own self-experience, independent of their experience with others.

While Bufford and colleagues did not suggest that grace to self and shame are opposite traits, they noted that grace to self can be described by its "inverse"—shame.[33] Furthermore, they found grace

---

29 Hodge et al., "Experiencing Grace."
30 Hodge et al., 381.
31 Bufford, Sisemore, and Blackburn, "Dimensions of Grace."
32 Rodney L. Bassett, "An Empirical Consideration of Grace and Legalism within Christian Experience," *Journal of Psychology and Christianity* 32, no. 1 (April 2013): 43–69; Timothy A. Sisemore et al., "Grace and Christian Psychology—Part 1: Preliminary Measurement, Relationships, and Implications for Practice," *Edification: Transdisciplinary Journal of Christian Psychology* 4, no. 2 (2011): 57–63; Jill Diane Spradlin, "Shame, Grace, and Spirituality: A Comparison of Measures" (PhD diss., George Fox University, 2001).
33 Bufford, Sisemore, and Blackburn, "Dimensions of Grace," 60.

to self was significantly related to mental health symptoms; coping; and existential, religious, and spiritual well-being. In a study involving grace interventions in Christian church communities, Bufford and colleagues found grace to self was also positively related to self-forgiveness.[34] It appears that grace to self is associated with conditions that promote health and lay a foundation for healthy development. As mentioned previously, offering grace to self is not necessarily an act of approval of parts of self that are not esteemed or might require additional growth. Grace to self is certainly not the denial of a value-based critique of behaviors on the basis of beliefs about God, others, or self. Grace is a complex gift that transcends what one likes or dislikes about self-related experiences. Moreover, we posit that grace to self is the glue that makes self-cohesion possible and reduces self-division.

The gift of acceptance, communicated through the virtue of grace to self, has an impact on the way persons are able to steward themselves and related experiences. Self-accepting and potentially graceful processes do mediate how effectively the faith and social support of sexual minorities help them manage distressing experiences.[35] Grace to self, it appears, plays a role in how people approach self and engage God and others. One might conceptualize grace to self as necessary for the perception and experience of God's grace. God's grace for all persons lays the foundation and motivation for grace extended to others and to ourselves. Grace to self may be a catalyst for the reflective movement toward a more integrated and cohesive self in identity development among sexual and gender minorities. It may actually promote an intentional process of development that leads to the integration of two aspects of personhood that are most complex for sexual and gender minorities—religion/spirituality and sexuality/gender. Grace facilitates a particular way of holding self that resists self-division and shame, and it may actually facilitate healthy relationships with God and others.

---

34 Bufford, Sisemore, and Blackburn.

35 Dean, Stratton, and Yarhouse, "Becoming an Intentional Church"; Dean, Stratton, and Yarhouse, "Mediating Role."

Holding Sexual or Gender Identity and Faith

In our previous work,[36] we discussed ways in which Christian sexual minorities manage their sexual and religious or spiritual identities. Through our interviews with forty-six Christian sexual-minority students,[37] we came to use a metaphor of students moving various boxes into their undergraduate residence halls, preparing for their developmental experience. If we see their numerous boxes as different aspects of identity, these particular students were attempting to maintain their grasp on two very large and heavy "boxes," both significant to them—their sexual and religious or spiritual identities. As they wrestled to carry these two boxes, they experimented with different positions of holding them, fearing they may drop one and spill the contents for everyone to see. Or worse yet, they might break fragile contents if they hit the sidewalk.

We initially thought students would be tempted to set down one of these boxes, particularly given the seeming tension between them and the varying messages they receive both from those who think they should set aside their faith and those who think they should let go of their sexual identity. Surprisingly, only two of the forty-six students chose to rid themselves of one of the boxes. Twenty percent of the students kept both boxes, dealing with one at a time. They would emphasize one box while setting the other down. Then after a period of time, they'd pick up the other box and set the former one down for a while with no way to integrate the two experiences. It was definitely an either/or split, not both/and, when it came to navigating sexual and religious or spiritual identity development.

Approximately three out of four students negotiated some way to maintain their hold on both sexual and religious identity boxes, to some degree working to integrate them. One group held both boxes close together, close enough that the boxes were in regular contact.

---

36 Yarhouse et al., *Listening to Sexual Minorities*; Stephen P. Stratton et al., "Updated 'Holding Patterns': The Intersection of Sexual Identity and Religious/Spiritual Identity" (presentation, Kentucky Counseling Association Conference, Louisville, KY, November 2019).
37 Stratton et al., "Updated 'Holding Patterns.'"

We called this contentious holding pattern a "two-box" method. Attempting to integrate the two boxes in this way meant the individuals lived with dissonance and conflict between the two. Seemingly, these students had not developed a cohesive internal structure complex enough to manage their sexual and religious or spiritual experiences. Granting grace to self appeared to be more complicated than in any other integrative pattern. They lived in more of an unsettled space. Consequently, this "two-box" group had the worst mental health outcomes of all the students interviewed.

In contrast, there were students who reported a more robust internal self-structure that helped manage these complex aspects of selfhood. Self-division was intentionally minimized in their self-reports, and it appeared to be confirmed by better management of communal stressors. These students had negotiated a way of holding both boxes until they developed a more secure integrative arrangement, characterized by less internal conflict and greater psychological health. They described a more coherent self-structure that appeared to create the conditions for grace to self and an accompanying sense of stability.

Some of these students metaphorically emptied the contents of both boxes into one box. They said they could not separate their faith from their sexuality as each could only be understood within the context of the other. Other students put one of the identity-based boxes inside the other box, thereby submitting one to another. Some of them used their faith to order their sexuality, while others depended on their sexuality to order their faith. Both ways of managing with a superordinate or ordering aspect of self appeared to be associated with increased stability and decreased psychological distress.

These "holding patterns" are in actuality different forms of stewardship of sexual and religious or spiritual aspects of self. For the students in our studies, these "holds" came to be conceptualized as cognitive and emotional regulation methods, affording a felt sense of internal security and stability. The more integrated and coherent the self-structure of these students, the more they spoke with intentionality about grace toward themselves. Those in more integrative patterns also appeared to have more satisfaction with their social support systems. In contrast, less integrated and complex internal structures were associated with more psychological distress, and unsurprisingly, those sexual minority students reported decreased social support.

For this group, holding patterns were not necessarily static or immutable.[38] Though students may have developed a robust and intentional way of holding sexuality and faith, their apparent developmental achievement was not inviolable. Internal or external processes (and usually some degree of both) could cause reduced satisfaction with a previously more settled experience with sexual identity and religious or spiritual identity. In those situations, we watched students enter into a period of renegotiation, needing to develop a way of holding themselves and their experiences that fit new, complex conditions.

There was evidence in student interviews that persons of this developmental age may move from the more stable "one-box" or "two-box" integration methods into less stable methods when faced with internal or external "crises."[39] We posit that this "identity moratorium,"[40] related to settling and unsettling integration, could be a way of developing internal self-complexity. This moratorium appeared to come with an unwillingness to throw out any part of the self-experience. We came to believe that more reflection on self in varied and often unsettled relational contexts could potentially result in more resilient self-structures, possibly suggesting greater self-cohesion. But again, we suspect that grace to self needs to be present to manage distress. This process occurs in an interaction of self and environment or context. We suggest that self-cohesion grows most effectively in the graceful interplay of self and others.

---

38 Stratton et al.

39 James E. Marcia, "Development and Validation of Ego-Identity Status," *Journal of Personality and Social Psychology* 3, no. 5 (1966): 551–58; James E. Marcia, "Identity in Adolescence," in *Handbook of Adolescent Psychology*, ed. Joseph Adelson (New York: Wiley, 1980).

40 Marcia, "Development and Validation"; Marcia, "Identity in Adolescence."

Closing Thoughts on Stewardship of Sexual and Gender Identities

For the Christian navigating sexual or gender identity and faith, intentional stewardship starts by recognizing that one's sexuality or gender experience is an ongoing, sanctifying journey within a communal context. We believe grace is embodied when the communal experience of faith, sexuality, and/or gender can be discussed, explored, and integrated with respect to personal meaning-making and purpose. Shame, if present, can be metabolized in these conditions, and appropriate guilt can motivate contemplative action. A self in relationship is then able to choose God's call for these vital aspects of human personhood.

Stewardship is facilitated by self-cohesion and characterized by a graceful approach to self and experience. It will be reflected in an individual's sense of self-worth, feelings of coherence or consistency, resilience, self-regulation of emotions and actions, and self-acceptance (i.e., a nonshaming, nondividing approach to self and experience). Indeed, grace may be seen as a quality of healthy self-cohesion, just as mature cohesion yields a grace that is not "cheap," but "costly."[41]

Grace toward self is the catalyst for intentional engagement of the intersection of faith, sexuality, and gender. Identity development for all persons—but especially for sexual and gender minorities, who face complicated formational processes—depends on the practice of extending grace toward oneself in ways that reflect the heart of God. Students at Christian colleges and universities need to have this reality embodied corporately in the communities in which they live and learn. If Christian communities intend to develop healthy and holy stewards of sexual identity or gender identity, a "holding" environment that models an embracing and intentional discipleship[42] is especially important. Discipleship in higher education communities occurs best in intentionally securing, intentionally relational, intentionally formational, and intentionally Trinitarian engagements.

41 Dietrich Bonhoeffer, *The Cost of Discipleship* (1959; reprint, New York: Touchstone, 1995); Bufford, Sisemore, and Blackburn, "Dimensions of Grace," 60.
42 Dean, Stratton, and Yarhouse, "Becoming an Intentional Church."

This last aspect of intentional communities is the theological picture of the kind of "holding" environment that Christian communities endeavor to provide when they want to embody a God-like presence for community members. Growing as a community is learning how to embody corporate acceptance, even when approval may not be possible because of doctrinal or other faith-based values. Modeling this complex variety of acceptance permits students to experience and then internalize the "holding" of others. In the embrace of relationships, students experience how to hold all aspects of their lives—those that they affirm and those that they do not. It makes tangible the reality that a Trinitarian God is intentionally inviting each aspect of self into a transformative relationship.

Dietrich Bonhoeffer in his classic treatise on grace[43] made an impassioned case that grace offered to self can become cheapened unless it is enacted in mutually accountable Christian fellowship that resembles the qualities of a relational God. For God's grace to self to be perceived appropriately and applied effectively, persons need to be in discipling relationships with others who are also intent on developing as Christians. Development toward self-cohesion requires the support and challenge of giving and receiving grace with communal others. Again, the motivation to do so is grounded in God's grace. One's capacity to live in grace with others and self appears to be an experience that can expand. For the Christian, it is participation in loving communion that forms the basis for living out God's personal calling to be holy and healthy sexual and gendered bodies. It is participation in loving communion that also aids in expanding the capacity to give and receive grace.

We hope it now becomes obvious how personal stewardship is strengthened by the relationships we form with others. These can be deep friendships in keeping with the language of spiritual friendships, discussed in greater detail by Wesley Hill,[44] and lived out in intentional communities, such as the Nashville Family of Brothers

---

43 Bonhoeffer, *Cost of Discipleship.*
44 Wesley Hill, *Spiritual Friendship: Finding Love in the Church as a Celibate Gay Christian* (Grand Rapids, MI: Brazos, 2015).

Monastery.[45] Others have taken formal vows in a variety of Christian communities as a reflection of vocational celibacy—a particular form of stewardship. Of course, this act of stewardship is not a call to be alone in community but is also a call to life together with persons who hold one another. There is also the possibility of expressing love by channeling love toward the same sex in service of the good of the same sex. Eve Tushnet, for instance, describes her volunteer work at a crisis pregnancy center as a way in which she loves women and expresses her love for women in tangible ways that are in keeping with church teaching.[46] Still others enter into mixed-orientation marriages in which one partner experiences same-sex attraction, while the other is attracted to the opposite sex. Laurie and Matt Krieg discuss their mixed-orientation marriage and offer insights and advice that would strengthen any marriage.[47] Finally, stewardship is strengthened by the relationship we encourage students to have with God—the One for whom they are managing the beautiful gifts of sexuality and gender. Relationships that these students have with God may be layered and complex given the messages they have received about same-sex sexuality or discordant gender identities, and there may be benefits to taking time to consider and process those many layers with the goal of helping persons see themselves as God does. From the perspective of Christian sexual or gender minorities, this also means entrusting to God their sexuality or gender and trusting that the One who created human sexuality and gender is actively and compassionately participating in the process.

We cannot end this chapter without noting that holding students who are developing as human beings is never a one-sided affair. When Christian higher-educational communities invite and hold students in the intentional way that we have described, the whole community has the opportunity to see the sanctifying journey of

---

45 "Home," Family of Brothers Monastery, accessed July 5, 2022, http://familyofbrothers.org/.

46 Eve Tushnet, *Gay and Catholic: Accepting My Sexuality, Finding Community, Living My Faith* (Notre Dame, IN: Ave Maria, 2014).

47 Laurie Krieg and Matt Krieg, *An Impossible Marriage: What Our Mixed-Orientation Marriage Has Taught Us about Love and the Gospel* (Downers Grove, IL: InterVarsity, 2020).

sexual and gender minorities as they walk with God and others. Without the chance to see how God relates to sexuality and gender expression, the Christian community has trouble understanding what self-development actually looks like in these students, and faith-based higher education develops a truncated vision of how to accomplish the goal of educating the whole student. Maybe more tragically, a failure to understand may mean that Christian communities miss a grander view of the holiness of God. Our sexual and gender minority students have much to offer. Christian higher education learns to be a steward of their corporate life, just as sexual and gender minorities learn to be stewards of their self-related experiences. God has a chance to transform us together.

Conclusion
Charting a Course Forward

Perry L. Glanzer and Austin T. Smith

Throughout this volume, our hope is that you have been both challenged by the imperative to steward your body as God's temple and encouraged by the possibilities for the work of student development professionals to help students learn to be better stewards of their bodies. Of course, while we have attempted to cover a variety of topics related to the stewardship of the body, not all topics of concern to Christians in student development have been thoroughly explored. Immediately, the topics of alcohol and other drug use and body image might come to mind (for some suggestions about how to approach alcohol with students, see chapter 9 of *Christ-Enlivened Student Affairs*).[1] We are, however, optimistic that based on the theological foundations presented in this book, we have provided a bearing from which student development professionals can begin to navigate conversations faithfully (for those whose campuses have yet to begin engaging in these discussions) or approach conversations from a new angle (for those whose campuses have been discussing these topics already).

In light of the theological foundations, the glimpses of the fallenness, and the vision of redemption concerning how we steward our bodies that we have attempted to provide in this book, we present a few final suggestions for our colleagues who live alongside and

---

1 Perry L. Glanzer et al., *Christ-Enlivened Student Affairs: A Guide to Christian Thinking and Practice in the Field* (Abilene, TX: Abilene Christian University Press, 2020).

invest in college students. First, we suggest that practitioners start by framing these topics within the context of stewardship. This manner of approaching the topics discussed in this book speaks to the realities that we are created in the image of God and that, as part of bearing his image, we have been given specific jobs rooted in the Genesis 1:28 creation mandate (to rule the earth and subdue it), and it addresses our call to be colaborers with Christ as his ambassadors of reconciliation (2 Cor. 5:18–20). Within the context of student development work, the language of stewardship reminds us and our students that our bodies, minds, and souls do not primarily belong to ourselves but belong first and foremost to the one whose image we bear. With this reminder comes the imperative to recall and partake in the work for which we were designed.

Second, one of the significant benefits offered to faith-based institutions is to have openly theological discussions with some degree of shared language and common core of belief. As such, we emphasize here that there is a desperate need for conversations and practice concerning mental health, sexuality, social media, and even fashion to be rooted in theology. In *Christ-Enlivened Student Affairs*,[2] we described three approaches to relating faith to the cocurriculum: Christ assumed, Christ added, and Christ animated. The first approach operates under the assumption that since practitioners are Christians, their practice is inherently Christian; the second takes practices common across the range of higher education institutions and then adds components of faith; and the third approach makes theology the foundation upon which practice is built (even if some of the practices are similar to those found elsewhere), and it seeks to order our identities and work within the larger biblical narrative arc. As we did then, we once again advocate that the third course of action is the most transformative orientation for faith-based institutions and practitioners.

Of course, as some of the authors in this volume have noted, faith is sometimes used to dismiss these topics as irrelevant (e.g., "I'm a Christian, so I shouldn't be struggling with anxiety or depression").

2 Glanzer et al., 224–27.

These attitudes are contrary to our call to be with people in their pain[3] and to discuss these issues and approach our practice through our theological convictions. As such, Christian practitioners should consider the theological foundations for any conversations and practices engaged for the sake of helping students become better stewards of their bodies.

Finally, student development professionals must remember that people must learn to steward their bodies. In our fallen condition, stewardship of the body is not our natural inclination; no child is keen to nap or eat healthy foods that they do not like without at some point learning the limits of their physical bodies or through the prompting of another. When I (Austin) was an undergraduate student, I took a course in ethology (animal behavior in the wild) and have since found the ethological definition of learning highly applicable in my work in student development. Specifically, this definition is that learning is "a stable, relatively permanent *change* in individual behavior that occurs as a consequence of experience."[4] This definition speaks to a few important considerations for learning to steward one's body: it becomes an ingrained part of how we live our lives moving forward, it has physical outcomes for the individual, and these changes are the result of a transformative experience. For Christians in student development, our task then becomes facilitating these transformative experiences. We should expose students to new ways of seeing

---

3 Jesus's example after Lazarus's death makes this reality quite plain (John 11:17–44). He knew that he would raise Lazarus from the dead, and yet, he comforted Martha and Mary in their immense pain and wept at the tomb of his friend (though there are different perspectives on the reason for his weeping—see John 11:35n69 NET for an overview of some of these perspectives). For those of us in student development work, we know that students sometimes just need someone to be present and mourn with them over their current circumstances, even though we might see more of the picture regarding what God is doing in their lives.

4 Edwin M. Banks and John A. Heisey, *Animal Behavior* (Chicago: Educational Methods/Chicago, 1977), 68, emphasis in original. I will acknowledge that I take this definition and expand it beyond the typical ethological usage; I broaden it to include mental (knowledge) and soul behaviors (virtues), while the ethologists are concerned only with physical behaviors, which is understandable since it would be difficult to examine the mental behaviors of a leopard, yak, or sea cucumber in the wild.

themselves as made in the imago Dei and provide a vision for living out stewardship. However, we must also remember Steven Garber's argument in *The Fabric of Faithfulness*[5] that belief becomes behavior through a weaving of convictions, character (informed by mentors), and community. As such, it is not enough to simply frame everything as theologically rooted stewardship; we must also model these behaviors with our own lives and work to create communities that support a commitment to bodily stewardship.

Observing the current trends in students' lives, we may quickly be disheartened by the numerous examples of fallenness. However, despite the choppiness of the waters, we have a consistent bearing through our faith in the death and resurrection of Jesus. In him, we see a perfect example of how one stewards the body—even in death—fulfilling the creation mandate. With Christ as our example, we have the opportunity to encounter students and help them consider their own identities as stewards of the gift of their bodies and the implications this truth has for how they faithfully live their lives.

---

5 Steven Garber, *The Fabric of Faithfulness: Weaving Together Belief & Behavior during the University Years* (Downers Grove, IL: InterVarsity, 1996), 37–38.

Discussion Guide

Part One: Foundational Christian Vision

Chapter 1: The Body in the Biblical Narrative: Foundations

1. In what ways does my campus discuss stewardship of the body, even if we don't actually use that exact terminology? Are there areas of bodily stewardship that we ignore in part or entirety?

2. How do we convince students that their bodies are gifts, even when they do not feel like they are?

3. Am I prepared to engage students who are suffering due to physical realities of pain, illness, or death in their own lives or the lives of those close to them? What is my own tendency when dealing with such realities? Do I tend to rush past grief to get to redemption, or am I more likely to stay in grief and forget that God cares?

4. Have I reflected on my theology of suffering and how it impacts the way I engage my students who may also be suffering? If I am unexperienced in this area, do I know to whom I will refer students needing support?

5. What are instances of bodily fallenness I have witnessed on my campus? Have there been any notable instances of redemption related to these examples?

Chapter 2: Savoring and Stewarding Food

1. Does my campus do anything to encourage students to consider what they eat and the various sources from which their food comes? Do we help students think about their seemingly minor choices about food and the larger impacts they might have?

2. In what ways, if any, does my campus promote the practice of hospitality, particularly through the use of food? Are there areas where we need to be better at this form of hospitality?

3. How do the ideas of being thoughtful about where our food comes from and the quality of the food we eat change when healthy and affordable options are not necessarily available?

4. How should our campus navigate the topic of stewarding food with students who are facing food insecurity? On the flip side, how does an overabundance of food for the majority of students (think free choice and unlimited access in dining halls) influence their "savoring" of food?

Chapter 3: Stewarding Our Limitations: Receiving God's Gift of Sleep

1. How might my campus best encourage students to adopt better sleep habits? Are some possible barriers to initiatives specific to my campus, and if so, how can these barriers be overcome?

2. Are there creative practices that I might personally adopt to help encourage better sleep habits among my students?

3. How well do the faculty and professional staff on our campus steward their bodies through sleep? In what ways, if any, does our campus promote healthy sleep habits among faculty and staff or encourage faculty and staff to structure their classes and activities to encourage healthy sleep?

4. For what are your students sacrificing sleep? How can I best engage with my students in conversations about whether or not these competing goods are worth the sacrifice of sleep?

Chapter 4: Sabbath Taking

1. In what ways, if any, have I pursued taking the Sabbath seriously? Are there any lessons I have learned about Sabbath taking from my own experiences that I can pass along to my students?

2. Are there ways we treat students as machines as opposed to people? How can Sabbath practices help us reimagine who our students are? Do I consider Sabbath when I determine workload, due dates, and so on for my students' assignments? Why or why not?

3. Where are places where I or my students need to lean into Sabbath rest? What holds us back from fully trusting God in these areas of life? What would it take for me or my students to be more comfortable turning this area over to God?

Chapter 5: Attuning and Attending: Exercise and the Body

1. Where are some places on my campus where we ignore theological perspectives of the body and focus primarily on the biomedical body? What are some ways that my campus can start considering the body in a theological light?

2. What are the messages my campus promotes about what it means to be fit? What is the source of such messages?

3. Are there any ways in which these messages might need to be altered, and if so, how could we best go about changing them? How do we simultaneously engage students at opposite ends of the extreme without leading any astray?

4. What are my rhythms in my life of work, rest, and play? What parts of these rhythms are healthy and can serve as an example to my students?

5. Are there certain aspects of my rhythms that need to be addressed? What are the implications of unhealthy rhythms in different facets of my life?

Chapter 6: Sex: A Positive Christian Vision

1. How does my campus currently frame conversations about sex? Whose job is it to talk about sex with students and in what context? Is it a topic we address, or are there reasons we tend to avoid it?

2. What are the implications of our current approach, and what does our current approach communicate to my students?

3. What messages about sex are my students currently receiving from influences outside our campus community? What are some of the most potent vectors of these messages?

4. In what ways do those outside messages agree with or diverge from the messages we hope they are receiving from their time at this institution?

5. How can we better create a campus culture that promotes healthy conversations about sexuality, rooted in a theological vision of sex, and that also brings in those who fall short of our community expectations with grace and forgiveness?

Part Two: From Fall to Redemption

Chapter 7: Fashion: Clothing Collegians in Christ

1. In what ways do you "stylize" your life? What does this communicate about how you view living well?

2. What do our students communicate to us and others through how they clothe themselves? Are there messages that need to be challenged? Are there any messages that should be encouraged? How might we have these conversations without coming across as legalistic or puritanical?

3. What does it practically look like for myself and my students to "put on Christ" in relation to our fashion choices? What idols might we have to "put to death" in order to best clothe ourselves in Christ?

Chapter 8: Your Body and Your Mind: Social Media

1. What are my habits regarding social media? How might my habits look similar or different from my students, and how might these similarities or differences influence how I speak with students about this topic?

2. How do my students' and my social media practices shape who we are? Have I seen examples of this formation in my own experience?

3. What counterliturgies and spiritual disciplines might be most accessible to my students, forming them toward the Kingdom of God? What practices can be implemented on my campus

(or among the students under my purview) to help promote presence?

Chapter 9: Beyond Anxiousness

1. What are some of the most common triggers of student anxiety that I have observed on my campus? Are these influences something that can be mitigated by the institution? If so, what can we do to help manage the degree of anxiety students experience?

2. What are some ways my campus can help instill students with coping skills to help them manage anxiety? How can we best root these coping mechanisms in a biblical worldview in a way that is meaningful rather than trite?

3. Where do I feel anxious in my own work with students who are struggling with anxiety? Do I observe—in myself and my colleagues—tendencies toward empathy or frustration when dealing with those who seem stuck in anxiety? Why?

Chapter 10: Depression: The Role of Student Affairs Leaders in Supporting Struggling Students and Helping Them Build Resilience

1. How confident do I feel in my ability to help students struggling with depression? Am I able to identify the major symptoms? Do I know when to pass students along to professional counselors?

2. What might it look like to take an approach that acknowledges the realities of depression and speaks to those realities from a place of biblical truth without being dismissive (e.g., "All you need is Jesus")?

3. How does our faith change the way we understand topics of depression and resilience? What role does our faith play in how we respond?

Chapter 11: Mental Health and Spiritual Disciplines

1. What spiritual disciplines, if any, are currently discussed, promoted, or incorporated on my campus? How, if at all, are these disciplines framed in relation to mental health?

2. Where are opportunities for celebration and gratitude on my campus? How frequently do we purposefully gather together, and what is the tone of such gatherings?

3. Are there any disciplines not discussed in this chapter that you have found helpful in your own life? How might these disciplines be framed to promote mental health among your students?

Chapter 12: Sex with a Person's Mediated Body: Pornography

1. How would I describe the current state of conversations on my campus related to pornography? Is this something we discuss, and if so, how? If we don't talk about this topic much, what are some of the barriers to these conversations?

2. Do I feel adequately prepared to have conversations with students on my campus about pornography use? In what ways, if so? If not, what would I need to know in order to be able to have these conversations?

3. What should be the role of rules when addressing topics such as pornography? How might the way we communicate and enact rules help students develop or hinder them from developing a more complete and compelling view of personhood and flourishing?

4. How does your view of rules fit within a framework that emphasizes redemption?

Chapter 13: Stewarding Diverse Sexual and Gender Identities

1. In what ways, if any, does my campus currently help students navigate questions around sexuality and gender? What do we do well, and where can we grow?

2. In what ways can my campus better walk with students through the process of self-acceptance (as a reminder, this is different from approving of or rejecting) so that they might better engage their faith in light of their experiences?

3. How will these conversations need to be navigated in light of my institution's doctrinal beliefs?

4. How can I be a better resource to my sexual minority students? What do I need to learn, and who might I consult for advice, as I seek to help these students move toward greater self-cohesion and extend grace to themselves? Are there places where I can provide discipleship or opportunities for community?

Contributors

Stephen T. Beers is the vice president for student development at John Brown University. He has served as the president of the Association for Christians in Student Development and is serving as a senior fellow of the Council for Christian Colleges and Universities. His publications include *The Soul of the Christian University*, *Funding the Future*, and *Making a Difference*.

Andrew Borror is a PhD candidate in theological ethics at the University of Aberdeen and the Theology, Medicine, and Culture research fellow at Duke Divinity School. He works at the North Carolina Study Center, teaching Scripture, theology, and Christian ethics to undergraduates at the University of North Carolina at Chapel Hill.

Steve Conn is the dean of students at Letourneau University, where he is blessed to work with amazing students and colleagues. He lives in Hallsville, Texas, with Cortney, his wife of twelve years, as well as his children Carson, Mckenzie, and Parker.

Robert Covolo is a cultural theologian residing in Los Angeles. He serves as a professor of theology and culture at Fuller Theological Seminary, as a pastor at Christ Church Sierra Madre, and as the director of vocational discipleship at the Center for Faith & Work Los Angeles (CFWLA). His book *Fashion Theology* (Baylor University Press, 2020) pioneers the relationship between Christian theology and fashion studies.

Janet B. Dean is a professor of pastoral counseling education at Asbury Theological Seminary, an ordained elder in the Church of the Nazarene, and a licensed psychologist in Kentucky. She has coauthored several research articles on faith and sexual/gender identity and the book *Listening to Sexual Minorities: A Study of Faith and Sexual Identity on Christian College Campuses.*

Justin Whitmel Earley is a lawyer, author, and speaker based out of Richmond, Virginia. He is the author of *The Common Rule: Habits of Purpose for an Age of Distraction* (InterVarsity Press, 2019) and *Habits of the Household: Practicing the Story of God in Everyday Family Rhythms* (Zondervan, 2021).

John D. Foubert serves as dean and professor in the College of Education at Union University. His major research areas include sexual assault prevention and the harms of pornography. His most recent book is *Protecting Your Children from Internet Pornography: Understanding the Science, Risks, and Ways to Protect Your Kids* (Northfield, 2022).

Perry L. Glanzer is a professor of educational foundations at Baylor University and a resident scholar with the Baylor Institute for Studies of Religion. He has authored and edited numerous books, with the most recent being *Identity Excellence: A Theory of Moral Expertise for Higher Education* (Rowman & Littlefield, 2022) and *The Dismantling of Moral Education: How Higher Education Reduced the Human Identity* (Rowman & Littlefield, 2022).

Jonathan Grant is the vicar of St. Paul's Symonds Street in Auckland, New Zealand—one of the largest Anglican congregations in the Australasian region. He holds a ThM from Regent College, Vancouver, and is the author of *Divine Sex: A Compelling Vision for Christian Relationships in a Hypersexualized Age* (Brazos Press, 2015).

Lea D. Hart is a PsyD student at George Fox University and holds an MA in clinical psychology from George Fox University and a bachelor's degree in psychology from John Brown University. She also currently serves as a graduate resident director at Linfield University in McMinnville, Oregon.

Julia D. Hejduk is the Reverend Jacob Beverly Stiteler Professor of Classics and associate dean of the Honors College at Baylor University. She has written numerous articles and books on ancient Latin poetry as well as essays on faith and society for journals such as *Public Discourse, Church Life Journal, Christian Scholar's Review,* and *Homiletic and Pastoral Review.*

Connie Horton serves as the vice president for student affairs at Pepperdine University. Her career in higher education has spanned three decades and included faculty, counseling center director, and administrative roles. Dr. Horton, a licensed psychologist, led the effort to develop RISE, a faith-based resilience-skills development program for students.

Lisa Igram's twenty years of experience in higher education include a variety of curricular and cocurricular experiences. She serves as dean of student wellness at Biola University, adjuncts for Talbot School of Theology, and is pursuing a PhD in New Testament at the University of Aberdeen, focusing on the value of embodiment for spiritual growth.

Lisa Graham McMinn (PhD sociology) is a spiritual director who taught sociology for twenty years at Wheaton College and George Fox University. She coordinates the spiritual direction care in the PsyD program at George Fox. Her relevant books include *The Contented Soul* (InterVarsity Press) and *To the Table* (Brazos Press).

Austin T. Smith is a PhD candidate in higher education studies and leadership at Baylor University. He previously worked as a resident director at Pepperdine University and received his MA in higher education and student development from Taylor University. Additionally, he serves as the associate editor in chief for *Growth: The Journal of the Association for Christians in Student Development.*

Felicia Wu Song (BA, history, Yale; MA, communication studies, Northwestern; PhD, sociology, University of Virginia) is a professor of sociology at Westmont College. Prior to her most recent book, *Restless Devices: Recovering Personhood, Presence, and Place in the Digital Age* (2021), her research focused on virtual communities and the evolution of "mommy bloggers."

Stephen P. Stratton is a professor of counseling and pastoral care at Asbury Theological Seminary. He is a licensed psychologist and counselor educator whose research interests include Christian contemplative practices and the intersection of faith and sexuality, particularly during the college years.

Mark A. Yarhouse is the Dr. Arthur P. Rech and Mrs. Jean May Rech Professor of Psychology at Wheaton College, where he also directs the Sexual & Gender Identity Institute. He is a licensed clinical psychologist and the author or coauthor of several books, including *Understanding Gender Dysphoria: Navigating Transgender Issues in a Changing Culture.*

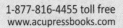
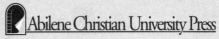

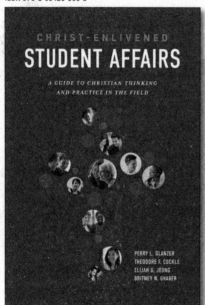

A CALLING TO CARE

Nurturing College Students toward Wholeness

TIMOTHY W. HERRMANN and KIRSTEN D. RIEDEL, editors

ISBN 978-1-68426-160-4

Reviving the timeless call of educators to nurture and care for college students in a culture that continues to care less.

Despite the widely differing perspectives held by those who work in higher education, there is one goal upon which all educators and educational leaders agree: students should leave college stronger than they came. Join this unique blend of experienced practitioners and researchers in considering how we can best nurture our students toward health, wholeness, and purpose.

1-877-816-4455 toll free
www.acupressbooks.com

Abilene Christian University Press

A FAITH FOR THE GENERATIONS

How Collegiate Experience Impacts Faith

TIMOTHY W. HERRMANN, KIRSTEN D. TENHAKEN, HANNAH M. ADDERLEY, and MORGAN K. MORRIS

ISBN 978-0-89112-344-6

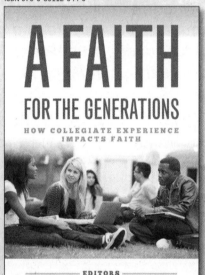

The reshaping of our cultural and social landscape continues, creating unprecedented opportunities. But one question remains: Is a life of faith worth embracing?

A Faith for the Generations explains how a Christian campus, a classroom, or even a simple mentoring relationship can flourish in passing on faith to today's emerging adults.

1-877-816-4455 toll free
www.acupressbooks.com

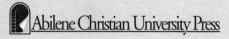
Abilene Christian University Press

REIMAGINING THE STUDENT EXPERIENCE

Formative Practices for Changing Times

BRIAN JENSEN and SARAH VISSER
Foreword by DAVID S. GUTHRIE

ISBN 978-1-68426-280-9

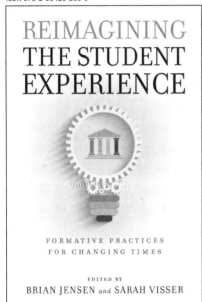

REIMAGINING
THE STUDENT
EXPERIENCE

FORMATIVE PRACTICES
FOR CHANGING TIMES

EDITED BY
BRIAN JENSEN *and* SARAH VISSER

Understand the times.

RESPOND FAITHFULLY.

Higher education stands at a crossroads. However, there is a way forward that recognizes our current realities while also embracing the possibilities of what higher education could be. In this volume, Jensen and Visser have brought together a collaboration of diverse voices from among those devoted to Christian higher education. Offering a professional, robust vision of human flourishing, *Reimagining the Student Experience* invites educators, administrators, chaplains, and university professionals to think deeply about their journey with students, from their arrival on campus to their pursuit of faithful living.

"*Reimagining the Student Experience* is an essential read and a reminder of the kingdom work we engage in daily."
—**SHIRLEY V. HOOGSTRA,** President, Council for Christian Colleges and Universities

"This volume is an ideal resource for both veterans and new arrivals to the challenging privilege of helping young people set the trajectory of their lives."
—**SHIRLEY A. MULLEN,** President, Houghton College

1-877-816-4455 toll free
www.acupressbooks.com

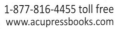

Abilene Christian University Press